THE
DARK STAR

First published 1951

THE DARK STAR

by

AIR CHIEF MARSHAL LORD DOWDING

By the same Author
TWELVE LEGIONS OF ANGELS
MANY MANSIONS
LYCHGATE
GOD'S MAGIC

www.whitecrowbooks.com

CONTENTS

"And now call on the Love Ray and send it out over this sad Dark Star, and let the love of the Most High drench and purify every darkest corner of the Earth plane. Let the light from the Holy of Holies shine forth in brilliance. Let fear stumble and die. Let hope rise triumphant. Let hatred fade away in the blinding glory of His everlasting day, and in His keeping may we walk in peace. Amen."

CHAPTER 1

INTRODUCTION

For a person like myself it is difficult to know when the time has come to write another book. To the professional author the problem is reasonably straightforward—he acquires, or creates, sufficient material, and the howling of the wolf outside the door provides any additional stimulus that may be required.

I am not compelled to write by economic necessity, though it would be hypocritical to suggest that I am indifferent to such material rewards as fall to the lot of authors in these hard times. My hesitation is due to my slowly increasing knowledge of my own ignorance. I don't in the least echo David when he said, "Lord, let me know my end, and the number of my days, that I may be certified how long I have to live." That would be a most uncomfortable piece of information, so far as I am concerned. And yet it would be convenient in a way to 'job backwards' from that date and work things out so that I should leave behind me the most up-to-date approximation to the ultimate Truth, which I shall have reached in this little span of my everlasting life.

In a way, I become less and less inclined, as time goes on, to write at all, for fear of misleading where I only wish to help; but it is more apathy than ignorance that I wish to combat, and, right or wrong, I can perhaps provide some thoughts for my readers to ruminate upon, and then leave them to draw their own conclusions, which are the only conclusions worth having.

Additionally, during the past two years and more I have found myself withdrawn from the active type of work in which I was engaged during the period covered by my book *Lychgate*. The small Circle which was the focus of that work has been interrupted—temporarily, as I believe—and I now have the leisure to undertake a task which might be impossible under a greater pressure of work.

My plan of operations, in so far as I have a plan at the present stage, is to try to throw some light on the conditions of human life after death while the persons concerned are still not too far removed from Earth conditions for us to be able to follow their progress. The mass of material available on this subject from all sources is enormous; but the volume of evidence available, so far from facilitating the task of producing an ordered picture of the future life, has the contrary effect, because of the apparently fantastic inconsistencies and contradictions with which it abounds.

I think that this is one of the chief stumbling-blocks of Spiritualism—one of the chief reasons why educated and intellectual people who have had their attention attracted to a study of the unseen, either through phenomena which they have observed or by personal experience of communication, fall away, lose interest, and return to the materialism from which they have made a brief excursion.

They may say, perhaps, "I have read Vale Owen's book. Barring a certain percentage of people who go to Hell and exist in varying conditions of darkness and pain, people as a whole seem to lead a life which would not especially appeal to me. They wear robes and ornaments coloured by their state of progress, they attend Halls of Instruction, and are treated to periodic manifestations from which they derive aesthetic satisfaction combined with spiritual benefit. All right! It doesn't happen to appeal to me as I am now constituted, but I have an open mind. It may be that this is the road we all shall follow, and when I reach that stage I shall enjoy it like the rest and shall recognise and admit my present limitations.

"But then I pick up another book—*They Survive*, by Geraldine Cummins—and I find people—ordinary, decent, respectable people—continuing to live almost exactly as they did upon Earth. They live in comfort in replicas of their Earth-houses and consume Earth-meals. Some of them go fishing and catch enormous salmon, and old ladies are not above squabbling about the testamentary disposition of their Earth-property.

"This concept is roughly borne out when I pick up *The Living Dead Man* by Elsa Barker, but here the picture is enlivened by characters who spend their time play-acting and deceiving Spiritualists on Earth, while others have their minds set upon reincarnation, immediate or after an appropriate interval.

"The next book I take up informs me, on the highest spiritual authority, that reincarnation is an ignorant superstition which is entirely contrary to truth; and, lastly, I am shown a series of messages indicating that humanity passes years, if not centuries, as drifting semi-conscious ghosts in a grey mist.

"No. If you Spiritualists want to attract the attention of reasonable, educated, thinking men, you must present them with something better than this hotchpotch of conflicting and contradictory ideas. I am too busy to occupy myself with such puerilities; and, besides, I have a reputation for sanity to maintain." In my opinion, everyone who calls himself a Spiritualist ought to be able to cope with this line of argument; not necessarily in discussion with the hypothetical representative of 'common sense' whom I have conjured up, but with his own intellectual self. Most Spiritualists are justifiably critical of the Churches in their refusal to face the hurdles of conscious survival and the possibility of communication, but there are many hurdles in the race, and, if I can see a crowd of clerics jibbing and refusing at the first obstacle, I can picture another group of Spiritualists doing very much the same thing at the next.

For the above-pictured states of being are all true, in the sense that a place must be found for them in any satisfying system of cosmic philosophy.

I don't happen ever to have made psychic contact with a recently deceased Eskimo; but if I did I should be prepared to find him living in a commodious igloo by a sea teeming with seals and fish. I should not expect to find him living with South Sea Islanders, nor they with him.

I hope to show in the course of this book that all the above states of being, and many others also, are 'true' for certain souls at certain stages of their evolution. By this I mean that they represent accurately the conditions in which these particular souls find themselves at any given time.

It may be said, "Oh, but these people are living in the Planes of Illusion. They only imagine these things." This may be true enough; the same might well be said of us, living in this world of 'solids', which are but aggregations of dancing atoms, themselves consisting only of electricity—living in our own distorted conceptions of space and time. But just as this world is real and solid to us, so the Astral world is real and solid to its inhabitants.

We have, of course, to beware of the practical jokers and of those who deceive with deliberate and sinister purpose; but, making allowance for this, we have a vast quantity of evidence upon which we may base our opinions. And, if I give you my opinion, please don't think that I expect you on that account to accept it; you must form your own opinions for yourself and hold them flexibly until such time as better evidence may be forthcoming to induce another tentative change. Dogma is the curse of all systems of thought; once a system or religion gets bogged down in a printed book, once the pundits and priests lay down that you must believe such and such a statement or be guilty of heresy, then that system or religion has begun the process of ossification which will end in death. A typical instance of this sort of thing has just emanated from the Vatican (I write in early 1950). Among Catholics for hundreds of years past the 'Assumption of the Blessed Virgin Mary to Heaven' has formed a subject of discussion. By this is meant, of course, that her body never came to decay upon Earth, but was translated and reunited to her in soul Heaven.

This is not at present an article of faith, but Pope Benedict XIV in the eighteenth century went so far as to declare the Assumption to be "a probable opinion" the denial of which ought to be considered blasphemous and impious It has been stated in the Press that in December 1949 the Vatican gave out that, after consulting all Roman Catholic bishops, Pope Pius will proclaim this as a dogma, probably during the present Holy Year. The proclamation will be made *ex cathedra*, and when the Pope so speaks he is infallible, and the dogma must be accepted unquestioningly by Catholics as part of Christian revelation.

Now, I don't for a moment maintain that the translation of a human body without its undergoing the process of corruption is impossible; on the contrary, I am inclined to think that it was the rule in the very early stages of humanity, before the development which is symbolised in the Bible by the story of Adam and Eve, and I should expect that it may become the rule rather than the exception in the dim corridors of Time which humanity has yet to traverse; but what I say is that it is a process which in present ages is very, very uncommon, and (I say it in all reverence) the question is one upon which divergent views may be held without the slightest effect upon the spiritual development of either party.

So in this book I shall present you with no dogmas; I shall merely try to fit together the thousand pieces of the jigsaw puzzle and see if you like the picture I build: but no, that is not a good metaphor, for if you do a jigsaw puzzle at all, you know that you have done it right; and we shall not know in this life whether we have done our puzzle right, nor shall we know in full for ages after, for we do not come to all knowledge merely through the act of dying.

You may wonder a little, perhaps, at the title of this book. *The Dark Star* was a title given to this Earth not infrequently by those by whom our Circle was inspired.

According to our teaching, there is life everywhere in the Universe, and a basically similar life in the Sun and Planets of the Solar System, though the physical envelope varies with the mass, temperature, and atmosphere of the globe in question. Our terrestrial bodies, for instance, would be quite unsuited for life on Jupiter; for one thing, our legs would break under the terrific pressure of gravity. Nevertheless, as I have said, we are taught that life is homogeneous, and transfers of individuals can be, and are, made on occasion between planets.

Not only have volunteers come to help Earth-humanity, but individuals on Earth who find the road too stony may in certain circumstances transfer, between lives, to somewhere where the going is a bit easier.

It would seem that the Law of Limited Freewill operates with less restriction on Earth than on other Planets, and this accounts for the spiritual darkness and turbulence of our conditions. On the other hand, we may perhaps infer that those of us who 'make the grade' in our Earth-lives generate in the process qualities of spiritual endurance and strength beyond what is attainable by those who have come to the top of the hill by gender paths.

All the same, the sight of Earth from the outer regions is not a pleasant one. A phrase from Vale Owen's book sticks in my memory, "the hell-broth surrounding Earth".

The influence of the Planets upon the Earth is generally realised and accepted, if not so generally understood: it is not unreasonable to suppose, then, that Earth, in its turn, exercises its influence on other Planets, and that this influence is neither pleasant nor welcome.

Now, don't accuse me of dogmatism because I have written the above. This has been our teaching, and you don't have to accept it, even provisionally, unless it strikes you as reasonable. All I have been doing is to explain to you what lies behind the title of this book. You will find the expression used in the Blessing which precedes the first chapter.

Some hundreds of years ago the view officially held was that the Sun and the Planets and the Stars went round the Earth roughly once in twenty-four hours, and that the Earth was the centre of the Universe.

This was indeed a dogma, and one could get into pretty serious trouble for questioning it. Nowadays it is safe to say that nobody worth mentioning believes this literally. But still there are millions of educated people who believe it metaphorically.

They think that the attention of God (however they envisage Him) is focused exclusively upon this little ball of mud, and upon its unique and incomparable inhabitants. That the countless millions of suns, with their billions of planets, were created for our delectation, even though they may be millions of light-years beyond our cognisance in the deeps of Space. That, because life in its terrestrial form could not perhaps exist on any other heavenly body, it therefore exists in no other variety of physical form.

If there are any readers of this book who have held these ideas, I beg them to adjust their spiritual eyes to a longer focus, and to start out on their search for Truth clad in the cloak of intellectual humility. It is written that Jesus thanked His Heavenly Father that He had hid these things from the wise and prudent and revealed them unto babes.

I often notice a characteristic impatience, among those who have themselves accepted the broad basis of the unseen Truth, to convert by the very force of their fervour, scientists, priests, and philosophers. Of course there is no inherent impossibility in persons of these categories "becoming as little children" but the process is not a normal one with them. In my small experience, nothing is gained by trying to cram unwanted matter down unwilling throats (except perhaps in the case of sick horses), and it is better to wait for those who come with an open mind, even if it be "secretly by night". "Sow the seeds" say my invisible friends, "no matter if you never see the blossoming. That is not your affair." There is another point, too, which must be kept in mind in this connection. The "wise and prudent" assume (if they condescend to inquire at all) that spiritual truths can be conveyed to them in one short and simple demonstration; and that if they cannot be so conveyed, then there is nothing to convey. Nothing could be farther from the truth. It is true, of course, that the actuality of psychic phenomena is capable of being demonstrated in a straightforward manner, and the same can be said of the fact of survival and the possibility of communication; but the mysteries behind the portals cannot be communicated to an unprepared mind. Spiritual knowledge is of necessity a plant of slow growth. Would-be proselytisers must remember this, and not be too much disappointed if the seed will not germinate in unploughed ground.

CHAPTER 2

BRICKS AND MORTAR

I think that, in order to get any sort of picture of the unseen world and the events that occur therein, it is very necessary to form some mental conception of the various grades of matter and the slow but continuous process of change from one to the other. Spirit is the ultimate constituent of everything in the Universe—of God, of the angels, of you, of me, of the animals, of the trees, of the stones, of the fairy folk, of electricity, of everything you can think about, and of the thoughts with which you think about them. So it is obvious that Spirit must be capable of taking on an almost infinite variety of forms.

Now I would like you to accept, not as a dogma, but as a working hypothesis which will account pretty well for the conditions which we find to be operative in our little parish of the Universe, that God, or the Infinite Intelligence, or the Central Directing Power, or however you like to think of Him—or Pure Chance, if you are frightfully intellectual—has decreed that pure spirit shall slowly descend through all the grades of materiality into dense, gross physical matter: stone and metal and water and air and all the things which we can touch and see, and which we, in our ignorance, believe to be completely inert and lifeless. This process is called Involution.

After matter has reached its lowest point in the descending scale it turns the corner and begins to climb back as slowly as it descended, through the mineral to the vegetable, through the vegetable to the animal, through the animal to the human, and thence up through all the stages of life unseeable by us, back to the First Source from which it started. This return progress is called Evolution.

It will be seen that we are some little way past the lowest point, and it is our business to associate ourselves with the upward stream. But we are not forced to do so; we have freewill, and we can, if we choose to do so, associate ourselves with the downward current. But we find that the results of this association sooner or later involve us in pain, and, as we strongly object to pain, we label this down-going current 'Evil', and learned divines are provided with a life-time's occupation in discussing why God permits pain and evil. It would be just as sensible for us to discuss why God permits fire to burn him who thrusts his hand into it.

Now, I want to put before you an almost childish simplification of the process of involution and evolution. I want you to think of pure spirit as an enormous length of very fine wire. Take this wire and coil it tightly round a knitting needle. Remove the knitting needle and coil the coil round a pencil. When you remove the pencil you have a coil with a double twist; coil this round a kitchen poker and you have a 3-twist coil. Continue the process with a desk-ruler, a rolling pin, and a beer-bottle, and you have a 6-twist coil. Coil this round a telegraph pole, and you have created a 7-twist coil. (I am not suggesting that you should actually try to do this. You will mid it difficult to overcome the spring of the wire, and even more difficult to remove the telegraph pole without incurring the hostile criticism of the G.P.O. authorities. I only want you to imagine the process.) The 7-twist coil represents physical matter, and it can be restored to any of its previous states by the process of uncoiling it through one or more stages.

The process in Nature is infinitely more complicated; one is not dealing with a simple thing, like a length of wire, but with lines of force of incredible complexity; and furthermore, each state of matter which I have described above has sub-states of condition which have very different properties. For instance, we all know three states of physical matter: solid, liquid, and gaseous—ice, water, and steam. Comparatively few people know that there are other invisible and impalpable forms of physical matter between the gaseous and the ultimate physical atom.

Theosophists tell us that there are in all seven grades of physical matter, and that the 6-twist and 5-twist (and so on) forms of matter each has seven varieties. If that be so, then there would be in our universe forty-nine different grades and varieties of matter. I think that this is probably a fact, but I am not in a position to be too definite. Anyway, I am confident that the picture is not grossly inaccurate.

It is not important, in our present stage of development, that we should be inquisitive about the details of existence in the upper reaches of evolution. We are not capable of fully understanding anything beyond the physical, with our three-dimensional minds, and even then a good deal of what we think we understand about the physical is erroneous or incomplete. What really matters, if you are to follow me in what I am trying to put across in this book, is that you should get a reasonably clear idea of the various bodies which encase our True Selves and go to make up our Personalities. Put aside the idea of body and soul, and even the idea of body, soul, and spirit. Things are not so simple as that.

In the first place, we have each of us an etheric double that is to say, a replica of the physical body in etheric matter. The etheric double has very important functions to perform in maintaining and restoring the health of the physical body, and is active in its recuperative functions when the higher and non-physical bodies have vacated their normal abode during sleep. There are various methods by which one may come to believe in the existence of this etheric double; perhaps the most effective (though not one which I should seriously recommend) is to have a limb amputated. Although the physical limb has disappeared, the etheric double has not, and the illusion of sensation often persists for years in a limb which is no longer there. This is due to the intimate connection of the etheric double with the nervous system. A friend of mine lost a leg in the First World War, and wore an artificial one.

He told me that in cold weather, when his remaining foot was uncomfortably cold, his wooden foot by contrast felt as if it were in a pleasant glow of warmth.

The next-finer body is the Astral, which is not composed of physical matter at all, but of the 6-twist matter of the astral or emotional world. (The word Astral means starry, and refers to the luminous appearance of 6-twist matter when viewed clairvoyantly.) It is very important to differentiate between these two bodies. The Astral body is not the same as the etheric double, though many writers fail to differentiate between them. I claim no special virtue for my nomenclature, but if a writer, incarnate or discarnate, refers to what I call the etheric double as the Astral, he must produce another name for the Astral, or else he will plunge his readers into confusion.

This is why the matter is so important. When a person dies in bed from illness or old age, death is a gradual process, which may not be complete for twenty-four or forty-eight hours after the time when a doctor would certify that death has occurred. During this process the finer bodies leave the physical, and float near the latter till the 'silver cord' (which is a very real thing) is broken. Those interested are referred to a small book called *Private Dowding* (nothing to do with me), where the process was watched and recorded by a clairvoyant over a period of two or three days. The book is published by J. M. Watkins, 21, Cecil Court, Charing Cross Road.

The important point is that during this quiet process the etheric double is discarded with the physical body, and both return in due course to their constituent elements.

But when people, and especially people who are completely ignorant of these matters during life—when such people, I say, are instantaneously killed in battle, or in a bombing raid, or by an accident, it sometimes happens that they fail to release themselves from their etheric doubles. Of course they don't know what has happened, they don't even know that they have etheric doubles, but the result is that they are liable to find themselves in what is called an earthbound condition; that is to say, they are not free (as they should be) in the Astral world, but are bound to the physical by the etheric double.

This is a very distressing state of affairs, which will be extensively referred to in later parts of this book. The symptoms are often those of wandering aimlessly in a grey mist, not knowing what has happened, and very often not knowing even that they are dead.

Every war leaves such poor derelicts behind in their thousands, and modern war, with its bombing of cities, produces its victims by the million. It is one of the most rewarding functions of constructive Spiritualists, if they are permitted to play their part with the invisible host who succour these poor people in their distress.

Let us now suppose that a normal death has taken place, and that the released person has shed the etheric double and is free in the Astral world. The Astral body is now the 'outer skin', so to speak, and the person begins his Astral education. His body, the landscape, and Astral matter in general appear solid to him—in fact they are solid to him, just as much as physical matter is solid to us. He still has his freewill, and is not compelled to do any work or to learn anything. He may, from force of habit, feel that he needs to eat and drink and smoke, etc., and can continue so to do until he finds out that it is not necessary. He has no need of food or clothing, shelter or artificial warmth or money, or any of the things which compel a naturally lazy man to work in this Earth-life. So he can just loaf if he likes to, and a great many people do.

The special characteristic of Astral matter is that it is very easily moulded by the power of thought, especially in the upper reaches of that very variegated state of being.

Hence the extraordinary variety of the Astral world, and the apparent contradictions in the accounts of the next world to which I have already drawn attention.

When I say that nobody is compelled to work or learn, of course I don't for a moment wish to suggest that nobody does. This is, in fact, the ultimate lesson of the Astral state, whose so-called 'Summerland' is so attractive to earth dwellers.

This corresponds to Paradise, and not to Heaven. Heaven is not reached until the soul has discovered that there is no permanent satisfaction in the ability to gratify every wish, to create beautiful houses and gardens and clothes by the power of thought. The more easily treasures are obtained the less they are valued. Sooner or later people find that the only real happiness comes from unselfish work for others, and they find also that they cannot do this satisfactorily without going back to school and learning how to do it.

This seems to me to account logically for the 'Halls of Learning' and the bright surroundings and the aesthetic clothing of those whose existence in the upper levels of the Astral is reported to us.

But of course there are other levels. Man is born with a 'clean conduct-sheet' and an unblotted copy-book: we all start level as innocent little children; but before very long we begin to blot our copy-books and incur entries in our conduct-sheets, and little by little we make ourselves into a different sort of persons. Strangely enough, it doesn't matter nearly so much what we do, as the frame of mind in which we do it. So long as I keep struggling against my besetting sin I am the sort of person who does not want to commit that sin, and if it is a sin which has its roots in the physical necessities of life, I shall probably have little difficulty in cutting clear from it in the Astral. But if I give way to it and cease trying to resist, I become the sort of man who wants to commit that sin, and I shall still be that sort of man even after I am dead, and so I shall go of my own free-will to 'my own place', where I shall associate with people of like mind to myself.

People think of a stern Judge sitting on a throne who sends poor weeping souls down into Hell. Not a bit of it! People who go down to Hell go down there of their own freewill; it is their own place, and they cannot be comfortable at any higher level until they have got the desire for wickedness out of their systems. It is the people who live in Hell who make it such a very unpleasant condition. On Earth people are all mixed up together, saints and blackguards, philanthropists and thieves, givers and takers; but in Hell one has to live exclusively with people of one's own kind, and that is not nearly so nice! In my first book, *Many Mansions*, I quoted an opinion from X, the 'Living Dead Man', on the subject of suicide.

He wrote: "I can only say with regard to suicide, that if men knew what awaits those who go out by their own hand they would remain with the evil that they know." I am now sorry that I quoted this passage without comment or deprecation of its sweeping nature, because I fear that it has given unnecessary pain to a number of people, several of whom have written to me on the subject.

The more one learns about occult subjects, the plainer become the two lessons: "Never judge another human being, living or dead"; and never generalise. No two cases are ever precisely alike, and we can never know the full circumstances. I believe there are cases of suicide, committed from a cowardly fear of facing the consequences of misdeeds, which exact a proportionate retribution. But there are all degrees of culpability. In some cases the suicide is the completely innocent victim of an obsessing spirit, and in others it may even be a noble and unselfish act, as when Captain Oates went out to certain death in the blizzard in order that Captain Scott and his companions might have a better chance of survival.

Still, it might not be unreasonable to suppose that on the average the act of suicide might be expected to lead to a period of time spent in an earthbound condition.

Lastly there are the 'sleepers', People who have made up their minds definitely and stubbornly that they will find no state of consciousness beyond the grave are apparently sometimes successful in proving themselves to be right by some process of auto-hypnosis. I suppose it amounts to this, that they refuse to wake up into a condition which they believe not to exist. In any case, I understand that there is a small percentage of such persons, and that they sometimes remain unconscious for hundreds of years of our time. I don't suppose it matters to them very much, really; they wake up eventually, and they have all eternity to catch up in.

I have spread myself rather over these various categories of people living in the Astral, because, as I said in the first chapter, I want to try to provide a reasonable explanation to cover the extraordinary dissimilarities of the various pictures of the afterlife. There is just one more item, however, with which I wish to deal before I pass on, and that is to point out that the Earthbound fall broadly into three categories: those who are forcibly held to Earth by crime, those who are held by accident and ignorance, and those who are not held at all except by their own wish.

This latter condition is sometimes that of peasants who go on living in their own farms and cottages without any wish to leave the physical neighbourhood; so much so that to the clairvoyant eye it is difficult to see who are the 'living' and who are the 'dead', The plan of progress of human evolution is that all souls shall graduate in the Astral. During this process they master the emotions of the Astral body, discarding the lower emotions, such as hate, anger, fear, lust, and selfishness in its broadest sense, but retaining and building in to the aura of the True Self the worthy forms of emotion such as love, veneration, and the appreciation of beauty in all its forms.

Then comes what is called in our Group 'the Second Death', This phrase is used by other teachers in quite a different sense, and I lay no claim to special rightness in our use of it. But, if people use the words to mean something different, they should coin an expression which will cover this very important transition from the Astral into the Mental world which is constructed of 5-twist matter.

The Second Death is not a painful or an alarming occurrence. It is a graduation ceremony at which the unwanted remnants of the Astral body are laid aside and return to their constituent elements, just as the body of flesh did at physical death.

This is not the view generally held by Theosophists, who maintain that the abandoned Astral body drifts about as a 'shell' for a long time, with some vestigial remnants of the former occupant's consciousness, and that it is with these shells that Spiritualists normally make contact when they think that they are talking to their departed friends and relations. I shall not pursue this matter at the moment except to record my personal opinion that the abandoned Astral body is normally broken up at the Second Death.

Those interested will find an account of the ceremony (which is probably subject to wide variations) on page 101 of my book *Lychgate*.

The Mental body has now become the outer 'skin of the onion', and the soul proceeds to deal with this body as it did with its former outer skin in the Astral.

The main task in the Mental world is to subdue and discipline the lower mind and to develop true intuition in supersession of intellect.

You all know how the lower mind rambles along and builds its own chains of thought, regardless of any control by the individual. Many people never even try to control their lower minds, and let them go off day-dreaming and wool-gathering *ad libitum*; such people have no idea how difficult the process of control is until perhaps they try an experiment in meditation or concentration, when they will find how impossible it is to exclude random and unwanted thoughts from the mind without a long and severe training.

There is no need to await arrival in the Mental world to begin this training. The sooner it is begun the easier it will be, and the work done will not be wasted even in our Earth-lives.

I haven't much direct information about life at the Mental level; outwardly, I think, there is not very much difference from the Astral state. Soon after her 'promotion' my wife wrote:— "It's very wonderful here. I am living in a beautiful home—you could call it a mansion. This will seem a bit crazy. Many people share this home. I have a suite of rooms; yet I can feel completely alone or, if I want company, immediately there are people there.... Life over here is so natural—the earth dirties your fingers, but it isn't damp or gritty, and it doesn't rub off and leave a stain. The pores seem to absorb it, and yet we haven't got pores such as you know.

"You remember how I was always revitalised by lying on the ground or working with growing things. I am still sustained by Mother Earth." That was written in 1943, and in the seven years which have since elapsed nothing seems to have happened to make her more remote from me or to prevent her from manifesting as opportunity offers.

Well, then, sooner or later the soul arrives at the stage where the Mental body is shed. This event is called the Third Death, and is similar in general to the Second. I am not very certain of this, but I think that the Third Death occurs at the stage where the human form, as we envisage it, is transcended, and that beyond this point the Ego, or the True Self, or the Individual, as it is variously called, stands divested of its outer bodies in the material of the Upper Heaven.

I feel fairly confident, however, that the Individual is not of a homogeneous composition, but is itself built up on a nucleus which is known as the Monad, with the addition of matter of the layers higher than those of which we have any detailed knowledge. I shall return to this subject when I discuss reincarnation, but for the time being all I want to impress upon you is that the goal of this life, and, in fact, of life in the lowest three spheres, is the attainment of egoic consciousness—the realisation of the spark of divinity within each of us—the differentiation between the Individuality and the Personality, with which we insist on falsely identifying ourselves.

You and I and all of us are something incalculably more glorious than the Bill Smith or the Hugh Dowding or the other aggregations of bodies which go to make up our Personalities, and if we can live our successive lives in the realisation of the complete unimportance of the transient Personality and the supreme importance of the immortal Individuality, we shall each be contributing our quota to human evolution and hastening the time when peace shall come in all the world.

Some people feel so homogeneous in their Personalities that they find it difficult to accept the idea that they have, in fact, a number of different bodies. Such people may perhaps be helped by looking at it in this way: We start with the indisputable statement that it takes two to make a quarrel. And perhaps I may also assume that, even if you cannot define it, you have felt the existence of the real interior you which puts up a fight, good or bad, winning or losing, against some other part of you which wishes to do or say or think something which the real you instinctively knows to be unworthy. Supposing, for instance, that some hobnailed lout in a bus stamps agonisingly on your foot. Automatically, and without any conscious volition on your part, a great red surge of anger goes out towards the offender. That is your Astral body going into action on its own account. If you are a civilised person you will take charge of the incident and accept with civility any apology which may be offered. But perhaps it may be very hard to be civil; at any rate, it is a Battle between you and something else which is not you.

In the same way, you may suppose that I went to the Parish Church at the beginning of this year with the New Year's resolution of listening with attention to every word of the prayers, of the psalms, of the hymns, and of the sermon.

Before five minutes have passed I have caught my mind sneaking away on some side track initiated by some entirely trivial cause. I haul it back again and admonish it for its inattention, but before very long it has escaped again.

This isn't the same thing which you had to fight in the bus; there is no emotional flare-up involved; but I am having a fight, nevertheless, with something that is not I. I am fighting my Mental body.

I have gone into this matter of the lower bodies at some length, and I hope it has not been too boring; but a proper appreciation of the facts is of enormous importance to humanity if the octopus of materialism is ever to be conquered. It is also essential for a due comprehension of the rest of this book.

CHAPTER 3

YESTERDAY AND TOMORROW

In this chapter I shall attempt some sort of picture of the history of the Earth, not only in this phase of its existence, but in the deep recesses of the past and in the dim aisles of the future. Remember that the matter of which the Earth as we know it is composed is 7-kink matter, such as I described in the preceding chapter, that it originated in Pure Spirit in the incredibly remote past, and that it will ultimately return again to its source.

The Eastern teaching, on which the beliefs of the Theosophists are founded, regards the Earth-system as a chain of seven globes, lettered from A to G, and hanging so that the middle globe, D, is the lowest, C and E at the next lowest level, then B and F above them, and A and G at the highest level, which is i-kink matter; so B and F are in 2-kink, C and E in 3-kink, and D in 4-kink matter.

While they are in that position, the Divine Attention, which we may conveniently imagine as a spotlight, is focused in succession on the seven globes from A to G.

This complete process is known as a round. When it is A's turn again to receive the spotlight, the whole chain has sunk by one level of matter, so that A and G now consist of 2-kink, B and F of 3-kink, C and E of 4-kink, and D of 5-kink matter: and so the second round is completed.

In the third round D is down in 6-kink matter and A and G in 3-kink; and in the fourth round (which includes the present time) we are living on D globe, which is on the 7-kink or physical level, and the other globes are on correspondingly higher levels (C and E at the 6-kink, B and F at the 5-kink, and A and G at the 4-kink).

At the end of this round the chain will start upwards again on its return journey, and by the end of the seventh round the whole system will be back where it started.

Don't try to take this idea too literally; it cannot be more than a sort of diagram to bring the incomprehensible to within range of the mind's eye, but you may be glad to have read this when you come across the expressions rounds, chains, globes, etc., in the course of your reading or discussions with other people.

Also, the whole picture will dynamite you out of your existing ideas of time if you are a follower of "the worthy Bishop Ussher, who worked out Adam's date as 4003 B.C.

The whole duration of the process above described is called in India a 'Day of Brahma', and its duration is four thousand three hundred and twenty million years.

During this period there will have been seven rounds, during each of which seven globes have had their share of the Divine Illumination, so there will have been forty nine periods of illumination when the 'Day' comes to an end. If we assume, for lack of any more precise information, that all periods of illumination are approximately equal, the period in which we now find ourselves would last for nearly ninety million years, and our Globe (D) is due for another three periods of illumination before the 'Day' is ended.

Now we can breathe a bit more freely and feel that we have got a bit more elbow room—feel that we need not despair if all the problems of humanity are not solved during our lifetimes. There is plenty of time, and everything will inevitably work out eventually in accordance with the Divine Will. But the important point is that man still has his limited freewill, and, in accordance as he exercises that freewill in the supposed interests of the Lower Self, to exactly that extent will the pain and sorrow and misery of humanity be increased. It is therefore stupid and wrong to adopt the attitude that everything is bound to turn out well, and that therefore we have no liability to do anything about it ourselves. Man can progress smoothly and happily by allying his will with God's. In opposition he will evolve nevertheless, but through darkness and agony and humiliation.

There is another point, too, which is elucidated by this conception of the evolutionary plan. The words 'eternal damnation', so freely thundered by Calvinistic divines, are not a true translation of the Greek of the New Testament.

Aionios krisis are the words; and they should rather be translated 'the judgment of the Era'. It will be understood that humanity is continuously passing through the mill, the liberated spirits being roughly balanced by the young souls coming up from the animal state, and therefore, at any particular time when the 'closure' is applied, and the spotlight of illumination moves on to Globe E, a high percentage of humanity will not have completed its schooling and will fail to pass the final examination, or the *aionios krisis*. These people have not merited eternal damnation, or anything of the sort. All that has happened is that they are young souls, and have not had time to 'make the grade'. They fall into the 'Long Sleep', or the state of *Pralaya*—to use the Eastern phraseology—and wait for the spotlight to come round again. Time is a purely relative conception, and we are constantly being shocked by the results of applying our three-dimensional notions and trying to do fractional arithmetic in Eternity.

To show that this conception is not exclusively Oriental, you may be interested to know that Vale Owen gave me a great deal of help and instruction in the early days of my work in our Circle. This is an extract from a contribution of his in September 1943: "There is a great upsurge of power: many can be swept on this tide to that point of concentration where they become aware of the power of the Spirit."

Another way of putting it is that they are ready to be brought into conscious contact with the Master and to step on to the path of discipleship. (Smiling.) It sounds odd, but the Earth is returning to whence it came and, while it is a long way off in Earth time, nevertheless it is quite near, and the purpose is to awaken as many as possible before the Long Sleep begins." That is all that I propose to say about rounds or Days of Brahma, or of any period outside our present era of ninety million years odd, or whatever it may be.

To revert to Oriental teaching; during this present Era of Illumination seven root-races will appear upon Earth.

We are part of the Fifth Root-race. The middle of the Fourth Root-race was the middle point of the Fourth Round, and therefore the point at which Spirit plunged most deeply into dense physical matter.

The home of the Fourth Root-race was the continent of Atlantis, in which humanity reached a high degree of material civilisation. The marvellous civilisations of the Incas in Peru and of the Toltecs in Mexico and the Maya civilisation of Central America were all pale vestiges of the great developments of the Atlantean continent. But the Atlantean priesthood became exceedingly corrupt, and used the Ancient Wisdom (which had come down to them from the times when men and angels walked together) for selfish and oppressive ends. They became, in fact, Black Magicians, and the evil that they did had the effect of causing volcanic catastrophes which resulted in the submergence of their continent beneath the waves of the Atlantic. The last island of Atlantis, called Poseidonis by the Greeks, sank beneath the sea nearly ten thousand years B.C. Survivors principally remained on the American seaboard, which was not submerged, but parties under various 'Noahs' spread to various parts of the world.

One such party landed in lower Egypt and, over a period of a thousand years, built the three oldest and greatest Pyramids. The pyramid was a normal Atlantean structure.

I am afraid I have started rather in the middle of this story, but I started from the middle point of the round where the Spirit had reached the point farthest from its source.

To go back to the beginning, I don't think we need bother much about the first two root-races (it is convenient for me to say so, at any rate, because I know very little about them). They weren't solid in our sense of the word; they contained a preponderance of etheric matter.

I think that this may have been necessary because of the enormous differences of temperature which must have existed in a cooling globe with a thin crust. Life as we understand it would have been constantly exterminated by volcanic activity, and it is not unreasonable to suppose that etheric bodies would have been able to tolerate a very wide range of temperature, and perhaps the periodical evaporation of all the water in a district.

So let us start with the Third or Lemurian Root-race, which inhabited the continent of Mu, or Lemuria as it has been named in quite modern times.

This continent was where the Pacific Ocean now is, and the people of Mu may be considered as the true parents of the human race as it now exists. It was the first race where the sexes were separated, and the allegory of the Garden of Eden represents its development from its predecessors where individuals were 'androgyne' (a word which means man-woman) and were bi-sexual.

Adam and Eve were the symbols of the divided parts of an essential individual. Some day in the dim and distant future all our halves will join up again. You have all heard of soul-mates: they exist for every individual, but very seldom encounter one another on Earth, in spite of what our romantic novelists tell us.

Mu means mother, and Mu was indeed the mother of world-civilisation. It sent out two streams of colonisation, one through Cambodia through Burma to India and thence to Sumeria, Babylon, Assyria, etc., and the other through the Americas to Atlantis; so that, in fact, Atlantis was colonised from America, and not vice versa.

After the destruction of Atlantis, the party which landed at the mouth of the Nile (mentioned above) found that they could understand the temple-writings of the other occupants of Egypt who had come round the world the other way via Asia.

There is a fascinating pair of books on this subject; they are called *The Lost Continent of Mu* and *The Children of Mu*.

They were written by an American Major called Churchward who, while visiting India, was 'adopted' by an old Hindu priest, who quite obviously had Karmic links with him from previous incarnations.

This priest taught him a good deal of what I am passing on to you now, and he also taught him to read the temple script, so that when the Major subsequently visited some of the ruined Maya temples in Central America he was able to decipher a good many of the mural inscriptions from knowledge which he had obtained in India. There is a third book, too, in the same series, but it contains a good deal of repetitive matter.

I do most strongly recommend these books if you can get hold of them. The copies I read were in the library of the Theosophical Society, but I have no doubt that they can be obtained elsewhere also. They were published by Rider & Co. in England.

Don't be put off from forming an unprejudiced opinion of your own by scientists and archaeologists who say that twenty thousand years ago men lived in caves and chased mammoths with stone clubs and indulged in unsocial practices. Of course they did; and there are savages living in similar conditions today. An archaeologist of the future, grubbing about among aboriginal remains in Tasmania, would be hard to convince of the contemporaneous existence of New York skyscrapers unless he had some quite independent evidence of their existence. In those remote times the 'civilised' areas were comparatively small oases in a savage world, and the means of transport were so lacking that civilisation and savagery could exist close together without either having any impact on the other.

One other point. There is a fairly definite point (surprisingly late) in geological time behind which no human remains are found in caves or fossil-beds. The scientific deduction from this is that the human race did not previously exist. But, unless I am completely at fault in the picture which I have drawn for you, the explanation is that the earliest races were etheric, and their successors were more or less jelly-like, so that they would leave no solid bones behind them to form fossils.

The same line of reasoning accounts for the almost universal appearance in all religious myths (including the Old Testament) of the existence on Earth of a race of giants.

Scientists dismiss this possibility with a light laugh, pointing out that the giants of legend would have broken their own legs by their sheer weight (cf. *Possible Worlds*, p. 27, by J. B. S. Haldane). This argument is perfectly valid on the assumption that the giant was built of flesh and bone, but falls to the ground if the composition of the giant was largely etheric.

Furthermore, the giant's mentality is generally represented as being rather weak, and no match for Jack's. This might echo the contempt of the new Third Race for the dying remnants of the Second.

The main buildings both of Mu and Atlantis were destroyed or submerged with the continents; but there are all sorts of structures in Central America and Cambodia and India—and in the British Isles, for that matter—which scientists can neither date nor explain. The Ancient Britons and the Irish and the Western Scots have strong roots in the Atlantean past. Stonehenge and Avebury were not erected by ignorant savages, and the Druids at their best practised a religion which would compare favourably with the practical religion of the average inhabitant of these islands today.

The great root-races have, of course, a great variety of sub-races and branch races, with which I will not confuse you now. Those interested will find detailed information on the subject in Theosophical literature. One must remember, of course, that a new root-race does not suddenly spring into existence. It is the subject of gradual growth, with a long overlap with the preceding race and even races; for there are still remnants of the Third Root-race on the earth, e.g. the Australasian aborigines and the Veddahs of Ceylon.

The probabilities are that the Sixth Root-race will eventually crystallise out on the western coast of North America: in fact, some people claim to see the beginning of the process today. I offer no personal opinion on the subject.

Another point. I think it is not unreasonable to suppose that the tempo of evolution may speed up in proportion to the development of civilisation and the spread of education—particularly scientific education. A hundred years of material progress nowadays is probably greater than a hundred thousand years of progress a hundred thousand years ago. If this be so, then it may well be that the duration in our time of the Sixth and Seventh Root-races may occupy only a tiny fraction of the time necessary for the development of the first two, and that therefore the 'Long Sleep' may be quite close upon us in Geological time.

I think that perhaps in the last two root-races our bodies may become more ethereal as we recede from the middle point of the Fourth Root-race, which is the point of the deepest immersion of spirit into matter. I think that we shall certainly cease to kill for food, and that the idea of eating the flesh of an animal will become as repulsive to us as is the idea of eating human flesh now. It seems not impossible that we may reach the stage of not eating at all, but of drawing our nourishment from the atmosphere.

However, I don't come before you as a foreteller of the future. I have been more than sufficiently didactic, perhaps you will think, in dealing with the past. I can but repeat: "Pick and choose for yourself. If you find that an idea seems to make sense, adopt it provisionally till something better comes along." I think that perhaps I ought to put in a word here about the fairy folk and Nature-spirits generally. It is a subject which is of no great practical importance to us in our daily life, and at the same time it is one which is met by the most violent scorn and incredulity on the part of the sceptic.

People who have a message to give to the world concerning the unseen habitually skate very lightly over the thin ice of the fairy world, lest they unnecessarily weaken their reputation for sanity, and so prejudice their power of bringing conviction in the transmission of other teaching which they regard as so much more important.

I have said that the subject is of no great practical importance to us; but that statement is true only in the sense that it is no business of ours to concern ourselves personally with the work of fairies and Nature-spirits, and in fact such attempts at association are not without their dangers.

But that is not to say that the work of the fairies is of no importance and interest to us. Far from that, if it were not for the work of Nature-spirits of various kinds, the vegetable kingdom could not exist, and without the vegetable there would be no animal or human kingdoms.

The two books which I would recommend for information about the fairies are *Fairies at Work and at Play* and *The Kingdom of Faerie*, both by Geoffrey Hodson, and published by the Theosophical Publishing House, 68 Great Russell Street, London, W.C.1. Geoffrey Hodson is probably the most gifted British seer today, and he has observed and recorded much of absorbing interest in connection with fairy and gnome life, and also with those greater entities on the fairy line of evolution who are known as Devas. For the fairies and Nature-spirits never have been human, and (I believe) never will be. They have their own line of evolution up to the Devas aforementioned, and at last that stream of evolution will blend with the human (by then become Angelic) at some remote point far beyond our present ken.

The most improbable thing about fairies and gnomes is that they are so exactly like our conceptions of fairies and gnomes on the rare occasions when they become visible to clairvoyant sight (for not every clairvoyant can see the fairies). Essentially they are formless little blobs of light when they are about their work of tending or nourishing the plants; but they have little minds and the power of clothing their thought-forms in etheric material. The question is, why are the gnomes continuously mediaeval in their appearance, and the fairies sheer pantomime—wings, star-tipped wands and all? I can only assume that their fashions became stabilised a long time ago, and the same thought-forms are kept in being from generation to generation by small children who can see a good deal more than we can. I don't put this forward as a very good explanation, but it is the best I can offer for the time being.

Conan Doyle incurred a good deal of ridicule by publishing his book *The Coming of the Fairies*, in which he reproduced and vouched for the genuineness of some fairy photographs taken by two small girls in the North of England. I can well understand the incredulity with which this book was received; but I for one accept the photographs as genuine and the account of the happenings as accurate.

The gnomes can make changes in their clothing when something takes their fancy. Brogues or boots and stockings are their normal footwear, but Hodson was wearing a pair of long canvas and rubber boots on one occasion when he was watching some gnomes. One little fellow seemed to be taking a great interest in him, and presently he went away, and came back wearing a very creditable imitation of the said boots.

The gnomes are interested in the performances of human beings without understanding any of their underlying motives for human action. They often make for themselves thought-forms of human dwelling-places, but there is generally nothing behind the facade. One little man was seen by Hodson to make several journeys from the lake carrying water in a tiny bucket to me cottage which he had made for himself, but he soon tired of the game, and went floating off across the surface of the lake just clear of the water.

Gnomes and other Earth-spirits are often employed in certain types of physical phenomena, such as the production of 'apports' (physical objects brought from a distance in a dematerialised condition and materialised in the séance room). They are mischievous creatures, however, and sometimes play tricks which are put down to fraud on the part of the medium.

Earth-spirits of one kind or another are generally responsible for so-called poltergeist activities; where physical objects are thrown about or damaged in a mischievous manner.

There are all sorts of different genera and species of fairy folk; it is a subject which awaits methodical classification.

But, broadly, the Earth-manikins are called Gnomes, the Water-fairies Undines, the Air-fairies Sylphs and the Fire-fairies Salamanders.

I have said that the fairy-folk evolve along the line of Deva life, and do not join in with the human life-stream until a very late stage in the evolutionary process.

I have nothing authoritative to say as to the form of life from which they evolved. It is held by some Theosophists that they have evolved from bird life. In my purely personal view it seems unlikely that warm-blooded creatures, who have developed to the stage of sexual and mother love with capacity for thought, and elementary reasoning powers, should undergo a process of apparent retrogression; but, as I say, that is only a personal opinion, and it is not a matter of any great practical importance.

CHAPTER 4

REBIRTH

I will now say something about reincarnation. For some reason, this is a great bone of contention among Spiritualists.

To many it is like a red rag to a bull—they say, "Oh, he's not a Spiritualist, he's a reincarnationist!" There are places where a 'reincarnationist' is never invited to speak. There are places where they almost say, "Here comes a reincarnationist. Heave half a brick at him." When I was invited by the B.B.C. to broadcast in the series entitled *What I Believe*, it was subsequently made clear to me that I had not spoken for Spiritualists as a whole —but I had fortunately disclaimed in my broadcast any right or intention to do so.

I can't understand why the subject should engender so much heat. Reincarnation is either a fact or it is not, and one would think that people would engage in the search for Truth with an open mind. But they "don't like the idea".

Very well; I don't like the idea either. When I have blundered and stumbled my way through three score years and ten of human life where, upon the whole, pain has predominated over pleasure and frustration over fulfilment, I don't like the idea of coming back again and yet again to learn the multiplication table and Greek irregular verbs all over again. I don't like the idea. So what? Is the great plan of human evolution to be dependent upon my likes and dislikes? I have just been re-reading what I wrote about reincarnation in Chapter 12 of *Lychgate*. I am not going to repeat it here, but I should like to say that it pretty well represents my opinion today, with one exception which I will come to in a minute.

As I said there, it is almost impossible to prove what I may call Long term Reincarnation. I mean the system by which the Astral body is shed at the Second Death and the Lower Mental body at the Third Death, so that the Individual is finally left free from all his lower bodies, to digest and assimilate every useful lesson of this most recent 'turn of the wheel'. For when this process is over, and the Individual builds a fresh Personality by enclosing himself in a new set of lower bodies preparatory to rebirth on earth, and when this new Personality emerges and grows to years of conscious awareness, it is not improbable that everyone who inhabited the Earth during his previous incarnation will have been dead for a long time; and though the new Personality may perhaps have memories of his previous tour of duty on Earth, there is no living person to corroborate them from an uninterrupted memory of the events. I say 'uninterrupted' because it is not unknown for two or more people to have common memories of a common previous existence; but that is not regarded as proof by other enquirers—it is regarded as a shared delusion.

I personally accept reincarnation as a brick in my edifice, for a variety of reasons. First and foremost, it 'makes sense'. It enables one to account for lives terminated at birth, lives spent as a hopeless cripple or a congenital idiot, criminal lives where the poor child never had a chance and all those lives which (to our eyes) could not be reconciled with Divine Justice if they represented our sole appearance on this earthly stage.

And if it is a fact that Spirit does indeed descend into gross physical matter, there must be some object in view, and it seems to me reasonable that this descent is made in order to gain experience. The experience to be gained on Earth is very wide and varied, and not to be collected in one lifetime, however long and eventful that may be.

Then, again, I have a natural inclination to trust my own teachers, who have, upon the whole, guided me accurately and well. Where mistakes have occurred, the fault has generally been mine. Still, I don't press this upon anyone else; it is a purely personal point of view.

But while, as I say, it is very difficult to adduce anything that can be called proof of Long term Reincarnation, there are various little touches of verisimilitude which pile up the evidence of probability and help to bring conviction to a mind like mine, for instance, which is already disposed to accept.

Here is a case in point. For a purpose which does not concern this discussion, our Circle was taken back in time on one occasion to an event which occurred during some westward sweep of Mongol tribes a long time ago. The Mongols naturally had to fight their way through the territories which they were invading, and the scene which was shown to us included a Battle between the Mongols, who fought on horseback, and the rightful inhabitants, who fought in chariots. The psychic lady who was describing the scene (whom I have dubbed L. L. in *Lychgate*) noted in great detail some of the equipment and weapons which she saw. Among other things, she was strongly impressed by the shape of the bows which were used by the charioteers, and she made a rough drawing after the picture had faded.

The bow curved back above and below the hand-piece, and then the tips curved forward again.

I said to her, "That can't be right. When you pulled the string the tips would be pulled round sideways and backwards, and you would get no sort of accuracy." L. L. was a little nettled. She said, "I don't pretend to know anything about weapons, but I saw these bows very clearly, and I was impressed to describe them and to draw their peculiar shape." So I put that little affair in the back of my mind as something a little unsatisfactory, something that had slipped a cog somewhere, something that might or might not clear itself up later on.

About two years later M. Jean Herbert, who was then the Chief Interpreter to the United Nations Organisation, sent me a small booklet on Hinduism, written in French.

This booklet had only one illustration—that of a Hindu god—Yama, I think his name was. He was carrying a bow precisely as described by L. L. But the bow was strung, and it could be seen that the string joining the tips passed through the wood of the bow where it curved back from the hand-hold. This would prevent the tips from being pulled round sideways, and would produce a weapon ideal for use from a chariot, where the lower part of a long-bow would be liable continually to foul the chariot-rail.

Now, all this is far removed from proof. If it be accepted that such a Battle did in fact take place in the past, there is yet no guarantee that the participants in the drama were the same individuals for whose edification the drama was reproduced. But such little touches as these do add to the probability of the picture's accuracy, and may bring virtual conviction where proof is out of the question.

Here is another picture from the 'Akashic Cinema.' The scene is the arrival of a powerful Nomarch (ruler of a Nome or subdivision of ancient Egypt). He comes on a visit of diplomatic importance in his

State barge. L. L. describes the scene, with the reception committee waiting on the jetty as the barge slowly approaches across the waters of the Nile.

Now, if I were making up this story I should describe a powerful slave standing at the prow and another at the poop hurling their ropes to gangs of slaves waiting at the jetty to tail on to the ropes and bring the barge alongside. But not a bit of it. What happened was that the slaves dashed waist-deep into the water and caught hold of the rowers' arms extended through the oar-holes almost at water level, thus bringing the barge gently alongside the jetty. Again nothing even remotely resembling proof. Gilbert speaks of bringing artistic verisimilitude to an otherwise bald and unconvincing narrative. Here is artistic verisimilitude indeed, though the narrative was otherwise by no means bald or unconvincing.

As I explained in *Lychgate*, these pictures are not given to us for the satisfaction of curiosity, still less for self-glorification from the reflected importance of the roles played in past time. The main object is to instil into our minds the unimportance and impermanence of the Personality once the particular life in question is ended. Additionally, lessons may be learned regarding the action and interaction of individuals of the same Group in successive lives, and the perfect and inexorable working out of the Law of Karma may be studied.

There is another variety of vision which I think is very rare, but which would probably bring absolute conviction to the persons concerned. That is when two or more people go back in time and become the veritable actors in the scene into which they are plunged.

An account of such an experience is given in a booklet sent to me by Major Stuart-Menteth. It is entitled *Rebirth or Reincarnation*, by Arthur Hastings, costs sixpence and bears the address 19, Palace Gate, W.8.

I quote only one extract which reads as follows:— "I was walking with a friend along the terrace at Battle Abbey, and, when I lifted my arm to brush aside some briars, I 'stepped back' into what appeared to be another existence. In this existence I was conscious of a feeling of guilt allied to a consciousness of temporal power which would preclude any possibility of earthly punishment. I also became conscious of the fact that I was wearing a loose-fitting black coat and red hose, and had a sword at my side. A woman was with me in this experience who also (like my actual companion at the time) had her hand in the crook of my arm. It seemed to me also that this woman was dressed in black and white."

The experience faded within a few seconds, whereupon I turned to my companion and said, 'You were dressed in black and white,' to which she replied, 'You were dressed in black and red.' This experience took place in 1936." This experience must have been absolutely convincing to the two people concerned, since they both went back in time, acted in the scene (as opposed to being onlookers or listening to a description) and recognised one another in the setting in which they found themselves. On the other hand, it is of no evidential value for the purpose of convincing a sceptic.

I think one must be very chary of accepting the 'been there before' feeling as a proof, or even an indication of reincarnation. An alternative explanation of this not uncommon experience is that the person concerned has visited the scene in his Astral body, probably during sleep, and probably during his current Earth life. Nevertheless, true reincarnation memories do remain in the minds of certain people.

Before I leave the subject of Long term Reincarnation I should like to tell you about a correspondent of mine who had reason to believe that in a former life he had been Robert the Bruce. So convinced was he of this that his notepaper was printed with the heading *Robertus Bruce II Rex Scotorium* (Sic.) Down each side of the paper were recorded his lesser incarnations, of which the Duke of Argyll alone remains in my memory. He wrote to ask what I thought of his remarkable antecedents.

I replied that I had no reason to doubt the truth of his statements, but that, granting that they were correct, I should still advise reticence on the subject; because the ignorant would laugh at him for making ridiculous claims, the wise would laugh at him for taking credit where no credit was due to him in his present Personality, and schoolboys would laugh at him for not knowing the genitive plural of Scotus. I should like to put it on record that he sent me an entirely unruffled and civil letter in reply, and made me feel just a little bit ashamed of myself.

As regards the conflict of opinion in messages from the other side dealing with reincarnation, a very reasonable explanation is given on pages 98 and 99 of *Lychgate*, and I shall not attempt to repeat it or to paraphrase it here, but on p. 99 I make the statement that souls do not normally reincarnate from the Astral, and I wish now to modify that statement in the light of further experience. I believe that the process of what I may call Short-term Reincarnation is a good deal more common than I supposed at the time when I wrote *Lychgate*. I think that this quite often happens when children die in infancy; and perhaps adults, too often yield to the compelling pull of Earth and the physical body, especially if they have led very material lives, so that they are uncomfortable in their Astral bodies.

This Short-term Reincarnation is much easier to prove than is the Long-term variety, because the child may often bring, back memories of people and scenes and events of the previous life which are capable of verification. I think that a careful investigation in India would produce a considerable volume of evidence of this kind.

There is one specially well-documented case.

Shanti Devi was a nine-year-old Delhi girl who for six years had been telling her parents that she remembered many facts from a previous life in Muttra, where her husband was a cloth merchant.

So persistent were her demands to go home that her parents mentioned the matter to some friends who knew Muttra, and many of the geographical and historical facts mentioned by Shanti Devi proved to be correct.

Relatives of the man claimed by Shanti as her husband heard the story and persuaded him to visit Delhi. Shanti was not told of the proposed visit, yet when one day a stranger knocked at the door, Shanti immediately embraced him, crying, "My husband has come back to me." Of three children accompanying the husband, Shanti then recognised her own son, born to her in her 'first life'. A searching cross-examination demonstrated the accuracy of many of her assertions concerning her life in Muttra, e.g. that her name was Ludgi, that she had been born in 1902, that her son had been born in 1925, and that she had died in the same year at Agra.

This remarkable story attracted wide attention, and at a mass meeting of Delhi citizens a committee of responsible and influential Indians was appointed to investigate the matter. On arrival at Muttra station Shanti recognised from among a large crowd her husband's brother, mother, and cousin, and greeted them with a colloquial phrase common in Muttra, but unknown in Delhi.

She then found her own way successfully to the house where she had lived, and showed herself familiar with all the details of its interior.

The investigating committee produced a report in pamphlet form which was translated into English, and a few years ago Mr. H. S. L. Polak of the Theosophical Society was kind enough to lend me his only copy.

Unfortunately, this has now been mislaid, and the above is an abbreviated version of the same story taken from the *Morning Post* of

April 22nd, 1936. The story gave rise to a series of letters' to the Editor which lasted till the middle of May, and produced several other parallel accounts of similar occurrences.

Mr. Polak has made a collection of these and other reports of reincarnation stories, which he has very kindly placed at my disposal. Space is not available to give them all in *extenso* (even if the consecutive reading of a number of these stories would not be rather tedious), but I will briefly summarise them, so that the reader may realise that there is a considerable volume of evidence awaiting the interested inquirer.

An English schoolboy who remembered his life as a Roman youth (*Morning Post*, April 25th, 1936). This was not a case of Short-term Reincarnation, and so could not be proved; but it was checked by a visit to Italy and the boy's intimate knowledge of certain Italian cities.

Mr. Shiva Dayal Mukhtar was murdered in the Cawnpore riots of 1931. A five-year-old child in Premnagar claimed to have been Mr. Mukhtar. He remembered being decoyed to the house where he was murdered. He remembered his wife and children, and claimed them as his own (*The Leader*, Allahabad, 30.4.38).

A three-year-old girl named Lata saw a photograph of her grandmother lying on her deathbed, and claimed it as a photo of herself in a previous incarnation.

When her mother Kashabai had occasion to beat her, she turned to her aunt and said, "When Kashabai was my daughter-in-law I treated her very well. Now she thrashes me." She remembered numerous details of her previous life and birthplace. She also remembered a happy nine years as a contented cow (*Occult Review*, Jan. 1930).

A three-year-old boy announced that he was one Gopi, a bania of a neighbouring village. He had died as the result of a snake bite, and had left a wife, son, and daughter, and some treasure buried in the house.

He was able to identify the woman and children, but the house had been sold and the money discovered by the new owner (*Western Mail*, 13.2.30).

Ramluki, daughter of a Brahmin named Pandit Ganga Vishnu, at the age of three claimed that she had lived in a village called Maglabad and had three sons, the eldest of whom was named Sitaram. As she grew older she became more and more insistent on visiting Maglabad, and finally went on hunger strike till she was taken there, where her memories were found to be accurate (B.U.P., *Daily Express*, 28.5.28).

A full account of the Shanti Devi story summarised above can be found in an American book called *Metempsychosis* by John H. Manas, published by the Pythagorean Society, 152, West 42nd Street, New York City.

I have heard numerous other stories of children who have apparently brought back with them memories of an immediately preceding life, but they are only stories, and, as I have no verification, I do not feel justified in publishing them.

There is a good deal of affirmation (quite non-evidential) from the other side that immediate reincarnation is a common occurrence, though no memory of the previous existence remains, and I have come to think that this is quite possibly a fact.

Lastly, it is stated and believed by Theosophists and others that there is another type of Short-term Reincarnation. I refer to those advanced and dedicated Spirits who voluntarily renounce the 'Heaven-time' between lives, which they have earned, and reincarnate at once to help their brethren along the path of evolution. This idea is perfectly acceptable to me, though I have no evidence one way or the other concerning it.

One would be inclined to believe, if the process of reincarnation is logical according to our ideas, that each life would be just a little better and more successful, ethically and morally, than the last. I have good reason to state (from what we have been told and taught in our Circle) that this is by no means necessarily the case, and that the comparative virtue of a succession of lives, if plotted on a graph, would look rather like a hospital patient's fever chart, though of course there is an average improvement over a long term of years.

The fact is, of course, that we must never take it upon ourselves to judge any other human being. The Law of Karma is justice inexorable and precise. It takes into consideration all those unknown factors which lie beneath a human exterior. We see only effect, and that dimly. The Law of Karma deals with causes also.

One more word on this subject. There is a view of reincarnation which is termed metempsychosis, and is held fairly widely in the East. According to this teaching, human souls can in certain circumstances be reborn in animal bodies.

This idea will be extremely repugnant to Western minds, as indeed it is to my own. But I think I ought to say that I have collected a number of statements (though none of them are in the least evidential) to the effect that this does, in fact, occur in some cases, particularly after a specially unsuccessful life-period. It is represented as being a sort of rest-period—*reculer pour mieux sauter*, as it were—rather than any sort of a punishment. (I shall give some instances later on in this book.) I am certainly not prepared to accept this idea on the evidence which I have at present. All I say is that I shall keep a little compartment of my mind unclosed to this idea.

We might perhaps find some day that it fits unexpectedly into the scheme of things.

It is an interesting fact that reincarnation and its necessary corollary, the pre-existence of the soul, were widely held and generally taught in the early Christian Church up to the sixth century. But when the Church formulated the doctrines of 'special creation' and 'original sin' it became necessary to eliminate the teachings of Origen and Clement of Alexandria, who, with other Christian Fathers, had taught 'pre-existence' and 'reincarnation', After one or two unsuccessful attempts on the part of the Church to eliminate these teachings, the Council of Constantinople, convened by the Emperor Justinian in the year 553, issued the following Decree:— "Whosoever shall support the mythical presentation of the pre-existence of the soul and the consequently wonderful opinion of its return, let him be anathema." And so the conjunction of Church and State prevailed, and the idea of the continuous existence and progress of the soul was pushed into the limbo of forgotten truths.

The unmathematical conception was formulated of a creature finite in the past and infinite in the future, and this conception-is stubbornly maintained unto this day—it is as sensible to imagine a stick with only one end! To finish this chapter. I have on my mantelpiece a framed picture cut from an American magazine. It represents an eager circle of relatives sitting round the room waiting for the will to be read.

A dry-as-dust attorney adjusts his glasses and reads as follows: "In view of my firm belief in reincarnation, I do hereby direct that my entire estate be held in trust, pending my return to this earth."

CHAPTER 5

RESCUE CIRCLES

Now I must begin to try to give you pictures of people in various stages of their life after physical death; and I shall start with some descriptions of the sensations of people who have experienced a sudden death and do not know what has happened to them. I have described a number of such cases in *Lychgate*, mostly of men in the fighting services killed in action. You will find a few more in a little paper covered booklet of mine called *God's Magic*, published by the Spiritualist Press, 49, Old Bailey, E.C.4.

I don't think it fair to readers generally to quote extensively in one book from another of one's own, but *Lychgate* and *God's Magic* don't seem to have reached quite the same circle of readers, so, with the kind permission of the Spiritualist Press, I will reproduce three of these cases.

We had just finished our healing circle when Chang (a Chinese guide) told us that he had someone for us to awaken.

> *L. L.* "It is an American flying boy; he can't see us or anything yet. Will you conduct the conversation? I shall be too far away." (From this point L. L. was in a semi-trance. She spoke with a strong American accent and her face worked in accordance with the emotions of the boy.)
> *Boy.* "Say, what's this? Where am I?"
> *Self.* "It's all right. You have been brought to us so that we may help you."
> *Boy.* "Oh, never mind about me! Help the others— help the others. I've just seen one of them have his leg snapped off by a croc."

Self. "It's all right. The others are being helped.
(But he was difficult to pacify. He wanted me to go and help them.)
Can you see me now?"
Boy. "Sure, I can see you. But you keep on acting funny; kinda shimmering like a bad movie."
Self. "Yes. I want you to look closely at us and you will see that we do not look solid and real to you. And when you can see that we are not real, then you will be able to see the others who have come to help you."
Boy. "Say, where am I?"
Self. "You are in England."
Boy. "Well, that's a good one! We were flying over.... No, I mustn't tell you; but one of those Japs got us and we couldn't stay in the air."
Self. "You came down out of control?"
Boy. "We were on fire. But we all got out except Tubby. Tubby was in the tail. A damned death trap that is! Sorry I can't tell you where we were flying."
Self. "Never mind about the Official Secrets Act now; it doesn't affect you any more. I tell you again that this is England—just near London."
Boy. "Say, I've always wanted to visit England, but I never thought it would be like this. But who are you, anyway?"
Self. "You've been brought to me so that I may help you."
Boy. "Yes, but who are you?"
Self. "Well, you've heard of the Battle of Britain. Did you ever hear of Sir Hugh Dowding?"
Boy. "Why, yes; sure I've heard of him. I know old Dowding."
Self. "Well, I'm old Dowding. I really am. Come on now, put your hand on my shoulder."
Boy. 'How can I put my hand on your shoulder when you keep jumping about? "(Of course I hadn't moved.)
Self. "All right, then. Smack me on the back. A good hard one." Boy (tries it and encounters no resistance). "Gosh! Are you a ghost?"
Self. "No, I'm not a ghost."
Boy. "Am I a ghost, then?"
Self. "No. What has happened is that you and I are in different worlds."
Boy. "How do you mean, different worlds? You just said we were both here in England. (Suddenly he realises, and his face puckers up into an expression of agony.) Why, I haven't been all that bad; I don't have to go to hell!"
Self. "No, no, no. You aren't going to hell. We're just trying to wake you up so that you can go and join all your friends."—-A pause.

Boy. (with a sudden flood of delight). "Why, MAC.
How in hell did you get here? (To me). I'll be O.K. now. Mac's a great
guy. Mac taught me to fly."
Another long pause, then—
Boy. (his face lighting up with indescribable awe, reverence and joy.
Speaking very slowly). "Today shalt thou be with Me in Paradise. Well,
I'm no worse than the thief, and I guess I will be. (He talks to Mac for
a little, then—) Say, I understand now. Mac got his too. (Sees Tubby.)
Why, Tubby, how did you get here?"
Tubby. (apparently so called because he is very tall and extremely thin).
"We're all here. We've been here all the time, but we couldn't see one
another nor see you; we could only hear your voice." (Now they can
all see one another and are talking together.)

After the healing circle on March 30th, 1944, James (who com-
manded a squadron in the Battle of Britain) says: "We have a crew for
you to wake up. It shouldn't be a difficult job. My heart is very much
in this because some of my friends are among them. They are not here
yet: as a matter of fact they are walking along the road outside. They
will come in here."

L. L. "Here they are, seven of them. The leader seems to be a squadron
leader with fair, wavy hair. Now they are looking at a big picture on
the wall. They can't see us yet. They think they are in Germany. One
of them says: 'They seem to be quite civilised people here. I mean to
say, this is a very nicely furnished and homelike room.' "They move
over to the piano. One of them wishes to play. I say, "You won't be able
to open it," and I go across and open the piano.
L. L. "He didn't like that! He says, 'Gosh, this house must be haunted.'"
She describes some other members of the crew, a ginger haired lad
and a little dark Jewish-looking boy.
Now they are beginning to see us. They can't understand the new
dimensions. With ten people in it the room ought to be crowded, but
it doesn't seem to be. Five of them are sitting on the music seat, meant
to accommodate two. Now the leader begins to talk to me. He says,
"How is it that you are talking English?"
Self. "Because I am English."
Leader. "Where are we, then?"
Self. "This is Wimbledon, do you know it?"
Leader. "I should just say I do!"

Self, "All right, then. You have just been walking along the Worple Road."

Leader. "But how did we get here? We must have come down over the Ruhr."

Self. "You have been brought here that we may help you."

Leader. "But who are you?"

I go to the mantelpiece, take down a picture of myself in uniform, and hold it beside my face.

Self. "Do you know who I am now?" Yes. They all recognise me now. One says, "I remember you when you came to inspect us at Biggin Hill."

Leader. "How can you help us?"

Self. "Oh, just by talking to you and helping you to realise your position. Do you see me clearly? Do I look natural?"

Leader. "Yes, of course you do."

Self. "Very well, then. Shake hands." (I hold out my hand.)

Leader. "I can't get hold of it. Why don't you grip my hand?"

Self. "All right, I will. Watch very carefully" (and I slowly close my hand through his without his feeling anything).

L. L. "He didn't like that!" Just then the dark lad comes up behind and gives me a terrific smack on the back. He utters a shrill Cockney yelp as his hand encounters no resistance.

Leader. "Look here, Sir, are you trying to tell us that we are—that this is death?"

Self. "Yes. That is exactly what I have been trying to get you to realise."

Leader. "But how can we be dead? We are just as we were before."

Self. "Yes. Now you can see what a ridiculous little barrier death is. This death of which everyone is so frightened. (Now he can see James. I introduce them.) Talk to him and he will be able to explain much more than I can." The tail gunner says: "I remember a Hun fighter coming up behind and knowing that something was going to happen. Then I remember no more until we were in the road outside." James explains that they were all blown to pieces instantaneously in their aeroplane three or four days previously over the Ruhr.

Now they can see all their other R.A.F. friends who have come to meet them and they all go off together.

May 22nd, 1944.

L. L. "Here are two R.A.F. boys wearing 'Mae West' jackets. One has hurt his ankle and is nursing it.

He is very dark, with a black moustache. The other, very fair, is smoking a cigarette. The dark one is cursing freely: his companion says: 'Stow it. Come on. Lean on me.

Hop a bit and see where we can get to.' Here are two more coming along. One is a tiny Cockney."

The Fair One. "Where is Galbraith?"

The Tiny One. "We can't find him."

The Fair One. "The deuce we can't. He is the only one likely to know where we are."

The Tiny One. "I think I know where we are. I think we are in Germany. Look, the river isn't far away; but we can't have been over here very much, there's not enough damage." Now the fair one has seen us.

The Fair One. "I don't understand this. One moment we are out of doors and the next we are in a house."

The Dark One. "I don't care. Here's a chair." (Sits down.) They can all see us now.

The Tiny One. "Wait a minute. I'll try and find out what the old chap's writing."

Self. "Yes. Come and have a look over my shoulder."

The Fair One. "Just a moment. You are speaking English. Can you tell us where we are?"

Self. "You are in Wimbledon."

The Fair One. "Will you help us to get back?"

Self. "Where do you want to go? "(But they won't tell me, for Security reasons.)

Self. "As a matter of fact I know where you want to go."

The Fair One. "It's strange, but I don't want to move." They go on asking after Galbraith, who was their navigator. I ask L. L. "Is James there? James, what happened to Galbraith?"

James. "Galbraith baled out." (I tell them this.)

The Tiny One. "That's a good joke! What should he want to bale out for? Nothing happened to us. We're all right." James explains that the machine blew up. It was blown into halves. Galbraith was able to escape by parachute.

They overhear but don't understand.

Self. "Galbraith got away with it, but you four didn't."

The Fair One. "What do you mean? We're here all right.

Self. (to Tiny). "Give me a smack on the back, will you?

The Tiny One. "Watch me!" (Tries.) "Oh! so you're made of india rubber, are you?" (Tries again.)

The Fair One. "Stop it now! Yes, thanks, I see."

The Tiny One. (dancing about). "We're spooks, we're spooks, we're spooks!" They begin to see us looking shimmery and unreal. I tell them to look round and I tell them who James is.

They see him.

The Fair One. (saluting James). "Reporting for duty, Sir." Now they see all the great crowd of the Boys.

The fair one can't see me any more, but thanks us nicely.

He says: "There's nothing to worry about. We're exactly as we were."

The Tiny One. "If we're spooks, Tyndall's leg isn't broken, is it?"

Self. "No. He will find he can use it if he tries."

The Tiny One. "Go on, then. Get up, you lazy lump!"

The Dark One. (recognising a friend). "Why, hullo, Bill! You see we couldn't let you fellows steal a march on us. We've caught up—we've caught up!"

Now, I shouldn't like anyone to get the idea this is the only way in which these lads are awakened to their new life, or that we are the only operators of this particular method.

Quite a number of people are engaged in this work, but for some reason or other it is very little known. Also you must remember that every little drama, such as I have described, is watched by numbers of unseen spectators who see what is happening and apply the illumination to their own conditions.

At the time when our circle was in full activity it was perhaps natural that most of those brought to us for help should have been war casualties, and that among them airmen should preponderate. But of course there were tens, and perhaps hundreds of thousands of civilian war casualties in this country alone, and when we add to these the casualties from the bombing of Germany and Japan and other countries, both Allied and enemy, it will readily be imagined what a tremendous task lay (and lies) before the celestial 'rescue squads' in coping with this vast drifting population of bemused and earthbound souls.

Of course I do not for a moment suggest that everyone who was killed by a bomb became earthbound; but it is no use shutting our eyes to unpleasant facts, and it is an unpleasant fact that a great number of such people did become earthbound. I have no reliable knowledge as to the rate at which relief is reaching these people; but the important thing to realise is that living human beings can do a great deal to help, and I here quote a few instances where a clairaudient friend of mine was able to help some of these people and release them from their unhappy, aimless drifting. (I use the word 'earthbound' in this connection to indicate a state where the etheric double has not been shed at death, and the victim is consequently between the two worlds, seeing the physical but being unable to communicate, and not seeing the astral or its inhabitants and so being cut off from that world also.) The main point is, I think, that all those who recognise the possibility of spirit help, and reach out for it, find that help, and the drifting crowds which are described below were drifting and lost solely because they had not asked for help.

It is very important that this idea shall be disseminated as widely as possible. It doesn't matter so much even if people won't accept the truth now; but sooner or later they may find themselves in this distressing predicament, and then they will be glad to find that they have in the back of their minds the idea that, if they cry out for help, help will be forthcoming.

Always at death there is somebody to meet the soul as it leaves its physical body—maybe a relation or a close friend, or perhaps some one of the invisibles with whom it has a special tie. But it does not follow that the messenger can make himself seen or heard; that depends upon the extent to which the new arrival had developed his spiritual sight.

Here follow verbatim extracts from my friend's script: a condensed version has appeared in the February 1949 Number of *Light*.

I boarded the bus to go up to town. I went up the bus stairs and took the front seat. There was no one else 'on top'—at least that is what any of us would have said. I had hardly settled when I sensed a new voice; the words were perfectly clear, though I knew my ears did not receive them, and the tone was unutterably sad.

"I used to like the front seat like that woman does.
It's better right at the back now. I don't feel it quite so much when no one takes any notice of me. Oh, how tired I am of this endless journeying—always trying to get somewhere, and never getting anywhere. I wonder why, why, why?"

"Where do you want to go?" my mind asked.

The voice was full of surprise: "Did you speak to me?"

"Yes. I heard you say you never get anywhere."

"It's most curious. I seem to have been on this bus for days—weeks—years—I don't know how long. I never get anywhere. If I do catch a glimpse of my home or office it's horrible, and I come back here again at once. Nobody takes the least notice of me anywhere. They don't even seem to see or hear me. You are the first that has heard me since I, don't know when. Why can you hear me?"

The clippie came. I said, "A sixpenny, please," and answered her cheery bit of chat.

She went, and I was aware of a sense of shock in the voice.

"That was not your voice? Why do you speak in two voices? I don't understand." But I understood by now, unexpected though this was. I am not a bit psychic, but I was under such influence that I was most acutely psychic for the time being, and—oh, joy —perhaps able to help this poor, unhappy traveller.

"I think if you listen you may be able to hear another voice," I said. "I have a friend here whom, like you, people never seem to see."

"Do you mean a spirit? I don't believe in spirits. Uncanny idea."

"You won't find this uncanny. Listen." As I expected, my known companion took up the conversation." Can you hear me?"

"Yes, but I can't see you. Where are you?"

"Don't you realise that people can't see you?"

"Seems like it, but I can't understand why not."

"You don't know what's happened to you, then?" Suppressed agony of terror was in the voice now: "For God's sake don't tell me I'm dead—I can't be dead. I know I'm here, so I can't be dead."

"No. You aren't dead, for, as you say, you know you are here. But your body is, as people say, dead"—a terrible groan of anguish interrupted. "Don't worry. You're better off than you realise; you're not in the very least dead."

"What's the good of saying that, if I'm only a ghost?"

"You needn't be 'only a ghost'; you can be a free spirit. Try to see me, and I'll lead you to a real end of your journey, and heaps of friends."

"I can't! I can't see anything but that wretched woman sitting there not looking at me at all—"

"Shut your eyes and try to look."

"If I can't see with my eyes open, how can I see with them shut? Don't torture me with such talk."

44

"Didn't I tell you your body was dead? What's the use of trying to look through dead eyes? You've got spirit eyes, if you'll only use them. Shut those dead eyes and try to look."

"I'll try. I'm desperate, so I'll try any stupid thing.

No, of course I can't see anything at all..."

"Go on trying."

"Of course I can't. Oh yes—I can see a light, a very dim light. It's getting clearer. It's a tall sort of light.

There are several. Oh!! They've got faces! Is that you? Oh, what a kind face! I never saw such a kind face—and you're looking right at me. Oh, how beautiful! Of course I'll go with you! How utterly beautiful".

And the voice faded away.

I had to wait a little time on a side street while companions I had joined kept an appointment. Great blocks on this street were hollow or missing, and I wondered who had lived there.

"I did. We had a flat there. Lots of us lived round here. Can't find it now. We're bombed out, and there's nowhere to go."

There seemed a multitude of desolate voices joining in: "No home— nowhere to go—no shelter —no one to help—no one listens—no one bothers—no one hears—"

"I can hear," I said. "I can help you. Can you hear me?" I was in the middle of a jostle I couldn't feel. There were voices all round: "Here's a woman who hears!"

"Come on, here's some help!"

"Tell us what to do and where to go? It was too much for me.

"Listen," I said. "Listen to this voice!" They thought it was instructions over a loudspeaker, and listened eagerly, but the clamour broke out afresh over shutting their eyes to look.

"Utter nonsense!"

"I guessed it was all hooey."

"Never mind, do it to please this woman; she can hear us, anyway."

"I shan't do anything so unreasonable."

"I've done it! And I can see People! Tell bright people with lovely kind faces—holding out their hands! Oh-h-h-h!" I don't understand why some of these wanderers are utterly alone, and others in crowds.

Perhaps if the same raid, or the same kind of calamity, precipitated them all unprepared for any such change out of this life together, they may have been able at least to wander together. I don't know, but many were in crowds, and called to each other. Many more seemed to be in crowds of solitary ones.

Perhaps most were utterly unaware of anyone else in their condition.

The hardest of all to deal with were the hopelessly terrified, who seemed no more than whispered dreads drifting round with an insistent beating fear in their stifled cry of "Dead—dead—dead—dead." I tried again and again to make them listen to me; the "Dead, dead, dead," continued in a frozen monotony of horror.

I gave up reasoning and shouted (if you can imagine an inward shout), "Shut up a minute! Stop saying 'Dead, dead'! Stop, I say! How can you be dead if you can say 'dead'? Stop and tell me that!" It was hard, but eventually it succeeded, though some would go off again and again into their awful crying before they could be persuaded to look.

Others cried only, "Fog, fog, fog" or "Lost, lost, lost". The side streets were packed; crowded. Some were looking for a car or bike; said they didn't know what had happened to theirs, they must go on searching.

There seemed little that was evil about them all, and little that was good. They just had no clue to what had really happened to them, or that there was any help to be sought from any but the crowds of deaf indifferent people hurrying up and down and taking no notice whatever of their pitiful entreaties—if they still made any.

I did not find one who expected to find any spirit help, though there were several with minds closed against such ideas. I can only suppose that all who looked for help would be able and ready to recognise friends and helpers, and would never wander lost like this. One was terribly frightened of listening to a spirit; had 'never had anything to do with spiritualism' and considered spirits 'most dangerous'. Another said explicitly that he had 'closed his mind to the idea of spirits' and was not going to open it.

He seemed to feel that any shadowy semblance of existence which remained would collapse if he opened his mind.

Oh, how relieved he was when at last just in common courtesy to a request—however absurd—he opened his eyes and saw love and help and reality! Two of us went to the Zoo. I almost felt hands tugging me in, and was surprised, for I did not expect to find wanderers there. But there were many, very many. The crowds of cheerful people, perhaps the children, perhaps the animals, seemed to make them feel not quite so desolate and forsaken—for all I met there were alone. I must have been a very unsatisfactory and abstracted companion, for almost all the time I was either carrying on or listening to other conversations.

There were several trying to find some grim sort of satisfaction in making rude remarks to people crowding round the cages; it was often comical to sense their confused surprise when they knew that had been heard.

On the Mappin Terraces I was eating an apple, and heard:

"Oh, you greedy woman! That goat needs it much more than you do. You look like a monkey, munching like that. I wish you could hear me say so, grinning to yourself there. I expect you were a monkey in your past life, if the truth were known."

"I don't think so," I replied. "Monkeys are so intelligent. I think I was only a sheep."

"Good heavens! She heard me! Did you say that to me, Madam?" I answered something to my human companion, and the voice went on in still more surprised alarm: "Now she's talking in another voice! Did you speak to me just now?" My spirit companion took over. "Yes. She can hear you."

"Who are you? I can't see who is talking now."

"I am a spirit who was once that woman's husband."

"Oh, then you're another dead person like me—just wandering round forever. Why did that woman hear me? Nobody ever hears me now."

"She has reached up and got in touch with us. It has made her sensitive."

"I was frightfully rude. Why isn't she angry? She just looks amused— rather pleased, in fact."

"She isn't angry because she is so glad to meet you. And she honestly thinks monkeys are very distinguished ancestors."

"Glad to meet me! Why? She can talk to that girl or anybody else she likes; why should she be glad to meet me! But I can tell you I'm glad to meet you! This is the first time I've found anyone to talk to for years, I should think. You've no idea how thankful I am to hear you, although I can't see you. This is a real treat."

"Would you like to see me?"

"Like to! Of course! Is it possible?"

"Certainly. Try shutting your eyes and looking."

"What an idea! Sounds a topsy-turvy notion, but I'll try gladly; I'll try anything once. . . . Oh, this is extraordinary! Do you look like a tall sort of light? Why, yes, you do! I can see a face! Excuse my saying so—I have never seen such a kind face! Oh, how glad I am to meet you!"

"Describe me. The woman will be interested. She can't see me."

"You have fine clear-cut features, shining with light. Hair rather thin on top. Expression very wise, and very hopeful and happy, and eyes more kind and loving than I have ever seen. Does she remember you like this?"

"He was not very hopeful or happy," I said. "But I know he is now."

"And I did not look very kind either—" But our new friend broke in again: "Are you wearing a lab coat? You look like a scientist."

"I hardly know what I'm wearing, but I was a research chemist."

"My work was research! I was a biologist. It's why I hang round here—more interesting than most places.

This is marvellous. You are evidently thoroughly satisfied with what you are doing. Can you do any research now?" I am doing research at this moment. I have never before been able to see or speak to people in your case, and there are evidently very many. I have just been learning a lot on the subject, and think we have here an opportunity for research more worth while than any we have dreamed of. Care to join me?"

"Do you mean to say there are others wandering lonely and wretched as I have been?"

"Very many indeed, but in much more pitiable state than you."

The day wore on, and others of my friends from Beyond were near, ready to lead all those we met who were wandering. Here and there in busy thoroughfares and near badly bombed places it was impossible to gauge the numbers of the crowds who jostled my mind. I do not think time was measured for them in hours and days, as with us, but in seemingly endless monotony. They had looked for nothing on the other side of death, so they found nothing.

The life which had appeared to them everything was left behind, and held nothing for them any more, yet it was the only place their minds were opened to perceive. Some were spirits of culture and ability, but for some reason their outward sight—turned down to earth—seemed all-sufficient for them, and they had never really thought of looking for any reason for life itself.

That concludes the quotation from these scripts.

I should not like it to be supposed that any one of these poor people is really lost or abandoned. The ruling spirit of the Universe is Love, and all these people—yes, and all the people down to the deepest Hells—are watched over and their progress is noted until the time comes when they have learned the needed lesson, whatever it may be, and are fit to be raised up into the next stage in their journey towards the light. It is the greatest mistake to suppose that any suffering, of whatever nature, is imposed as a punishment in the sense of vengeful retribution. It is only that every cause has its specific effect, and the misuse of man's freewill has painful effects, as the result of which man evolves slowly towards the light of wisdom.

I know no more now about the conditions in Hell than I have indicated in my previous books; it is not a subject upon which a healthy mind will wish to dwell; but it is, I think, important to know how much human beings, living in their physical bodies, can do, and do do, to help in the evacuation of those who have served their time so to speak, and are ready to move up out of the darkness.

Time and again it has been said to me, "The regeneration of mankind must come through man It is, I think, the chief failing of all the main religions of the world that they ignore the possibility—nay, rather the imperative necessity —of human cooperation in the work of the Angels and Messengers of God in raising those who are ready to rise from the lowest strata of the Astral.

This work is going on, but it is almost unknown to the world, and completely ignored by the Churches. I remember that I was speaking (at Bristol, I think) some years ago, and I described a single instance which had come the way of our Circle. Afterwards a man came up to me and told me that for fifteen years his Circle had been engaged almost exclusively in that work.

I was privileged to visit one such Circle the other day, and I kept rough notes in my indifferent shorthand in semidarkness, and reconstructed afterwards as much as I could of the events and dialogue. A trance medium was occupied first by the controlling Guide, and later by the 'patients' in succession. A gramophone was played to cover the periods intervening between the departure of one patient and the arrival of the next.

Here follows the result of my labours.

Present, Question Mistress (Q.M.), two other members, trance medium and self. Medium had a bad cough.

I was present by invitation in place of a permanent member absent in U.S.A. for a short period.

Opening prayer from Circle and from Ramamen, leader of the Circle. "You say, why do not we do it all? Why should we turn to you for help? There are many cases which we can deal with, but there are others whom we cannot reach except through the minds of earth people." Gramophone played Handel's Largo during change of occupants of the medium. "Now we will commence to do the work which the Master wishes us to do to help those in the darkness. I will do my best with what the instrument gives."

Case 1.

Why am I here?
To talk with some friends.
Have I to undergo more punishment?
No. You have come among friends: now you have passed through your unhappiness.
I killed my wife—I stuck a knife in her because the little one was not my own.
Don't think about it: have you been in the dark sphere a long time?
It seems a long time.
What is your nationality?
Italian. You do not blame me. No?
It is not for us to blame. You would be happier if you brought yourself to be kind to your wife.
Oh, no, no no no no. I have suffered.
Try to forgive her.
No.
I know how difficult it is, but be a strong man. Try not to think too hardly about her.
I would do it again. I think I will go back.
No. Do not go back to that place.
Has the little one gone?
You would not find the little one yet. You will not meet them till you are ready to meet them. We wish you well, and that love may come to you again.
No more love.
Well, kindness, then. God will be with you, and help you to understand. What is your name?
Toni Rosetti.
You are going on to better things, and you have got over that. Our prayers will be with you to help you. God bless you.

Case 2.

Have you any friends?

No friends of yours? What are friends? They are no good.

You are among friends now.

What is the catch? I thought there was no catch, but I soon found out differently. I thought my crime would die with me. What is this game? I thought there was a catch in it. You are not my class, you are not my sort.

It is character that counts. We know that there is no death.

If I had not of come here you would not have known nothing.

Look at your hands (the medium's).

What's happened to them?

This lady has lent you her body so that you may speak with us.

I don't want to use this lady. It's another catch.

No, it's a truth;

I've never been a woman.

Life is just.

No, it's not just, I know it isn't just.

Yes, it is. Later you will be able to see the records.

(What is your name? I am going to call you Bill.) You will see why you have got to go through different lives.

I don't understand.

(Medium coughs violently.)

What's up with her?

She has got a bad cold. Won't you try to move on into a happier state?

No. I have got pals there. Come out of it.

What is your name?

Bill Kennard.

Won't you try to move on? (He is a bit doubtful but ready to try.)

Good luck to you!

I need it.

Case 3.

I don't know what I have come here for; if Bill gets hold of me he'll murder me. I am one of his women. Oh, I'm in such trouble! No, I wasn't with him just now. It's a trap, so as I will go to him. Oh, I am in a mess! You see, I did die, and then I lived. I was a cleaner in the church.

The parson was very nice to me: I was only a common girl. I thought it was better than having a missus over me.

51

I liked the parson and he liked me. We didn't live together.
I wasn't that bad. He tempted me. What could I do with a kid?
Did he get away with it?
The parson got away with it. I was found out.
Won't you try to go on now?
I wont go anywhere where Bill has gone. I don't know where I am going now.
(Floods of tears.)
Are all men the same? I thought he was a good one. I couldn't make a fuss, for the sake of the Church.
What is your name?
F—S—.
Did you have a mother? Look around and see if there isn't anyone you know here?
I see a tall light.
There is someone in that light. Look and see if it is anyone you know.
Oh! it's my Aunt Lettie.
(Such a joy in her face.)
I am coming, Auntie!

Case 4.

(Medium coughing.)
I thought my cough had got me. Hi! Give me a drink.
(We give him some water, of which he does not approve.)
Haven't you anything better than this?
You didn't get anything better where you have come from, did you?
No. That's why it's Hell. Wanting drink and not being able to get it.
What is your name?
Sam Murray. Has Bill been this way? If so I am going after him. I bet he's getting a drink; if so I'll have it off him. (To me.) Have you ever had to sleep out?
Yes. I was a soldier and sometimes had to sleep in the open.
I don't mean that: have you ever had to sleep out because you had nowhere else to go? Have you ever had to pinch for a living?
Q.M. (a trifle gratuitously). Yes, he has at sometime.
We have all done all these things at one time or another.
(Finally Sam Murray agrees, without much difficulty, to go on with the 'big man' who has brought him.)

Case 5.

(A caricature of a haughty and affected female voice.)
I was invited to come here, or else I should not have come.
Who are you? I would like an explanation. I was mingled with the common herd, and I was brought here.
Will you please understand that it was not by my wish that I was brought here at all; I am not interested.
We are here to help you.
Have I been brought here for something worse?
No, not at all. We want to try to tell you about eternal life.
That has been my downfall, not knowing about eternal life.
(Q.M. tries to explain how no life can ever come to an end.)
You know that sounds rather like a fairy-tale. Where have you had your knowledge from?
From people like yourself who have come to talk to us.
(I take over here because she will not descend from her pedestal of insufferable conceit and condescension.) I ask her to trust the man who has brought her, and tell her that she can make no progress till she has learned the virtues of humility.
Q.M. then tells her who I am, and that I was a leader in the Battle of Britain. She is absolutely amazed.
And he has condescended to come here?
Which makes us all laugh. We explain that one can take neither rank nor riches across the Valley. Nothing counts but what one has made of oneself during life.
Her whole tone and appearance gradually changes, and she says in a gentle voice:
O God, make me humble. Teach me to be humble.
She won't give her full name only,
Countess Alice. *If he can do it all can do it.*

Case 6.

A friendly visit from an ex-patient, Sister Sympathaca.
A nun who killed her baby and herself. The priest would not own up.
I am so grateful. The baby is grown up now. I was in misery.
(Kisses Q.M.'s hands.)

Case 7.

*Please show me the way. Do I have to say I'm sorry for what I have done?
I was desperate; what could I have done? Have you ever gambled?*
(Q.M. indicates that she does not consider it a sensible or profitable occupation.)
*What is the end? Suicide. I did my wife in first. She never knew that
I had lost all. We were going to have had a baby. I thought death was
the end, but found that it was not. I have not got her, let alone the baby.
Oh, why are we not told these things?*
I said that he very probably was told at some time or other, but in
any case if a Spiritualist had tried to tell him the truth, he would not
have listened.
*Even if I had not accepted it, it would have remained in my mind.
Not if I had known it when I threw myself through that window. I was
brought up in the Church, but left it.
My name is Harold Smart; I was too smart.*

We told him that his baby was alive, though never born on earth,
and that someday he would meet his wife again with the child.

I have kept in touch with this Circle, though I have not sat in it again.
They have had some very moving and romantic experiences.

The most extraordinary was the case of a racehorse owner who had
had a troublesome jockey put out of the way. He had a very favourite
horse called Starlight, and he (in the body of the medium, of course)
was telling the Circle about its gleaming chestnut coat, when he suddenly stretched out his arms and called, "Why, Starlight!" And out of
the air came a contented little whicker such as a horse makes when its
master comes round to the stable on a Sunday morning with a pock-
etful of sugar. (Or should I say used to come?)

The conversation was rather more consecutive than as recorded by
me. The scrappiness is due to my defective note taking.

I would invite attention to Case No. I, where the efforts of the Circle apparently failed.

The man would not have been brought to the Circle at all unless he
was nearly ready for a change of heart. He would turn over and over
in his mind what he had heard at the Circle, and so, in spite of an apparent failure, it is quite possible that the man was later brought to
forgive, and ask forgiveness from, his wife.

It is really rather dreadful to think of the vast numbers of human souls in an earthbound condition, or worse, who need help, and the pitifully small number of living human beings who even realise that the need for help exists. Still, the work is being organised now, and recruiting is going quietly and steadily on, even if you don't see anything about it in your morning paper.

Cognate with this subject is the question of the relief of sufferers from obsession by alien entities. It would be more accurate to use the word possession, only the former word has come into general use, and so I will retain it.

In the time of our Lord the fact that human beings could be possessed by unclean spirits was universally accepted, and the Gospels contain many accounts of the casting out of these spirits by Jesus and His disciples.

Nowadays our spiritual pastors and masters are mostly engaged in explaining away the manifestations of the power of the Founder of the religion which they profess, so they explain that Jesus did not really understand what He was doing, and that the people whom He cured were only epileptics; or, if there be some who are unwilling to denigrate their Master, they will maintain that the age of miracles is past, and with it have passed those conditions which made this particular kind of miracle necessary. In other words, human beings are no longer possessed by alien entities.

I am not quite sure how long our learned theologians allow that the age of miracles persisted after the Ascension of Jesus—I presume they allow some latitude for the miracles of Paul—but I suppose that at some date in the first or second century the age of miracles came to an end and the cosmic laws which govern the evolution of humanity were abruptly altered.

What nonsense! The accounts in the Gospels of the casting out of unclean spirits are precisely borne out by happenings today, some of which I am about to describe.

Souls of all degrees of development pass into the Astral world at physical death. Those who have depended for their enjoyment of Earth life entirely upon the gratification of their physical senses are acutely unhappy in the Astral, because the physical desires remain, while they have no means of gratifying them.

Some of these souls (instructed by more experienced sinners) find that they can occupy the body of a living person, and thus experience at second hand the longed-for sensations of physical life. These excite their victims to excesses of drink or rage or sensuality, and wallow in the gross satisfaction of their appetites. Not infrequently they drive their victims to suicide or to murder, and leave them to face the consequences of a deed of which they were innocent in intention. This is perhaps the worst form of obsession; but there is a very wide range of variety in the attendant circumstances. Some spirits obsess from loneliness, and some obsess their own children in the belief that they are helping and protecting them. Some obsessions are entirely innocent and accidental—an inexperienced wandering spirit gets caught up in the aura of a living human being quite by mistake, and sometimes without ever knowing that it has passed through the gateway of death.

And so in this matter, as in almost all the things of the Spirit, it is very dangerous to generalise. Every case must be treated on its merits, and hardly any two cases are precisely alike.

Unfortunately, however, the possibility of spirit obsession is not generally recognised by the medical profession. The two (or more) personalities in a single sufferer are observed, and a disease of the mind is at once diagnosed. I have no statistics to quote, any figures I might give would be only the wildest guess, but I feel quite certain that many of the occupants of our mental homes have nothing wrong with their minds at all; they have an 'unclean spirit' and if that could be disposed of they could walk out sane into the world.

Now, I know perfectly well that Spiritualists and dowsers and enthusiasts and practitioners in the realms of the unseen generally are wont to make sweeping statements such as the above, without perhaps being in a position to adduce any very positive evidence to back their assertions. It may be that you will quote my own dicta about Reincarnation as a case in point. But in this matter of obsession the evidence that I speak the truth is being ground out week by week in London itself.

At the end of October 1949 I wrote an article in the *Sunday Dispatch* entitled *The Casting Out of Spirits* and drawing attention to the work of the Marylebone Spiritualist Association in this field: the bulk of this article is reproduced below.

Case 1.

"A large number of people in this country at the present moment are unwilling hosts to unseen guests.

They are obsessed by alien spirits.

"If these spirits can be evicted by persuasion or force the patient may make an immediate and complete recovery, though it may take him a little time to realise that he has been freed if the obsession has lasted for any considerable period.

"In Biblical times this phenomenon was well known, and the New Testament contains instances in which Jesus and His disciples evicted the obsessing spirit and restored the victim to sanity and self-respect.

"Today it is not fashionable to profess belief in the existence of discarnate spirits, and therefore many a poor victim goes to the end of his earthly days accompanied by an incubus which might be removed if a suitable technique were adopted.

"Here I want to mention a book entitled *Thirty Years Among the Dead*, by Carl Wickland. The book has recently been re-published in this country by Rider and Co.'" Dr. Wickland's wife was a trance medium, and his technique was to administer quite a mild shock of static electricity. This shock, though mild to the patient, had a severe effect on the obsessing spirit, which left its victim and entered into the body of the medium, who was close at hand; and by this means Dr. Wickland was able to converse with the spirit.

"In some cases the obsessing spirit was quite an innocent party. It had accidentally become entangled in the aura of the patient, and was perfectly willing to leave when the situation was explained. Some of the obsessing spirits did not even know that they had passed through physical death.

"Others were not really evil, but were earthbound.

That is to say that they were dependent on the senses of the body, and they had invaded the physical body of another in order to retain the sense-experiences to which they were accustomed.

"These could generally be persuaded to leave when it was explained to them how much harm they were doing to their unwilling hosts.

"And then there were other cases where the obsessing entity was definitely evil, deliberately invading the body of the victim and deriving satisfaction from the damage done and the distress caused. Such invaders had to be forcibly taken away by what we may call 'Astral Police', because they were open to no arguments and, if not restrained, would have slipped back into their victims as soon as the effects of the electric shock had worn off.

"Sometimes there might be a dozen or more unbidden guests in the aura of one host. You will remember the incident of the unclean spirit who said to Jesus, 'My name is Legion, for we are many'.

"I read this book [*Thirty Years Among the Dead*) some years ago, and it seemed to me very sad that no attempt to work on these lines was being made (so far as I could ascertain) in this country.

"Of course it is a work that must be done by spiritualists—that is to say, by people who believe in the existence of spirits who are normally beyond the range of our five senses. If you believe, for instance, that Dr. Jekyll and Mr. Hyde are two facets of a single mind belonging to one individual—if you believe that it is not possible to converse intelligently with a discarnate spirit through a medium, you will be inclined to regard the above-described technique as an offensive piece of quackery.

"Furthermore, the assistance of unseen co-operators will be essential in those difficult cases where the obsessing spirits are not amenable to reasoning or argument, and you cannot ask for the assistance of people whose very existence you deny.

"The fact is, of course, that this type of work demonstrates spiritualism in one of its best forms.

The participants ask nothing for themselves—not even the comfort of conversing with those whom they have known and loved on earth.

"The motive is service to humanity on both sides of the grave; for remember that the obsessing spirits are in almost all cases human, they are often quite innocent of intention to harm, and, at the worst, are more desperately in need of help than those whom they have victimised.

"Now, what I have to relate in this article is that this type of work has been started in this country, perhaps by more than one circle, I do not know. I know only of the personal experience which I have had in two visits to one such circle which sits weekly in London.

"They use a Wimshurst machine for the generation of frictional electricity. One member sits by this machine throughout the session, turning the handle as required.

"The second member has developed his natural gifts until he can see the aura of the patient with or without the assistance of the dicyanin spectacles developed by Dr. Kilner. A trance-medium and a secretary who keeps notes of the cases complete the party.

"The first case which I wish to describe I have chosen because it went exactly according to plan.

The patient was a grey-headed widow, quietly but smartly dressed, and having had (I gathered) some connection with the theatrical profession.

"She had been sitting by herself for the development of automatic writing, and was regularly receiving messages which she was satisfied came from her husband and personal friends. Suddenly an alien entity began to control her hand—a dominant character who refused to allow any but himself to communicate.

He had nothing useful or constructive to say, but would allow no other to write.

"This was naturally distressing to the patient, especially as the stranger began to intrude upon her privacy at times when she was not attempting to write.

"When she had described her symptoms the electrical treatment began. She was asked to hold one of the terminals, and the operator passed the other terminal repeatedly across her head from front to rear, so that little trains of sparks jumped across to her scalp. Then the treatment was continued down the spine and across the shoulders.

"After five or ten minutes of this the spirit was dislodged and passed into the body of the medium, where he was able to converse freely with the members of the circle and with the patient whom he had just left.

"It turned out that he was an American whom the patient and her husband had met in the Eastern States about 25 years ago. His story was that his parents were English and that he had never renounced British nationality; that he had come across the Atlantic with an American contingent in 1944, transferred to a British unit, and been killed in France by a German sniper.

"His involuntary hostess was indignant. 'Why did you pick on me? she asked. 'I scarcely knew you.' Well,' he replied, 'I saw you like an open door with a light all round it; so I went in. I didn't do you any harm.'" It was explained to him that he had indeed done harm to the lady; and, in answer to further questioning, he stated that for some time after his death he had hung around with a bunch of his friends, killed about the same time; but that one by one these friends had 'gone on' with a person who was always on hand to give them help when required and whom he called the Missionary.

"He said that his mother and a brother were on the other side, but that they had 'gone on' and were living together, so that he was now alone. Asked why he didn't 'go on' too, he said that he didn't want to leave the earth and its contacts.

"After a little more discussion he agreed to 'go on' with the Missionary and join his mother and brother, who had been brought to look on from a short distance away.

"He was asked to promise not to go back into the lady in any circumstances, and he said, 'What? Into that fire? Not likely!'" This bears out the statement in Carl Wickland's book that the shock which is felt only slightly by the patient has a much greater effect upon the obsessing spirit.

"At the end of my visit I asked to be given the shock treatment. It was very mild—scarcely even unpleasant. One felt a series of little pin-pricks in the scalp as the terminal was passed back over the head, and when contact was made with the head or body, so that the sparks did not jump, I could feel nothing at all."

I have chosen the above case for description because it was normal, in so far as any case can be called normal when the circumstances of no two human individuals are ever precisely alike.

Case 2.

"A Scotswoman in late middle age joined a 'Development Circle' in Scotland with a view to becoming a medium. She became obsessed by a malicious spirit, apparently of foreign origin judging by his speech and accent.

"This case was peculiar in that the services of the medium in trance were not required, because the patient herself was a natural medium. She sat down in a chair to tell us of her symptoms and the history of her case, and within ten seconds she was no longer speaking to us; the obsessing spirit had taken control and she was in trance.

"At first the spirit was very blatant and triumphant, boasting that he had prevented the development of a first-class medium and delighted with the pain and distress which he had caused to his victim.

"As soon as the electric treatment was started, however, he changed his tune and began to express penitence for what he had done, and to ask to be helped to break the connection which he no longer desired.

"But he was an unpleasant creature, and I formed the opinion that in spite of his protestations he was hanging on like grim death—very like grim death! "The patient had been in a mental home, and had been subjected unsuccessfully to the heavy shock treatment which is given in such places. Possibly this unsuccessful attempt had toughened the resistance of the spirit to electricity, because, except for the change of tone in his babblings, it seemed to have little effect on him.

"Patiently, minute after minute, the aura specialist and the medium continued to converse with the spirit, persuading him to leave of his own free will. We were told that there was a cowled monk with a St. Bernard dog who had come to meet the obsessing spirit and to take charge of him when he was willing to go. The spirit could not see the monk at first, but eventually he saw him and 'a fat dog'.

"This went on for nearly half an hour, and then, suddenly, he was gone—like a cork out of a bottle.

"The patient came out of her trance, and could not believe at first that the spirit was gone. (This, I understand, is a very common symptom.) She was in mortal dread of being sent back to a mental home for good by her relatives; but she was asked to sit in a waiting room with a member of the circle, and after about an hour was quite composed and able to leave in a taxi with her husband.

"At the time when I sat down to write this article I was in hopes that the evictions might prove to be permanent, but I am sorry to say that in this case the expelled entity later returned to his victim and, at the time of writing, is still in possession, though the fight has by no means been abandoned.

"The fact is, of course, that the Circle is building up its technique, as it gains experience, and it would be an unwarrantable exaggeration to represent it at present as being able to cope successfully with every case presented to it.

"In particular, those cases tend to be intractable where the possession is not complete, but where the entity can enter or leave the patient at will. In such cases it can avoid the shock treatment and even the séance room.

"Nevertheless, I have felt myself justified in drawing attention to this development because there may be people who themselves suffer, or whose relatives suffer, from this fearful infliction.

"Such people may address their inquiries to Miss J. M. Cocks, Hon. Secretary to the Council for the Treatment of Obsession, 42, Russell Square, W.C.I.

This Council is directed by the Marylebone Spiritualist Association, of the same address. There is no charge for treatment, but patients may contribute towards expenses according to the relief obtained.

"Possibly the time has scarcely arrived when this process should be pressed upon the attention of alienists, psychiatrists, and the medical profession as a whole, for it is not only necessary to accept as a fact the separate existence of those discarnate spirits who are the cause of the trouble, but it is also necessary to recognise the existence of and the conscious cooperation of agents of the principle of Light in the never ending fight against the darkness.

"In point of fact, they are the directors and we the co-operators, and this is scarcely a point of view likely to be widely accepted by professional men at the present time.

"The proof of the pudding is in the eating, and it may well be contended that the onus lies with the Circle of producing an adequate number of verifiable case-histories of people who have been restored to sane normality after orthodox methods have failed, before professional men can be expected to register anything in the nature of a practical interest.

"My own attitude is that, as in the time of our Lord, people are invaded by unclean spirits, and, as in the time of our Lord, these spirits are susceptible to eviction in accordance with the power and knowledge of the exorcist. The laws of nature are immutable; all that changes is the fashion which determines the type of window through which we look at them." I received quite a large postbag as a result of this article, and some new patients were secured for the Obsession Circle, but I did not receive a single letter from a doctor or psychopath on the subject of the article, though one doctor wrote from Scotland to ask where he could get a pair of Kilner glasses.

I have kept in touch with this Circle from time to time, and in February 1950 I paid them another visit with notebook and pencil. Here is an abbreviated record of three of the cases.

Mrs. S. was of mixed Spanish and English parentage, her father being Spanish. She described her symptoms to us, and among other things, she told us that she sometimes felt herself to be very heavy, as if she were made of iron. (This sensation of excessive weight is one of the signs of mediumistic powers—latent or otherwise.) She said that she was troubled with distressing dreams accompanied by a nasty feeling in the solar plexus. She had seen the face of one man dressed in the brown robe of a religious order. She was a Catholic, but not a practising one, although deeply religious.

Here the medium intervened to say that the monk was a Guide who was there to help her; also that it was her own father who was obsessing her. Part of her trouble was the result of her own intense prayer, which attracted 'the wrong people'. She had been prematurely advised to develop her mediumship.

At this point the electric treatment began, and there was an immediate outcry from the medium, "Oh, Senor! oh, Senor!" in a great state of agitation. "Why do you take me away from my child? I get cut in two." (By the electricity.)

Question Master: "Why don't you go with your friends? Haven't you met any friends or relations?"

"Yes. I have seen five of my family. They say to me, 'You go to earth to break down your child's health?'"

Q.M.; "They have a home to go to. Go with them."

"I cannot leave my daughter; but if you give me your promise that you will look after my daughter I will say goodbye, Senor. If you give me your promise I shall be happy. Then I will not worry my daughter—my darling child. I am not so strong myself. I will go away."

(This is one of several cases which I have encountered in which the obsessing spirit imagines that he is guarding and protecting the obsessed person.)

Mrs. H.—an elderly lady brought by a friend. She complained of bad dreams and occasional inability to swallow.

She felt as if she were being choked. The friend told me that she was very difficult to look after. She would suddenly start shouting, "O God! O God!" in the street.

She had been trying to keep her out of an asylum, but she couldn't keep on much longer, and seeing a notice about the Obsession Circle, had brought her along as a last hope.

The friend looked tired to death, and much more ill than the patient. Directly the electricity was applied the medium began to shout:—

"Listen to me! who do you think I am? I cannot be quiet, I cannot get any rest. I don't want anybody. O God! they are choking me! Oh, I am choking somebody else. I want to choke that lady. I want you to do something for me. I want to murder somebody. They killed me."
(All very confused.)

Q.M.; "Why did they kill you?"

"For my money. They throttled me. I don't want to leave this place where I am till I have choked somebody. I get my fingers on their throats and I squeeze, but they do not die—that's the worst of it."

Q.M.; "The woman you are injuring did not do you any harm."

"You're right. I have been in Hell. Hullo! there is somebody who has got a thing like a motor car. I'm going in it." Then he begins to cry, "Oh dear, oh dear, oh dear, have mercy on me." And then, as he goes, "God bless you." Then came Mr. S., a pleasant-looking, white-haired man who had visited the Circle before. I was shown a record.

The obsessing spirit thought of Mr. S. as a friend. He liked to accompany him when he went fishing, and so on.

This time, as soon as he was forced out by the electricity he explained: "He's a pally sort and so am I. He doesn't know who it was, but I taught him the tricks of the trade."

Q.M.: "What do you mean by 'the tricks of the trade'?"

"If I told you, you would wish you hadn't asked. Not before the ladies." Then he went on, "You told me to go away, and I did, but I don't know what happened. You didn't push me out altogether."

Q.M.; "You won't be able to stay. You're going to lose your grip. Sooner or later you will come into the light, but it won't be for a long time. Why don't you go with your friends?" The spirit explained that he did not want to leave Mr. S. because he liked him and was helping him.

The Q.M. explained that he was very much mistaken if he really thought he was helping Mr. S. Then there was some conversation about the conditions in which the spirit found himself. He said he had no proper body, but was "all thin and airy," and he also said, "It was all so cold." Finally he said, "I'm going to a better hole. (Which placed him as from World War I.) Goodbye. I don't think I'll come back." Then he pointed to me and said, "That chap's brought a lot of Air Force boys with him. I know one of them; his name's Robinson. He's brought his aeroplane. I'm going with him. I'm going up in an aeroplane. I'm not afraid."

Mrs. J.—an elderly woman, who described herself as 'emanating' lots of little black things. Questioned by the Q.M. as to what she meant by emanating, she explained that the little black things formed inside her and kept jumping off her. She also saw a little old woman wearing a cape down to her knees. She also said that she sometimes saw several replicas of the old woman at the same time. She explained that she could stop the appearance of the little black things by putting three hot-water bottles upon herself.

That cleared them all off, but they came back again.

Now, if you were to give the above description of this woman's condition to an ordinary doctor and ask his opinion of the woman's mental state, I can guess what he would say. And yet this woman was perfectly sane, and did actually see these things with clairvoyant sight.

As soon as the electric treatment was started, a quavering voice came from the medium.

"I'm a very old woman. I passed out in the country.

I want to cling on to somebody because I'm so old. I'm so tired. I don't want to hurt her. I am the lady with the cloak. There was a pond in our village; I thought I saw it again just now. I don't want to go to the workhouse. I was eighty-seven when I went out.

"I can see our Willie and Mollie and Dad. They say, 'You come up to bed with us and we'll look after you.' They are looking a bit younger now. They say, 'We've got a fire up here.' They've got a bed to put me in. I can't keep awake. I don't want to be a nuisance." And then, almost without a pause, another one in the medium.

"Oh dear! My name's Annie. I had nobody to look after me. I like to hear her say 'Go away'. I brought some black children with me; they look ugly. They frighten you.

"When the moon's up this lady belongs to the moon.

I pull out some stuff from her body: I make them up out of her body."

Q.M.; "What a silly game to play!"

"I didn't know I could do it." (She explained that she had watched a séance where ectoplasm was being manipulated, and copied what she saw.) "I have been very comfortable. I know I harmed her."

Q.M.: "How much longer are you going to play this silly game? Why don't you go with your friends? Are you going with them?"

"If you are not going to be happy I will go away. I promise you I will not do it again. They say 'No. You must go right away'. I am happier than I was. I will go away forever. I will say goodbye—again goodbye all."

It will be realised that an apparent cure is not always permanent. There are three possibilities:— The dislodged spirit may change its mind and return; there may be other obsessing spirits which have not been dislodged (there are sometimes many spirits obsessing the same patient); or the patient may be of the type that attracts wandering spirits and puts up no resistance to a would-be obsessor.

It is a regular practice in mental hospitals to give what is called 'shock treatment'. This is a very heavy current of comparatively low voltage, and has the most painful results on the patient through the terrific muscular spasms which it causes. I have no doubt that obsessing spirits may often be dislodged by this treatment, but as nothing is done to reason with the spirit and persuade it to depart, it returns in many cases as soon as the effect of the shock has worn off.

The current from the Wimshurst machine is of very high voltage and tiny amperage. As I explained in the article, it was practically imperceptible except when the sparks give a little pricking sensation as they jump across to the head. And yet the effect on the spirit is intense: witness the remark of the American—"What? Into that fire!" —and of the Spaniard—" Oh, Senor, I get cut in two." I do also wish to emphasise the point which I made in my article. It is not only the patient whom we have to consider. The obsessing spirits are human, and are often in much greater need of our help than are the patients themselves. For deliberate obsession is the highroad from the Astral to Hell. I should imagine that Annie, who manufactured the 'little black things', had gone a good long way down that road; and how happy will be the members of the Circle if, in addition to relieving the patient, it should transpire that they have been instrumental in arresting her downward course and turning her footsteps towards the light.

You may have noticed that I do not devote much space or attention in my books to the business of 'proving survival'. Perhaps you can understand me when I say that these matter-of-fact conversations with dead people in the course of the various processes which come under the generic heading of 'Rescue Work! bring with them an atmosphere of reality that carries with it absolute conviction.

Subconscious conviction, if you like. One doesn't stop to think, "Am I imagining this?" or "Is the medium cheating or making it up out of her own subconscious?" One is thinking all the time, "How can we help these poor people?"

CHAPTER 6

ASTRAL LIFE

Well, now, the dead people about whom I have told you so far have all retained the earth mentality. They are living on the earth level, seeing and moving among living human beings, even though they may be invisible and inaudible to the latter. As a general rule they do not see or contact beings much above the earth-level, and they have no abiding place of their own apart from the earth.

As I have said, I do not propose to attempt to give a picture of life in the various Hells, so I shall now try to deal with those people who have settled down to live in those median levels of the Astral where life is reasonably happy and comfortable, but where the conditions of Earth are retained with very little alteration.

The two most important recent books which deal with this stratum are *They Survive* and *Travellers in Eternity*, both received through the mediumship of Miss Geraldine Cummins, and edited with the assistance of Miss Gibbes, whose relatives play an important part in the latter book.

They are published by Rider & Co. and the Psychic Press, respectively.

At first sight they do not appear in the least to fit in with the accounts of the future life given (for instance) in Vale Owen's Life Beyond the Veil, or in R. J. Lees' books *Through the Mists* and *The Life Elysian*.

There is nothing to be gained by trying to twist facts to suit our fancies. All the books mentioned above bear the stamp of truth and sincerity, but the widely differing circumstances described by the two types constitute a stumbling block to the recent convert to Spiritualism, who is inclined to say, "They can't both be true." It is my task to attempt to show that they can both be true, as well as a number of other apparently mutually contradictory accounts of discarnate life.

They Survive was the earlier of the two books to be published, and parts of it are extremely amusing, particularly the section which deals with the Ross sisters: two elderly ladies who continue in their new life the friction and mutual criticism which was the regular feature of their association on Earth. The later arrival from Earth cannot forgive her sister for cutting her out of her will. As evidence of the persistence of character and personality beyond death, this section is very convincing.

The main purpose of the book is to adduce evidence of survival, and the compilers succeed very well in their task.

Twelve cases are described, some of which have been submitted to the Society for Psychical Research; but the thing that would probably strike a reader who is a newcomer to the study of after-death conditions is that all the actors, with the exception of one fifteen-year-old girl, seem to continue in very much the same sort of life that they led on Earth, and are not in contact (or at least in regular contact) with people of higher development and greater knowledge.

Travellers in Eternity is in a sense a continuation of *They Survive*, because it continues the story of Case II in the earlier book, that of Lieut. Nigel Gibbes, 8th Hussars.

Most of the characters in *Travellers in Eternity* are near relations of Miss Gibbes, and we must be grateful to her for suppressing her natural reluctance to publish intimate family affairs in order to give us a most educative picture of the conditions of life, in that particular family, in the early stages beyond physical death. In doing so she has made her relatives into public characters, and I am sure that she will forgive me if I discuss their affairs dispassionately and in contrast to the experiences of other people in other circumstances.

The central character of the book is Hilda, the wife of Miss Gibbes' brother Arthur, and the mother of Nigel, referred to in the previous book. The whole family revolves, as it were, about her, both in Earth-life and afterwards, trying by every device to save her from sorrow and anxiety, particularly with regard to the Battle experiences of Nigel in North Africa, where he was first wounded and later killed in tank actions.

Arthur and Hilda were a devoted and exemplary couple in Earth-life, but the book shows that there is no enduring tie between them, and that Hilda's real affinity is her brother Harold, who comes closer and closer to her, finally displacing even Nigel as soon as the latter has obtained a confident foothold in his new life.

They recreate the two family country-houses in their new world. The building is done by thought-power, and Hilda lives a sort of 'Alice Through the Looking-glass' existence, owing to her lack of concentration. During one meal the roof comes off and the dining-room ceiling slips off sideways into the garden.

They go on living an imitation of their Earth-life for quite a long time. Two years after Hilda's death they are still eating three meals a day; it is explained that this is really unnecessary, but that they can gratify their desire so long as it remains with them.

But they could not always be sure of their food. "My lovely Elizabethan furniture, the dinner-table, the glass and silver and dishes on it, vanished one day when Arthur was here and got into a bad temper. It really was most awkward.

You know Frank and Nigel like to enjoy a good dinner, just as they did on earth.. . . Well, when Frank and I saw their favourite dinner and wines fading into the air, they looked so dismayed and disappointed that Arthur and I burst out laughing, forgot the cause of our disagreement and so stopped further destruction." Hilda's main work was in the garden, but even here, when she allowed her attention to wander, the rosemary would come up smelling of garlic, the azaleas wouldn't stand up, colours got mixed and everything went wrong.

One thing that struck me as very odd was the occupation of Arthur. For one thing, it amused him to gain access to the historical records and find out all about mistakes which old-time generals had made and had succeeded in covering up. That was natural enough for a man who was interested in military history. But his other occupation was the catching of enormous salmon. (He even went to live in Scotland, so as to be near the fishing.) Now, this is the sort of thing that chokes off many an earnest enquirer. They say, "How can such things be? How can it be permitted to take animal life (assuming that animal life persists after death) just to satisfy the atavistic pleasure that human beings derive from killing things?" The answer, I think, may be derived from the story of the inquisitive gentleman in the railway train who saw on the rack opposite him a small box pierced with air-holes.

He said to the man sitting opposite him, "Excuse me, sir, but would you mind telling me what you have in that box?"

"Not at all, sir," replied the other; "it's a mongoose."

"And why do you keep a mongoose, if I may ask?"

"Oh, I'm taking it to my brother. He sees snakes." The inquisitive one pondered for a minute. Then he said, "But they are not real snakes." "No," assented the other cheerfully; "but, then, this isn't a real mongoose." That is the answer: they are not real salmon; not even real Astral salmon. They are merely thought-forms built up from the subliminal mind of the sportsman and temporarily animated by a fraction of his consciousness.

It seems a bit far-fetched as an explanation, but I believe it to be correct. Of course it is by no means an elevated type of amusement, and I should imagine that most decent folk grow out of it fairly quickly.

In Appendix II of a book attributed to F. W. H. Myers, *Beyond Human Personality*, received through Geraldine Cummins, the following extract is taken from an explanation concerning woodcock shooting in the World of Illusion.

"These woodcock may be described as thought forms conceived and shaped in the man's subconscious mind.

The sportsman's craving to shoot birds creates the birds.

They are merely alive in the sense that they are animated by the electrical waves of thought emanating from his mind and stimulated by his desire." I shall be referring again to this book later on.

Although the people in the book for the most part apparently wear modern dress, they are aware that "Guides or guardians wear white robes that glow or darken according to the mood and character of the man, woman or child they watch over." After about three years in the Astral, Hilda writes: "I have found my guardian angel, and I call him Methuselah! He said rather a wise thing: 'The life we live in others is far more important than the one we live in ourselves when we are on earth. The great teachers in the lives of their pupils produce an effect far beyond anything produced in themselves in the growth of their own self.' "They do also realise that there are distant levels to which they themselves will eventually attain. For instance, Norrie—Harold's wife—has 'gone on', and becomes increasingly out of touch with Harold, who was never her real affinity, but Hilda's.

Little by little one imagines that one can see these people's future beginning to crystallise. Hilda and Harold seem to be shaping towards creative work as twin-souls in the Flower World. They believe that they are to have one more life on Earth together, and then will be free from the wheel of rebirth, and will be able to go ahead along their own line.

It is interesting to note that Hilda, at any rate, despite her tendency to cling to Earth-habits and ideas, accepts the idea of Rebirth almost immediately. Like most people (myself included), she is inclined to be a trifle didactic about this deep and almost infinitely variable mystery, but many people pass right through the Astral, and even the next stage beyond, without accepting this principle, which, to me at any rate, lies at the root of all hope of long-term progress for humanity.

Arthur's fondness for research, too, begins to be turned to good use. Towards the end of the book Arthur is given a new job. Hilda writes: "He is in a very good mood, because he feels really important at last. He has a job! He has in a manner of speaking become a Recording angel. (Laughter!) I said so and he became quite amazed and said Don't talk rot.

His work is to study the pasts of certain Nazi leaders who are shortly coming here. He finds it interesting. Personally I should prefer to keep a butcher's shop to working on such horrible stories. The odd thing is it's the first time since his arrival in this world that I have seen Arthur looking as if he had really arrived in heaven! So he is very busy, and we all call him the Major-General. He has adopted that air of Major-General—at least that happy grimness of authority, lightened occasionally with a faint but kindly smile." So perhaps in the tomorrow of Eternity we may find Harold and Hilda as twin flower-angels, and Arthur as one of the forty-two Assessors, or perhaps a Lord of Karma.

Well, that's all I have to say about these two books. I think they are important contributions to our knowledge concerning a state of life enjoyed (for they do enjoy themselves) by an appreciable section of humanity. They are also thoroughly amusing to read, and nobody should miss the saga of the two Misses Ross. *The Living Dead Man*, by Elsa Barker, also deals to a considerable extent with people living very close to Earth conditions; however, as I have dealt extensively with it in my book Many Mansions, I shall not repeat myself here.

But there is just one thing that I should like to say about the book. When I wrote *Many Mansions* I was very much puzzled by the egocentric character of the writer. He was intent on collecting as much magic knowledge as he could, stamping it indelibly on his memory, and then "coming back with Power" to Earth as a great magician. I want to say that since then I have read two more books from the same source. They are called *War Letters from a Living Dead Man* and *Last Letters from a Living Dead Man*. (The 'War' was that of 1914-18.) I have only to report that all his' toughness' fell away from him while he was helping the war-dead, and he finished up as a completely selfless and respectable member of Celestial Society; and, if he wasn't quite so interesting in that capacity—well, you can't have everything! There are, of course, plenty of other books which deal mainly with the early stages of life on the other side of death. I might mention, perhaps, the Rev. C. Drayton Thomas' books, and particularly In the *Dawn Beyond Death*, which is interesting and amusing, besides being informative; but I have perhaps written enough to make my point that there is a type of book which may give the inexperienced and unobservant reader the idea that this is all there is to look forward to in the future life.

Of the books which deal with later stages of the life after death, one of the most important is *The Life Beyond the Veil*, by the Rev. G. Vale Owen. I have dealt with this book at great length in Many Mansions, and shall not repeat myself here; but there is a rough dividing line between this type of book and those which I have hitherto mentioned, and this is that the characters have for the most part discarded the habit of wearing clothes of Earth-pattern, and normally appear in robes and ornaments appropriate to their stage of advancement.

Other well-known books of this latter type are *Through the Mists and The Life Elysian*, recorded by R. J. Lees.

They have attained to the status of classics of Spiritualist literature, and, though they are written rather in the style of a Victorian novel, there is nothing surprising in that, because both the author and the amanuensis were Victorians to the fingertips.

I shall not devote space to reproducing any part of such well-known and easily obtainable books; but the point which I wish to make is that an inexperienced enquirer, reading one of these 'White-robe' books, and then reading *Travellers in Eternity* (for instance), might possibly be discouraged from further study and enquiry by the great difference in the conditions of life described by the two types of book.

Since the time when I acquired the leisure to study this engrossing subject of life after death I have read many books, good, bad, and indifferent; but I think I can say that I have read none from which I have not learned something, provided that the author has been honest.

Whether the author is incarnate, or is discarnate and writing through a medium, if he is making a genuine effort to describe conditions as they exist, we can always make some addition to our knowledge, and even the decision to reject certain proffered information as probably mistaken is a good exercise for the intellect and the intuition; for we must always keep at the back of our minds the possibility that our judgment may be at fault, and that we may have to modify our conclusions in the light of further evidence.

There is one type of book, however, which seemed to me to be altogether vicious. I refer to that in which the author claims to be in contact with some wholly imaginary Master or Adept, and puts forth his own personal ideas under the spurious authority of this entirely fictitious entity.

In justice to to British Spiritualism, I may state that such books are very rare, if indeed they exist, in this country.

There is a book called *Beyond Human Personality* (Ivor Nicholson & Watson), attributed to F. W. H. Myers and received by Geraldine Cummins, which is interesting because it can be compared with Myers' book *Human Personality and its Survival of Bodily Death*, written by him during his lifetime; and also because it takes the reader far beyond the point where most other books cease to follow the progress of the human being after bodily death. It is commonly accepted by several schools of thought that there is a point in the 'Mental' stage of human progress where form is transcended. Myers (if it is indeed he) takes us considerably beyond that stage. I do not feel called upon to say whether I accept this account or not; I have insufficient knowledge to form a judgment. I merely draw attention to its existence, and leave readers to form their own opinion, if they are sufficiently interested to pursue the matter.

The last book to which I wish to invite attention here is called *Onward Humanity* and is obtainable at a cost of eighteen shillings from Alec Bussey, 39 Palace Street, Norwich.

It is a combination of three volumes received successively, and I must say that I personally have read the book with very great interest. Mr. Bussey's father is one of the principal contributors, but by no means the only one; and perhaps the main value of the book is that it gives a good deal of the personal experiences of a group of people who have reached the upper levels of what is often called the Summerland without losing touch with the Earth. The things that they tell us from their own experience are of great interest for comparison with other accounts from people at a comparable stage of development in *The Life Beyond the Veil* and similar books. And I may say at once that there is a considerable measure of agreement.

But the authors by no means confine themselves to their own personal experiences; they cover a wide range of interesting subjects dealing with different varieties of Angels, life on other planets, the organisation of the solar system, pre-human incarnation, a contribution from Vale Owen's guide Zabdiel and another from Joshua, a forecast of the eventual system of world government, and many other items too numerous to mention.

Lest I be carried away too far by my enthusiasm, I had better mention here some of the defects of the book (or what appear to me to be defects). In the first place, the pedant will find that he has to make allowance for colloquialisms and lapses from the strict rules of grammar. I freely admit that it is petty to allow oneself to be worried by these. I know that many recipients of messages from the other side are very particular not to make any amendments, but to publish them verbatim as received. I think that this is a pity, because as likely as not the fault is really one of transmission, for which the medium is mainly responsible. Still, there it is; you will find some expressions which will grate on a scholarly mind.

In the first place, of course, one must allow for the high probability that conditions may vary widely on different parts of other planets, just as they do on Earth.

Two exploring Martians, for instance, might come to loggerheads over the question of whether Earth-dwellers lived in round thatched huts, or in houses a hundred storeys high, according as their travels had taken them to Central Africa or to New York. A single visit to Earth's surface might indicate that it was composed of jungle or desert or cultivation or ice or water. All this is obvious enough.

But there is another factor which must also be taken into consideration. None of the Earth-travellers who visit other planets see things as we should see them with our eyes. They see things at the Astral or higher levels, and therefore their accounts may be absolutely 'wrong' from our point of view.

In the instances given above I have assumed that the adventurous Martians could see Earth on the physical level; but there is no guarantee of this. Quite possibly they might come from the Martian Astral, and see us in our Astral Summerland. Their report then reads: "The Earthians live in uniformly peaceful and beautiful surroundings. They wear coloured robes and flashing jewels.

They all love one another dearly and the very idea of war among them is inconceivable." So one must make very large allowances for differing circumstances when one reads two apparently contradictory accounts of visits to the same planet.

I have a good deal of evidence that such visits do take place, and that in fact they constitute an important part of the training of the evolving soul. Nor, indeed, are such visits confined to the globes of our own so-lar system, but the longer the journey, the more elaborate must be the preliminary preparations.

More important, perhaps, from the evolutionary point of view are the expeditions in the shape of 'personally conducted tours' into spheres, or states of being, more refined than that which constitutes the soul's habitat for the time being.

But it would be useless to give a summary of the contents of this book; the difficulty is to think of any aspect of life upon which it does not touch in one place or another.

Try to get hold of a copy and read it for yourself. If you subscribe to a psychic library, ask the librarian to include a copy in his stock.

If you have a predominantly sceptical mind you will throw down the book with a grunt of indignation; if your mind is predominantly credulous you will accept the whole book uncritically as Gospel (which is perhaps more dangerous than throwing it down); but if you are at all like me, you will regard each fresh statement as a challenge to your intellect and your intuition. Of course you will have to let much of the book simmer indecisively in your mind for the time being, for you will have no yardstick against which to measure some of the ideas; but as you read and study other books and pile up personal experience, one by one the ideas which you have been holding in suspense will fall into place in your mind and will be (always provisionally) accepted or re-jected, as the case may be.

If I may sum up my ideas of the book in a single sentence, I should say that it brings into the field of intellectual examination questions of which the ordinary person does not even realise the existence as the subject matter for critical meditation.

CHAPTER 7

DISCARNATE ETHICS

Now I want to devote a couple of chapters to a collection of messages which have been received by Mrs. D. O. Roberts of 58, Whitehouse Avenue, Boreham Wood, Herts. I give her name and address with her permission, because she has failed to find a publisher for a series of messages which are in my opinion of such interest and variety as to deserve a wide circulation. She has courageously decided to publish the book herself. It is entitled *How Do We Live*, and contains eighty-eight letters. It is priced at 10s. 6d. and is obtainable from John Watkins, 21, Cecil Court, W.C.2, or from Mrs. Roberts direct.

Mrs. Roberts is not altogether a stranger to us, because she is the person who brought help to the earthbound spirits on the bus and at the Zoo, whose stories have been related in Chapter 6.

I find it extremely difficult to make a representative selection out of the hundred and more messages of this series which I have seen. The difficulty arises from their extreme variety, and whichever stories I choose for reproduction I shall still leave much of the ground uncovered.

This same variety makes it difficult to give any sort of general explanation of the apparent purpose of the stories.

They started, I think, by an organised attempt to prove survival by the concerted action of a number of communicators with uncommon names. The hope appears to have been that these names, or a number of them, might have been identified, and so the continued existence of the personalities concerned might have been accepted. Readers of *Light* may remember that in the May 1949 number there appeared an article by Mrs. Roberts entitled *Hands Across*. She gives short sample extracts from a number of letters, and a list of about fifty names, in case readers of *Light* might be able to identify any of them. At the time of writing, half a dozen names have been identified with varying degrees of certainty. As a matter of fact, I think it may have been the possibility that a number of these names might be identified which enhanced the difficulty of finding a publisher for the series. At any rate, that is not my object in picking out a few of these communications for reproduction—it is what is written which is, to me, more important than the writer.

It may be noticed that there is a tendency for a number of the messages to conform to a slightly unusual style of expression, with an abnormal repetition of certain favourite words. This is an interesting feature of the series, and is presumably due to some subconscious influence on the part of the medium; or it may perhaps be connected with the transmitting mechanism on the other side. For instance, one communicator at least could speak no English, and when he wished to refer to windmills and canals in Holland they came out as "towers with big hands and water roads So it appears that there must have been an effective, if imperfect, interpreter somewhere in the chain of communication.

If I may digress for a moment, this question of foreign languages in mediumship is interesting and worthy of study.

Several of the incidents related in my previous books have involved English conversations conducted by people who almost certainly knew no English (e.g. Heinrich in *Lychgate*, page 46).

Two or three people have written to me to point this out and to imply that as a result of this they are precluded from believing any part of the story. Well, of course, people must form their own judgments, but I am inclined to think that this particular judgment is just a little hasty. The mechanism of communication is so much more complicated than we suppose. There is an explanation of one method of Spirit communication in Volume III of *The Life Beyond the Veil*. In this method no fewer than thirty-six persons were employed.

It is fairly easy to understand that a medium in trance can write or speak some language like Chinese with which she is totally unfamiliar, the explanation being, of course, that the entity to whom she has given place is communicating in his own language and using the hand or the vocal cords of the medium for the purpose. But it is not so easy to understand how a German who knows no English can speak in English through a medium who knows no German.

Yet this can happen. And in one case, while we were doing rescue work, a German came through speaking in German which we could not understand: realising the situation, he spoke very slowly and only the simplest phrases, such as *Mein freund* and *Danke schon* which we could interpret. But the next week, through the same medium, he spoke to us in English, but rather broken English with a strong German accent—again perhaps accounted for by the employment of an effective but imperfect interpreter.

I recall, too, an odd incident which occurred in our own circle. 'L. L.' was not in trance, but was describing what she saw clairvoyantly. She stated that my wife was present, holding a dog in her arms. I jumped to the conclusion that it was Becky (a much-loved King Charles' Spaniel), but Chang said to 'L. L.', "No; it is a Cocker Es-pa-ni-ol". It seems obvious that he would not have found this queer word in either L. L.'s conscious or subconscious mind.

So don't be too dogmatic as to what is and is not possible in the mechanics of communication. Query every abnormality and improbability, by all means, but don't form your judgment too hastily.

I have picked out samples which give, I hope, a fairly representative impression of the whole; but there are two types of message from which I have included no samples.

One is that kind of message which purports to emanate from well-known persons comparatively recendy deceased, and the other category consists of a series of messages from a group of people who claim to be intimately connected with the writings of William Shakespeare, Shakespeare himself being included in the group.

These latter have no considerable connection with those aspects of Spiritualism with which I am dealing in this book. "Homer said the schoolboy," was not written by Homer, but by another man of the same name." And I personally feel that the spirit of this comment might be applied to the perennial Shakespeare-Bacon-Oxford controversy. However, I know that there are many people who take a very lively interest in the dispute, and, if so, they will now be able to make contact with Mrs. Roberts if they so desire.

Mrs. Roberts has seen this book in manuscript, and she tells me that she does not altogether agree with my views about the general object of the messages or about the Shakespearean communications. I readily agree that she is more likely than I to be correct, but I have dealt with the messages in the light in which they struck me.

Here follow selected messages.

I am going to start with a message from Richard Home.

It speaks of the original idea of trying to use these messages to prove survival by establishing identity, and the disappointment of the writer that the attempt had not succeeded in the way intended by the communicators.

He writes as follows:

We try to be wise in being patient, but it is hard to see opportunity wasted.

This true appeal to be tested was being made to try to help with establishing identity.

This could at least have been tried, but people are blind to any light which does not conform to their own preconceived notions of what is or is not true or important.

I think it is wise to wait for ill winds to blow good; this is generally the case when guidance is apparent, as it is.

This writing itself is guided by some spirit higher than I, and we all know we are being led in this enterprise, for not one of us thought of trying to write. Yet it is a simple idea, and easy with one who looks to find reasonable replies to questions which begin to prove the wish to understand how truth operates.

This is the line of wisdom which we must try to understand, and this true line is such a joy to us to follow.

We can see this lovely ray of light in the dark places, like a kingfisher trying to be the bearer of brilliant thought in dark and shaded places, over waters of swift thought.

I think it is lovely to think our spirits were evolved by the creator from such truly inspiring animals as this beautiful bird.

This is true wisdom, to see truth in everything that lives.

I wish we were able to reach others with such ideas. It is foolish of people to fear what only brings love and joy and hope and peace.

Richard Horne.

I like his remark "I think it wise to wait for ill winds to blow good and his simile of the kingfisher. I hope that he may be able to comfort himself by thinking that the writings have served their purpose, even if not exactly in the way that he expected.

The next comes from a Jew named Foulis Holber. One of his friends introduces him thus:— "Foulis was in a concentration camp. He tried to be more forgiving than this world. He is wise in loving, not in this worldly way." Foulis writes:—

25.11.48.

Let me in willing brotherhood try to use your pencil.

I wish it could acknowledge this debt of gratitude I owe to people of this country who have sheltered some homeless Jew.

I am a Jew, and tell you this at the outset because I now realise my people have had the truest opportunity that any nation ever had of redeeming their enemies; and now I can see that many have so redeemed those who ill-treated and tortured them.

Try to help them by loving the torturers too.

Think that they knew not what they did, as the Jews themselves did not know when they killed the Lord of Life.

They drew on their own heads the same fate; to redeem men of their sufferings.

I will try to explain how this was brought about, for a foolish cry could not have brought such a fate on a nation unborn.

It is because they were the kinsmen of Jesus, and believed they would have a king who would let them share his kingdom, and give them honour above all the peoples of the earth. So it had to be that they followed him, though the way was terrible indeed, for he tried by suffering to lead them to God.

They are too true still to be brutish, in spite of all that men have done to them; but their feeling that they are a chosen race is their very salvation, for it upholds them in all their sorrows. Often they know not how or why.

But it is the truth that Jesus is their king in a way beyond any earthly kingship, for he is also a Jew, and one of this truly loving race.

For this is true in spite of what men see of the Jews' greed and love of money; they are loving to their children in a way other nations have never been, and often they are ready to forgive those who despise them—often without a cause, for they instinctively feel the challenge of the Jews: "What think ye of Christ? Whose son is he?

"I will write again, for I have much to say.

Foulis Holber.

26.11.48.

Let me, in being able to write, be able also to love with sincerity all who read; for I shall know if with reading words they also understand, and try to love the people who have brought so much to the world, and suffered so much at its hands.

I think we try indeed to be in the nations what Christ is to each individual, but it is true there is no perfection of Love and Forgiveness, as with him.

Try to remember the beauty of what Jews have done in the world. This bible, which has helped to mould what is best in the behaviour of civilisation, as well as in the lives of individuals—even if they are unconscious of it. Think of its influence as a power of thought which is still unsurpassed in the literature of the world. It is the true treasure house of human achievement. This inspired book looks at the world's whole history in lovely thoughts which make clear the divine plan behind the bright thoughts that man can think.

I wish I had the gift of words to tell of the truly colossal temple which fills the world, that is the thought that men have built on truth they found in the bible. I think nearly everyone has laid a stone at some time in his life.

I think we try too to find a way of life which is truly harmonious in living peacefully with all who will welcome us in their land; and they are never the losers, for Jews produce still greater thinkers, and it is well known that they are broad-minded people with true feeling for the lands of their adoption.

I wish I knew how to think truly of those who try to be wealthy of this trash which is world wealth. It is only this true sense that their nation is royal that makes them try to provide a show of wealth. These have not understood what royalty really is; this is why they unconsciously turn to display.

This is the explanation of their wrongful extortion too.

They know in their spirits that the world owes them tribute, and in the crude ways of earth they take it wherever it appears to them to be due. For they rarely steal or commit violence; this they feel is unbecoming in a chosen people.

It is in ways which are hardly or not at all understood by people that the great tribal consciousness of a race will guide their actions, though often it is only mirrored in some superficial way.

I long to bring better understanding between peoples, for I thought this true thought in earth life; this is why I can express it now.

I wish I could see those who befriended me, but I am not high enough to do more yet than follow this thought that has proved to be true.

Foulis Holber.

Forbury Gibbon was a guard on the Tube Railway.
After opening with some generalities he continues:—

I was a tube conductor and never tried to help myself at the word of others, but instead gave orders to others how they should travel.

Now I am in a very different position, and cannot very well understand how I came to be in this plane at all, for I am not either loving or thoughtful, and did not particularly care for my work.

Perhaps this is right that I had an open mind. I did not believe in anything that mattered much, and never tried to believe in the teachings of others, so I may at least have had no hindrances, but the fact remains that I am truly on this plane, and it is a glorious thing to be so free and able to help others in this way of trying to love and not being, able to be angry.

For it is really the case that I cannot be angry if I try. I did try to be angry once, and it was no good, for I only laughed at my own attempt. I think it was really ludicrous, for no one is ever angry here.

I do not think it sounds to you as if it is a really colourful life in the matter of living emotions, but rather insipid and aimless. This is a tremendous mistake, for it is a life full of truly exciting events, and ability to make things such as the earth dwellers cannot possibly imagine.

We can easily make anything we care to think enough about, as it is in thought that we work. So I found I could not make much as I had hardly learned to think, so I tried to start thinking, and soon made a real thought form of a train which ran underground, and came in the tube railway, just as you have just seen.

Then I tried to understand why I did this, and it was because this was the kind of way in which I could serve.

For I can now travel on the Underground and help thinkers to travel in their thoughts, for it is the chief thinking place of very many.

This is a truly astonishing thing that men can think better as they sit, or even stand huddled, in the Underground in the stuffy air, but it is true that travel does really help some to think. The travel of their bodies stimulates the travel of their minds, and it is a real chance for them to think out their problems of all kinds, and try to find true reasons for their own journey through life.

I think this is a true Tube of life in darkness and noise for very many, but it leads into daylight in the end, and it is a truth that all tunnels have an opening. This is a true picture of life; into a tunnel in the dark, with no timetable or even Tube map to help, but only a trust that the train is in the hands of one who knows the right way, and can guide the train to air and sunlight and home at the end.

I think this is my message. Now I shall be better able to help my travellers as I have learnt another true vibration of earth in this writing, which is a teacher of how to put ideas into minds which are looking for them.

This is my name; Forbury Gibbon.

It is a strange idea that some people do their thinking in the crowd and clatter of the Underground, but one can quite imagine that it is so. Possibly it is the only part of the day in which they can be uninterrupted.

William Whiteley explains

"I worked in this hospital that this thing called shock is done in".

After some personal comments he writes:

I am a true type of helper of thought, for I held people's wrists when they received this treatment you call shock for mind troubles. I hated this, and thought this kind of treatment must be wrong, but I tried to love these sufferers, and the love I had made the guides better able to reach them in the horrible fright which seizes the spirit in this shock.

This is the true cause of the cures that sometimes occur; the guide is able to hold a bright hand, and the brightness is grasped by the terror-stricken spirit.

I cannot think it is a true kind of help. This is the nearest thing to 'kill or cure' that man has tried, but he is terribly reckless to his brothers. This is a truth he must one day face, for each is his brother's keeper.

I long to help healthy people to know how they can offer help to the truly unhealthy by only loving; then their guides can use love rays to bring them light. This is true to be taught to all, then love can find ways to heal.

I am William Whiteley.

Of course the shock treatment to which he refers is not the mild kind I have described in Chapter 6, but the terrible variety given in mental hospitals.

William Martindale comments on sickness and old age as blessings in disguise as an introduction to full consciousness in life after death. He has a great sympathy for the wandering spirits whose plight has been described in Chapter 6. This is because he was a stretcher-bearer at Dunkirk, and now continues in the same line of work.

This is hard to understand, but it is true that many are lost for a long time; but not to be endured as time, for time is not there.

I think illness is often the means of saving them from being lost at all, and they can be taught to look for help as a child, and to try to see, then they will have a true attitude of spirit when they die, and will find help easily.

I think it is better to suffer trouble in earth life than to be lost as this troop you met. It is true this long list of sufferers tried to help themselves in vain through the passersby, who could neither see nor hear them, though they could help by loving each other. This gives loving rays that make it possible to light the fog.

I think this is strange, but it is true. Love is the first thing that becomes visible to the spirit after death. These helpless spirits had not even looked to find love or they would have seen it.

I think the shock of sudden death is truly difficult for some who have not tried to love or look to be loved except in a purely natural instinctive sort of way.

I hope others may now hear of this, for this is love directly applied, and a far better means of finding these truly lost; for this too is true, they are not visible to spirits as they cannot assume a spirit form without some recognition that they are spirit, tacit or actual. This is true and terrible that many are really missing. I hope love can find them all, for many are searching.

I was a stretcher-bearer in the Red Cross, so I hunt for any in no man's land.

My name is William Martindale.

(It was this last war, in the truly horrible place at Dunkirk, I think, for I recognise the place in your mind.)

I now insert a message of a different kind. It comes from the same group, but from no particular individual. It deals with an incident which received much fortuitous publicity in the newspapers at a time when sensational news items were in short supply, at the end of 1949. The inhabitants of a haunted house had made application to their local vicar to exorcise the ghost, and this letter is addressed to him, a Bristol clergyman.

Apparently the B.B.C. took advantage of the temporary public interest thus aroused to stage a broadcast on psychic affairs, in which the subject was treated in a manner which appears to have caused distress to the invisible audience.

I did not hear the broadcast, so I am in no position to offer an opinion as to how far their distress was justified. It seems to have been real enough, however.

We hear that you mean to exorcise this ghost.

We can only be interested in this idea of exorcism from a spirit's angle, and not from the point of view of the dwellers in the house.

How can they hope to be happy afterwards if they have driven this poor woman away from her last home in the earth sphere?—for she will be homeless, and a sad wandering spirit.

But if they can take her into their home, and make her feel that she is free to dwell there until she can be told quite clearly by their own ideas towards her that she need not worry about being a helpless presence any more, then she may we hope look for some help in the spirit world; for many will be there only too eager to lead her.

We hear too that a ghost is by no means an unhappy thing to have in the house if not interfered with at all.

We fear that the recent broadcast was very unhelpful indeed; we know that there were many unhappy spirits disturbed by the unseemly mirth of man.

We hope this man's high love for all will help this poor woman to be welcomed into a better place than this lonely room she was inhabiting.

How can we lead her if she is only turned out into outer darkness?

I have included this message of set purpose, because I think it teaches a much-needed lesson. The poor wanderers who, for one reason or another, are bound to earth, are human souls in need of our sympathy and help. If those who make mock of them or who treat them as a sort of astral vermin would only make the effort to put themselves in their places (remembering that the contingency may not be so remote as they suppose), a kindlier outlook might be engendered and, if unable to help, they might at least refrain from adding to the distress of the poor wanderers by facetious levity.

I now propose to reproduce extracts from a number of messages on what I may call Discarnate Ethics; and I must begin by a disclaimer that I am necessarily in agreement with the conclusions to which their arguments tend.

But I also wish to disclaim any attitude of superiority or infallibility. It may well be that the communicators are right and I am wrong; only it seems to me that a release from the flesh and all its shackles has led some of our friends to advocate a line of conduct somewhat ahead of that stage of evolution to which humanity has yet attained. Maybe this is a good thing; maybe we should aim at a target which is yet out of range as the best means of improving our shooting.

But I am going to start with one with which I personally agree. It is by a public hangman who must have lived about the time when India was taken over from John Company.

You will notice a reference to a man "going back to animal again". Disregard this for the moment—I will deal with it later.

We try to find the kind of letter that helps someone each time, but it is not easy sometimes to find the kind of tale that is at all representative of any sizeable class.

However, here is a little tale which may interest some, for I was no humanitarian, but a truly brutal type of man, such as hardly ever is known, for I had the work of trying to hang these poor people that did wrong.

I had no idea how terribly wicked I was, and thought I did a brave thing that most would be too squeamish to do in ridding the earth of monsters of wickedness.

How awful I found my mistake, for I was met by one I had killed. He forgave me, and asked me to be his friend, for he had few friends as he had not made many, and these had left him when he had become a killer. But I was a killer too, so he hoped I could be friendly with him.

I had a terrible shock in meeting him at all, for I had no thought of such people living any more. In fact I had given little thought to anything that mattered.

I was just a man who felt impelled to be brave, and had chosen this dreadful way. I found my line at the expense of others. I now know the awful crime this is, to kill a man; especially in cold blood, and a man so terribly unprepared to die. For nearly all are quite un-prepared to look to be led, and wander unhappily looking to find help among hard-hearted people who care nothing for them. I had a true feeling that it was a bright thing to kill these poor people, but I was the worst killer of all. Though not so wicked as the men who told me to do this work, for I only obeyed orders.

I think no one who thinks the kind of thought I now have to think can be a doubter any more that no life should ever be taken in cold blood. This cold-blooded murder is always the worst kind of killing, for there is no sorrow or love to help the poor unfortunate man who has not been successful in finding a true purpose for his life, so needs love and help in being assisted to his line.

For all have a line to God, and this murder of men is the murder of God. However depraved he may be, this depravity is the failure to find God in any way at all.

This means failure to find loving purpose in life. This is the worst failure a man can make, for he has no hope of being an individual, but must give up and go back to animal again.

I know now that this is the case with several whom I killed, but I cannot help them, for I helped no criminals in earth life, so now I must stand helpless to be a comforter of them, even when I see them killed as I killed.

But I try to meet them, but this is hard for they cannot see me un-less they look for one to lead them. Some do, but some never think of any sort of help at all, but only of despair. This is awful, for they can see nothing but blackness if they look for no light. I try to be a bit of light, for I was almost despairing when I found what I had been doing to these poor spirits. But I cannot do much, for I am too weak to do much myself in such horrible darkness, for this needs strength and love to reclaim such spirits.

That is true that many mothers have met their poor sons, but some are in no helping condition, for they were despairing too. This is often the reason of their child's despair that they despaired; then the baby sees only blackness instead of love, and is the wonderer if there is any love in the world from the first.

I wish people would try loving such children, however unlovable they may seem, for this is the only way to help them to be their true selves, as all can but so few are.

I will try to help more now, for this is earth wave that I use, and I think can sometimes reach the wanderers, but I do not understand how. Perhaps I can be helped by many others who love these poor people, then we will meet them with more strength. I think I am the bolter of doors in the spirit world, for I try to bolt the doors of blackness and turn those away who wish to despair.

I hope I will now be more successful with this troop to give me help, though I do not understand how.

I was the man that did this terrible work long ago, for I had dreadful times myself, being helped by this man I had killed. He had only been a killer because he was chased, for he had robbed. But not because he needed things, but because he was brave too and had a longing to do some daring thing. This is how he found his line, for it is the same as mine. We both seek to do brave things; this line of courage makes us brave to be daring now in helping others who are brave in defying all help. But this is not easy, so please love us, to help too. This is all you can perhaps do. If there is a man who is brave and not helpful, try to let him know bravery is a true line to God, but he should be loving too.

I have the task to try to think of my name. It was Philip Folpery or Polperro.

Yes, I think, but I am not sure. I was so lost.

But I know I was in this London, and in the time of the king that was trying to be king of India, for he had no true right to India I thought, but I think he was successful. But I only thought this one true thought, so I remember it.

I am a very low spirit, but I try to love, and be higher by being a helper to these poor spirits who wander lost in darkness and fog. Be loving to them please.

Apart from the ethical problem raised by the question of capital punishment, there is also a very practical aspect from our point of view, though it is little regarded by our legislators, hereditary and other, when the subject is discussed in Parliament. The general view is that, whatever the theoretical merits or demerits of the case, we at least are well rid of some very dangerous characters as soon as we have executed upon them the sentence of death.

This is by no means necessarily the case, and it sometimes happens that we turn loose into the Lower Astral a strong soul filled with bitter hatred and determined to wreak his vengeance upon the Society which has driven him prematurely from his body of flesh. We may experience the effects of his subsequent activities, but fail to connect them with their true cause.

The better the mental development and education of the criminal, the greater his power for mischief after he has been killed. The Nuremburg sentences and their execution constitute a case in point.

Now comes a short essay on Justice. This seems to me to be an instance of that outlook which has run ahead of contemporary human development. I have no comments to make which will not be obvious to all my readers.

> We will speak of the question of human justice.
>
> It is truly monstrous to see men sitting in judgment on each other because the one was fortunate enough to find life easy—perhaps because he could see a reason for his life, or because he tried to think wise thoughts—and the other because he knew of no reason or love behind life, and did not think of looking for one.
>
> The judge sentences this poor ignorant man to prison, where any chance of his finding his reason is taken from him, for there can be no reason for such a life—in bare ugly buildings, in unnatural conditions which humiliate and deprive of self-respect—and without this most necessary of things in this life in the body, liberty; or love without which no man can grow gender.
>
> It is pure folly to judge men at all.
>
> It is why this man is unable to find his line which people should ask, for line that is found will bring a wish to serve and joy in service.
>
> This is a principle which is already understood, yet people still try to cheat each other of their chance to find a line of approach to God, and drive them to despair. This makes them revert to animal again; the human spirit has been crushed out by those who judge their brother.
>
> Henry Calverley.

Next is an essay on Patriotism. It takes the idea of sharing of personal property and applies it to nations; and, if the voluntary sharing of personal property seems to be still rather Utopian, the application of the principle on a national scale would seem to be still more so.

> Perhaps the idea of patriotism is not yet very clear in men's minds, for some consider their country is right if it is wrong, and others that

their country is always right but others may very often be wrong. There is however no country which can always be right, and perhaps no country which can always be wrong.

But as for patriotism, this should not wish for the country to be right or wrong, but to be the most understanding of others. For no country which does not understand the view-point of others can be considered a really good country; for this is the chief function of countries, to know each other's points of view and be a good neighbour, and thus safeguard the people it has in its territory against any encroachment or act of violence, for the neighbours do not envy it in any way.

We do not think this is an easy idea, but surely it is the thought on which foreign politics should be based. For no nation can be strong enough to fight all the others: and no country should wish to fight any other; and no country can fight any other without itself being a victim of warfare.

No country expects the disgrace of being a victim of defeat, but it generally happens to be one of the belligerents.

It is strange that everyone always feels confident that his country will win a war, even if it is not very righteous.

But what is a righteous war? We do not think there is any such thing. A nation attacked must defend itself.

But we cannot think it is an axiom at all, and are not at all prepared to call this a righteous war, but an unrighteous war because it attacks the undefended country which has sent these attackers out of its borders. This is a strange way of looking at war.

Men say, supposing they only fight the invaders. This is something not quite so imaginative, but not a great deal better, so let us suggest that war is never righteous, and these invaders should be treated as unasked guests. It is certainly not the habit of a housewife to withhold food from an unexpected guest. But, you may say, this guest is a robber; he will not be a robber if he is entertained willingly.

But how can a nation entertain invaders, for these are not guests or robbers, but fighters, and come to kill and destroy; this is a far worse problem.

We hardly like to suggest that it is a far simpler problem, but we think it is, for (a) They would not come unless they were in some way envious of the country they invade.

Which goes to show that this country is unfairly provided with this world's goods and its ways of living are too high and luxurious.

Or, (*b*) That in some way it is deemed to threaten the existence of others.

Now whether there are other causes of war I do not know; I may be over-simplifying, but I think most causes fall under one head or the other.

So I suggest that the patriotic thing to do is to be very willing indeed not to have any higher way of living than any other nation which is at all comparable in latitude or population; and also not any less than these either, because this would make the country's own people envious. The aim should be to be fair with all neighbours in the world family of nations.

Now how can this possibly be achieved? Man must work this out for himself, but I think we can suggest some principles.

First the country must not be greedy of course. We have dealt with this. Each country may work out its ration in comparison with all the other countries, and this would set a fair standard of living; and if it is a serious drop, we can consider ourselves patriotic for we make a real sacrifice for our country to be able to play its part in establishing world peace.

This idea is really new, I think, but I do not see why it should be, for it is obvious. Cannot the leaders of the nations see that it is so and suggest it at their councils? But we must leave this to man to discover, for human justice is a thing he says he values, so why does he not value it? Secondly every country should have adequate protection against invasion by insuring that it has nothing for which to be invaded. If it has empty lands it should welcome peaceful invaders from any country which has not enough room for its people, and can use the soil and enjoy the climate of these empty lands.

It is not for me to say where this should be done, but we can say one thing which is rather glaring; that Japan is so overcrowded and the U.S. and Australia have such vast desert spaces.

We think national sovereignty is to blame for causing many wars; it is not only held to be loss of face to be mistaken in judgment, but also to make a threat and not carry it out. The first of course is only a childish idea, and the second is the idea of the foolish parent of the child, who of course should never threaten at all. And would not if he knew that the child was a totally independent spirit that can always please himself whether he obeys or not. I see that this is not accepted, for little children must be supported, and even trained as people say, by their parents.

This is a strange idea to us spirits, but of course we have no care of physical safety at all, and can hardly judge on this point. But it is not exactly physical safety to hit a child, and this is the usual threat which is carried out.

Now what about the idea of hitting the other nation? We think such a threat is an absurd one and should never be made, and certainly not carried out, for there cannot be any question of not being hit back. For the nation that is hit will certainly retaliate unless it has become patriotic according to our ideas, in which case the invading nation will lose face.

Now we suggest that all the nations should see these things, for we think it is true idea that they can now perceive them, and we are hoping that many of the leaders do more or less see things like this. But why not the ordinary man in the street? Let him be a patriot and ask for less if his nation is greedy, and more if it is undernourished; but let him compare himself with all the others, and not with a more favoured nation only.

This is all we have to say, but we feel we could be patriotic if this is patriotism, and in no other way can we try to help our country. For we are English and wish England to lead in being a fair dealer with her neighbours.

The writer suggests that a country will only invade another if it is either envious or afraid of the latter.

Here, I think, he rightly suggests that he may be oversimplifying. In those countries in which all power is gathered into the hands of one individual, not even a pretext is needed for invasion and annexation. The weaker and more harmless the country, the more likely is it to be invaded.

The references to 'loss of face' and the over-population of Japan suggest that this essay may have been written by an Oriental—not that there is any harm in that, but nowadays those who "let the legions thunder past" may have little opportunity to become "plunged in thought again Peter Frisby's essay on Courage is the next on my list, and if you can read it with dry eyes, you are tougher than I am.

I think this is the true tale that I have to tell. I was most interested in things to do with people that did not be brave, and tried to be a true intelligent leader of timid people, for I was not brave, but had partly found I could be a person as brave as others by only trying to think I was the kind of person who tried not to show fear.

This I was afraid was real cowardice, but now I see it is not a true cowardice at all, but a true kind of bravery, as I had this idea that I would not let the cowardice master me.

Then came the war, and I had a terror of fighting, and longed to be able to escape, and tried in my mind to find some reason for this kind of escape. But I found no reason, so I told myself that I must not show fear, but carry on like other men as if I were not afraid. But this was so hard that I nearly gave up and developed a nervous trouble, but again I knew it was only a brave idea to be pretending I was not afraid, yet this idea still kept with me.

Then I made a decision I would try and see if I could inspire others to be braver if they knew I was afraid, but did not show it. So I let some of my friends know how terrified I was, and let them feel that they could help me and be braver this way, as I needed their support. This I found was a truly good idea, for I found I could not let them down, and they found they could not let me down, so this helped in both ways.

Then I got wounded and lay ill and nearly died, and I was in two minds to give up and be afraid of death, and nearly died in fright at the idea of dying. This would I now see have been a very sad thing, for such are not able for long to look for help; they are too frightened to think there is no cause for fear, and this makes them too hardly reached. This is a terrible condition, so do tell any who are afraid to die to look to be led, as there is always help for all in leading them to a secure place and being able to show them a haven of refuge from all their fears.

I did not know this so I became worse. And then I saw a fresh idea; that I had at some time to die; that it might be a high adventure, and that I might help others to be readier to die if I became interested in the thought of what came next. So I tried to face this illness, and think that if I died I would die in a brave spirit, and not because I was afraid to die.

Then I began to get better, and became the friend of some who really had to die, and did not bear to face such an idea, for they were young, and had not found a true satisfaction in living or any reason for their lives. So I tried to let them think I might be going to die too, though I knew by now this was not the case, and that I had a true confidence that this was a high adventure, and not a terror to be dreaded.

And I tried to think why I guessed this, and found a truly beautiful reason in this love of life. For I argued if life is so loved, it must be because it leads to a true conclusion, and that there is a true reason for it, and it is not the brutal truth that it is a thing of no value. For I had no true confidence myself; this was only a brave idea that I tried to grasp.

Then I was well again, and must fight again. It was worse now, for I had a glimmer of purpose in life, and did not wish to lose mine, and thought if I took away a life of all who were born I was in danger of destroying life, which now became for me a holy thing. I think I did not really think these things out; I only sensed them, for I hardly could formulate my ideas; I just had them.

Then I had a terrible task—to be in a firing squad, and shoot at one of my own comrades who had been afraid and tried to be this coward who ran away. I hardly knew what I did, for I had no true reason to guide me, but I tried to feel a confidence that I did a true thing, and I tried to believe that this was true; that a man held a treasure in his life, and that he should not be robbed in cold blood of this strange treasure that might be his.

Then I tried to help him in the thought I was in terror too, but I tried to feel secure that I was right if I was not brave, and I tried to love this poor man who tried to help himself and had failed as I had nearly done.

Then I became indignant, and this helped me to appear braver than I was, and I refused to shoot, and I said I would be shot myself first; and this was mutiny, and I was tried too, and in terror that I too would be killed. And it was a terrible time, and I was again on the point of giving up.

But I had this idea more firmly by now that life is holy and not to be taken in cold blood.

If it were not for this I would have tried to be again a coward and let them make me be able to say it was a true error that seized me and I would not disobey again. For I now had this brave feeling that I did not care, for I knew I was right and I made a resolution not to be a coward any more, but to be brave enough to do a brave thing if I saw it needed doing.

I had found my line, which was courage, and I think this was why I truly became brave, for I did not now feel afraid any more—except of course that I still loved life and hated to be bereft of my treasure.

This was the attitude I now took, and it is a bad one for a soldier, for he is not a good soldier if he decides for himself what he can consider right. This I tried not to see, for I had no idea that war was a truly wrong thing, but thought we were all fighting for true freedom, and that no one should refuse to fight and was a coward if he did. Then I began to see that war altogether was a wicked thing since it took lives of all young men who loved to live, and who perhaps were just as afraid as I to be bereft of their treasure.

This was a terrible thing to face, and alone in a prison in the Battle area in the true fighting which seemed to be calling me to fight too, and not shirk as I seemed to be doing. I tried to be sure, but it was a hard decision, but at I last I had a true sense that this was a right decision, and that I would not help to kill anyone again.

This I had to tell when I was led in front of my officers, and they thought I was mad, and that I must be suffering from shell-shock, and kept telling me to plead sick and ask for leave, for they did not want to kill me in cold blood as they had done to my comrade. But I felt a confidence that what I did was right in face of all men that knew more than I did, so I said I was not ill, only sure that it was wrong to kill, and that I could no longer fight.

Then they grew angry at my stubbornness and I was sentenced to be killed, and had to face this terror alone, for all my friends agreed now that I must be mad or a coward who was afraid to fight. This made it very hard, but I tried to feel confident though I had really little confidence in anything at all. It was only that I had caught a glimpse of my line and it called me to be brave.

Then I had to be killed, and it was a terrible thing, for I loved my life and was not even ill or being loved and pitied, but truly blamed and cursed. And this thing that is called death released me, for as soon as I was dead I saw how true I had been in this thought, and how sad was the sight of my friends trying to hate me. For I knew in their hearts it was only fear that made them try to do so; it was love I could see still trying to make itself visible even in my friends' hearts, for many pitied me truly and hated to have me shot.

This was a queer thing that one who had to shoot me was my best friend, and I saw he thought he had done his duty, but it was almost more than he could bear, but he was determined to do his brave deed too in killing his best friend in cold blood, because he thought it was the brave thing he must do. For he only thought of being brave, not of daring to be brave enough to do the right thing.

I loved him more now, and could see him loving and grieving over me, so I tried to be the true idea of being brave enough to do the right thing in his ear, and it helped, for he became a tower of strength in his family. And then he died, and now we work together and are the givers of ideas like this to any who grope for such ideas to help them to face danger and death, and these terrible things that men do to each other in the name of justice and discipline and all sorts of man-made words that have no real meaning, for they are not spiritual things at all, as we now see.

I love to be a helper in making this letter, and only hope it may be read by someone who is afraid to follow his best thoughts of what may be right in face of all terror and even death.

I think I can now add the name my people were ashamed of. It is Peter Frisby.

Yes; it was the last war; I think in France, but I can only see the things that last, and these details pass away soon when one is turned away from them. I loved my home; it was in this land in the country, in the lovely hills, in the beautiful lakes in this lake land. I think I may have been helped by these great mountains of strength, though I did not think it at the time; I was too bordering on fear to look to the hills that guide the life of men to climb.

"Loving Enemies" is written by an anonymous Frenchman; I have had to cut out about a quarter of it as it is rather long.

Loving Enemies. I never thought war a good thing. As a small child I thought it was foolish to kill strangers in cold blood, and not know how many we succeeded in killing, for it seemed more important for us to kill more than the enemy and we only knew our own losses. I could not understand how it could help either side that so many should be killed at all, for no one seemed any better for it, but only much more unhappy at the end.

I think I knew that we could not hope to be victors over our enemies without the conviction that we were right, yet the enemies seemed to have this same conviction, and how were we both to win? For this was so important—to win, and then we would be safe from our enemies.

I suppose it is true that a beaten side is not safe from its enemies, but I thought it better to risk being overrun by enemies without a war, and then we could always die for our country by refusing to obey.

I see now this would have helped very little, for it would not be loving the enemies, and this is the real warfare in the spirit world. It is not enough to be ready to give one's life for one's country, for it is the duty of everyone who loves his country or home and free-dom—to be ready to die if threatened with some tragic curtailment of liberty; but to love these tyrants is another matter. I see now how marvellous it is when someone does achieve this, for his spirit really can mix at once with those of his enemies and turn them into friends.

Even if they do not consider him a friend they can love his efforts on their behalf unconsciously, for they realise someone is wishing them well, and think it may be some kind spirit they can think of or remember in their youth; for most have some spirit that can soften their hearts and lead them into a gentler frame of mind. Some memory of a mother or a gentle friend of their baby-hood comes to their mind just at an uncomfortable time for the perpetration of a bad deed, for this spirit helps these other spirits in their gentle work of softening hearts and making tempers kind till their habit is gentler and kinder and they are disposed to come to terms with enemies.

I can really say this with conviction for I know by my own experience that this is so, for I really tried to love some enemies who were my prisoners in this last war.

I was not inclined to be loving to them to begin with, but one of them seemed to want to be kind to me. I wondered why this boy should trouble to be nice to me until he told me he was trying to love me because I was his enemy.

I was quite astonished because although I did not care for war I had no such thoughts myself, but tried to be a good soldier and keep my feeling out of it.

Many I think are like this, but not many had my good fortune in being loved by an enemy, for we became fast friends. He was a boy and I a man, but I loved him as a son, and I think he loved me almost as a father. He was not a real sort of pacifist for he did not think war was wrong at all and had not thought about how to do without it, but he really wanted to try this plan of loving enemies, and had the chance since I was his enemy when he became my prisoner—I was his gaoler, but he tried to love me for this very reason, and we were apparently widely different, for I was a Frenchman, and he was a Frenchman of another colour who had been made to fight on the other side of Africa. But I did not think of him as French or black when I grew to love him as my own son, for our love made us quite independent of such superficial distinctions.

But I now know that it was his love for me that started it all, for he tried this idea to see if it worked. He was just a simple native of this land where I met him first, but which I cannot name and neither can he, for these things have ceased to have any meaning for us, but our love is now a strong tie which we know will last forever.

One day this thing which was so likely to happen came, and we were both killed. But instead of finding ourselves in any unhappy condition we found we were rejoicing to be so free because the war was over. We looked at each other and saw that we were both alike, and this made us curiously happy too, for evidently, we thought, some marvellous arrangement had been made which made us alike in race and colour and everything.

One thing puzzled us both; where were all the others of our old camp? For we were with a lot of other people like ourselves who were jolly and happy because the war was over and we had all won. We could not quite see this, but we did not worry about it for this crowd was all so happy and quite unaware of any difference at all, though when we talked to them they told us they were of all sorts of different nations and races and colours and suchlike.

And different religions too; for some were quite amazed when they found I thought this was heaven and that I must have died, for they said this was a nonsensical idea, for when people were dead they did not exist any more. For of course they thought they still lived, and were quite prepared to enjoy life now that there was a chance.

It was a strange sort of enjoyment, for we all went hunting for someone to befriend, and these people were in all sorts of strange difficulties. We thought this must be the aftermath of war, and we were doing the usual sort of clear up that must always be done to find any lost soldiers in out of the way places; for we did not understand quite what we did, it was all so curious and strange. But I gradually came to the conclusion that I was quite right and that this was heaven; but not what I expected, for I think I had expected something much more uninteresting where good people sat round and worshipped or something of this sort. For I had been brought up a Christian in the land of France, but not made to believe too much of what I was told, or I might have found myself in this dull place.

We were now quite free in every sort of way except that we could not quite make out what had happened—but the war was over and we had won; this was quite definite.

I see now why this was so for we had all succeeded in loving an enemy and this had beaten war in us.

We were a large crowd of people. Many girls and boys who were quite young were with us who had made friends with enemy soldiers billeted in their homes, and some of the soldiers they loved. I think we all thought this was curious, but did not understand why not since we had won the war, so could now all be friends.

It never occurred to any of us to wonder how we could all have won, but I wondered how I could have been the victor when I found several of my own men who were needing help so badly; they were not able to see their way at all as the enemy they said had blindfolded them. I could not understand this at all, for I told them the enemy was completely routed, but they maintained that they were pursued all the time and were only able to get away by fleeing all the time in this foggy, dark wood. I tried hard to see what wood, and realised they were not in their right minds, for they talked of enemies all round them, and were looking at my friends and our party who were all winners of the war, and described them as a bunch of bad enemies.

I tried to reassure them, but nothing would convince them that these were not enemies, and of other nations than their own, so I had to leave them to skulk in this imaginary wood and hunt for others who could more easily be helped.

But I was now pretty sure I knew I was killed and wanted to tell my boy that this was so, but he already knew for he had been told by one of his fellow negroes that he was dead too and quite unable to make any living man hear him. We all tried this and found it was so, and were a bit frightened for a time, but we did not mind much for we felt so happy and had won the war.

We really were confident about this, and all of us equally confident too, for we all belonged we knew to each other in some way, and our side, whichever it was, had won the war....

We did not know what to expect as we were always finding new ideas. One fellow could not think what to do as he had lost his company and could not find his C.O. anywhere, but we did not mind about C.O.s and were all in a sort of equality that made officers unnecessary, so we tried to explain this to him. He would not hear us, for he did not want to be drawn into this kind of mutiny, and said it was dreadful, and that we should be shot for not having officers. We said we had won the war, but he said he was quite sure we had not, for he saw us in his old eyes and some of us were enemies. He could not see how we had all won the war, but we were sure of it, and he loved to be with us, so he found an officer among us and put himself under him and was quite content for he thought he was now correct.

This illustrates the kind of thing that fellows think when they are first killed. I do not know of any other particularly interesting idea, unless it was that we longed in vain to lead some who did not want to be led although they could not see, for they thought we were spies.

We did not succeed in finding any who could lead us as a group, so we tried instead to help ourselves, and find out what to do. This was not easy for we were very inexperienced, but this we had, that we loved enemies, and we tried to find a way to help enemies towards love, for we did love to help this war against war.

We did not know whether we could do much, but we tried to breathe loving thoughts wherever we saw the worst hate, and we succeeded. We soon found out that we were not on our own any more, but with a great host of such breathers; we had taken our opportunity and it led us to our real occupation for our heavenly life, for we had all found this idea of what we could do before in earth life when we had resolved to love an enemy.

The enemies we had loved were enemies in arms, and we now found these were not our real enemies. Our enemies were mostly our own neighbours who were in some way not loving to us and whom we did not like, and this was the root of being an enemy. Here is the enemy all should love, and not worry about those who are on the other side in holding some strange idea, or faith, or some kind of thought that makes them different; for these are only differences, there is no enmity here.

But when war comes it makes enmity general between all sorts of people, and at least we had tried to fight this, but we have much to learn about loving enemies.

We had to begin to think just how we had failed among our own friends and in our own lives, and how we had disliked people, but this we had—we had set out on our road.

The early part of this dramatic story perhaps comes under the heading of an idealism which goes beyond practical present-day politics, and is also a little illogical, because if "it is the duty of everyone who loves his country to die if threatened with some tragic curtailment of liberty then the duty of dying is presumably consequent upon the duty of resistance.

This problem of whether or not it is right to resist aggression is very difficult to solve satisfactorily from an ethical standpoint. My own practical answer, as an imperfect member of an imperfect society, is to resist aggression in all cases where I am able to do so.

But, ethically, I should say that it is not only permissible but incumbent on an able-bodied member of society to fight in defence of the lives and liberties of others.

It may be that this Frenchman's ideas conform to a code of ethics more advanced than mine, but certain it is that the support of high and shining angels has not been withheld from my countrymen and me while we have been engaged in physical struggle with the forces which were attempting to overwhelm our country and civilisation.

In any case, as soon as our French friend and his young protégé have got themselves comfortably killed, their ethical problems vanish, and they can continue the process of loving enemies without heart-searchings or other distractions.

The essay on Communism with which I conclude this chapter contains much food for thought. But first it is necessary to point out that what the communicating spirit means by Communism is not that which was meant by Karl Marx or Lenin or that which is now practised by Stalin. He says that this is "of course" the opposite of Communism; so you must try to make allowance for this lack of definition when reading the essay.

Communism. A Discarnate Spirit's Point of View

There is a true cry for some basis of love to help this pillar of Communism to stand in the temple of the nations, for it has no solid base.

This is truly a pillar of the nations, and one that the nations badly need, but the base is lacking, for there is none.

The true base of a beautiful strong pillar in the temple of the nations must be love. These pillars must be all different and all strong. Some are delicate and beautiful, some are massive and high, but all are necessary or the temple is incomplete. The roof is the brotherhood of man, and no whole roof is possible without every pillar.

This pillar of Communism is a central pillar and holds the centre of the whole structure. There is so little peace in the world because this central pillar is weak and ill-founded.

But this is not all; the other pillars are not helping, but are pulling the roof away. The other high pillar of the roof which is democracy is heaving the weight unfairly on this weak pillar, and even deliberately trying to undermine it, and this pillar does the same to them by clinging to the ground with surface roots, for it has no real root.

We have changed our image, but it will help the picture we try to draw, for trees interlacing are the best kind of temple. This tall great tree is in danger of falling, and these other trees want it to fall. But if it falls it will drag them with it, for they cannot occupy its place, or lace their boughs over the gap, but will be torn and broken with its fall, or even pulled over as well. This they know, but cannot see how else they are able to help this temple to be completed.

There is a way, for a tree can root more strongly if it has help equally all round. This is figurative of course.

If all other kinds of opinion can tolerate even its evil ways, this will help it to become more balanced and able to stand more squarely, and no longer feel the desire to cut off boughs that pull here or there, for it will be able to support all its superstructure.

It is the need of Russia now to be tolerated by other countries. There is a high purpose for her. This huge people has a great soul and a line of high inspiration for the world, but it has not found its true reason for being a people yet; it is still only a herd of persons held down by a highhanded tyrant who stands, in the name of Communism, to be a dictator to his brothers.

This is of course the opposite of Communism as most of the true communists know, but he cannot help this inverted role, for he inherits the high place that the truly tyrannous rulers of Russia held before him. He has taken the throne of Russia by murder. This makes his person the representative of these he has murdered, for their spirits do not rest easily; they are proud and seek to rule as they were accustomed to.

They could do no harm at all if they were loved by some of their subjects, for these could serve them for a time, till they had been rescued from this hell of illusion that royalty creates for its unhappy heirs, but hardly anyone mourned them in spite of the comparative blamelessness of the last family and the innocence of its children, for their ancestors held terrible sway for generations. This is the sins of the fathers being visited on the children indeed, but in a very special way.

Violent revolution is almost always a failure, for it only removes one tyrant to set up another. This is because the spirit of the first—often a powerful family spirit—takes control of the one who follows and makes him the first minister of the state, and wreaks vengeance through him on those who seem insubordinate. This is a blind sense of getting righted again, for they hardly know they are dead, but feel banished, or half imprisoned or in some sort of captivity, but trying to gain command again.

I think people will hardly believe this; it will seem to them far-fetched and highly improbable, but hell is terribly real to those who have lived a selfish cruel life. They live for long, even centuries some-times, in a sort of half dream trying to influence those who have been their friends or enemies, who are in their places. This is the fate of all bloody revolutions.

The kindred phenomenon of strikes following wars is the same kind of occurrence. Men are killed violently for some cause, as they think; but they do not know they are dead and wander round trying to find some cause for which to fight, and find a focus of discontent over some perhaps quite trivial cause, and come and foment disaf-fection till an almost purposeless strike breaks out.

The earlier wars were always on a similar scale, and workers had no power to strike, but there would be outbreaks of brigandage and robbery. Boys that do crimes after wars are easily the prey of these unhappy restless spirits that look for some daring thing to do to end this dismal wandering kind of war, so they find an adventur-ous young brain that has too little scope for healthy high-holding of his head up—this is not good English, never mind. This boy hears the temptation to do a thing and does it; he hardly knows why, but he has a feeling someone tries to dare him to. This may be his own brother or father or friend, for these poor fellows killed in war gen-erally wander long and unhappily before they can think they are dead, and call for help to be led to the spirit world.

No spirit can help them till they try to help themselves.

This is a true proverb as nearly all proverbs are.

But the spirits of these ancient royal houses are little likely to call for help. They were accustomed to be waited on, and never helped. It was their prerogative to be helpers if they chose, but not to need help; except of people to make them less helpful of themselves, or armies to fight for them. So they look for people to do all sorts of things that are unreasonable for them, or for groups of people with some grievance ready to be an army for them, for they see the mood that obeys or fights, and feel they achieve something as is unhappily the case.

Haunting that can be seen is an occasional accompaniment of such attempts, but rare because it makes the spirit very weak to make itself visible, and though it does not know this the effort is considerable, and only a strong resolute spirit will do this—though there are other forms of apparition which I do not know much about but which recur for long, and which is a different thing from a persistent attempt to command.

This is the state of Russia now. We think this kind of domination of the people can easily be recognised as the opposite of the true thing the beginners of Communism had in mind. Their theory is that all are equal while they live, and then, they think, there is the end; this is the whole history of man, to live and die. But his children can live better happier lives if he now lives better. This is a high ideal of unselfish service, for its aim is for the next generations, not for self. This should to some extent redeem this revolution, but its truth is so distorted that it is little help, for it gives no hope of liberty to the individual, but only oblivion. Though I think there is some idea of influence surviving.

This is the truest part of such a creed, (For this is a creed since it is believed and taught) for here is the surviving influence of the Tsars and their murderers making common cause to wreck liberty and love, since neither could find a place for either in their opinion that the common people needed neither.

This truly is a fearful idea that man must live and die, then cease. How can men live such high self-abnegating lives if they believe they have no hope of loving in eternity the love that they see here in their lives?

It is the tragedy of Communism that it denies the eternity of love. This is the real denial of God, for He was little to be found in the churches. They preached a rather similar creed to the Tsars, that man must be as he was created, and serve or rule without question or love that could truly help him, for it was only his accompaniment to increasing the population.

This is the terrible mistake of the theorists who plan the lives of men. They hardly think love is a force at all, though they appeal to it in propaganda; for the men must give these lives that are all they have to save their love and little ones, who must live and die the same.

This seems useless, to fight to save those who are in any case doomed to oblivion. There seems little point in being born, for this help is useless to them if they only have to give their lives in turn to save the next batch of cannon fodder.

It is true propaganda to urge men to fight for love, but if these men only thought they would see for themselves that here is the key, for it is love that leads them. Love is lovely in their eyes, for it is all that makes life worth living for most of them; they loathe fighting and do not love their work, but they love their loves and their little children who love both of diem.

Here is the basis of Communism, and Democracy, and all sound forms of living—for the family to live in peace and love. This is the true position for which man lives; to find love, and build it into something beyond the instinctive love of his animal ancestors, for he thinks truly his love is higher than this, and God-given. This is if his thought is that there is a loving God, for he need not think this to be able to find Love, which is the same thing.

I think this is hardly guessed though the Christian churches repeat often that God is Love, but even they think love is little use compared with arms, and fight to protect their god of love, as they call him. For no God of Love needs protection, for this is power invincible; the only eternal thing that man can find to help him in his life and death, for it is his love that makes him a living spirit. If he finds no love at all he will die, but he need not die; he can live.

There is a love possible for every man, for all can love some man or woman or friend, or even animal. It is the love that many men bear to their loving animals that leads them in this spirit world, and leads them truly, for it is truly a part of God, and not animal instinct, which is only for its own kind.

It is true perhaps that the love of man and woman is instinctive, but it need not remain so. The seed of love is earthy, and sown in earth life, but it can grow into the plane above and let its branches spread so that birds of living thought harbour in these branches. This is the simile to which Christians are accustomed; I think this is its literal meaning that they can prove if they choose.

The true pearl that is the priceless possession is the same.

This is the treasure for which a man is wise to give all that he has, even his life if it really is for this, but not if it fights against love and life by making physical war.

I long for more people to try risking all on this pearl, and letting the truth of the power of love prove itself.

For here is the truth we can see; the power of one enemy lover makes a bomb like an atom bomb. This is hardly believable by man because this power is spiritual and gentle and invisible, but here we see it in this spirit world splitting the atom of his personality and releasing power unbelievable indeed. It is true that we too can hardly believe it, for this is the help that God now gives; He returns to man his own weapons in spiritual form of good for evil, though He cannot compel man to receive them.

But there is power in plenty if man can only dare to love.

Even if a few dare to love there is power sufficient, for there is a huge storehouse of such power on this side, and there is little doubt that the heavens can open and drop these bombs of Mercy and love for men. Let them only beseech love to be their leader. It has the property of being the same to all whether it is called God, or only the love of helping the neighbour. But the highest form is love to the enemy.

This begins, as the proverb has it, at home, for enemy loving is free, and no malice that is a bane to a neighbour is love.

This is the first place to love enemies—the garden fence at home.

One of the most important thoughts contained in this essay is the idea that the semi-conscious influence of a dethroned and liquidated autocrat may actually operate in support of the tyrannies of his supplanter. This may be true enough where the dethroned potentate has used his powers tyrannically, but I should hesitate to accept the principle as applying to the Czar Nicholas and his family.

According to our teaching, those persons who are called to high office and responsibilities are ensouled by selected and experienced Spirits. I quote:— "For know that those who are born into such conditions, no matter how the Personality may confine, are indeed great; especially those who leave the Earth while still young.

"So here in the wider world, when the mistakes of the Personality are cast aside, they take up their great task of raising, through those mystic ties of love and affection for all which they symbolise, the myriads of the people who are struggling to see.

"Ponder that, my brother, and to all in such conditions send loving thoughts, even when they seem to fail most bitterly. Theirs is indeed a

Cross!" It is also a new aspect of an old phenomenon that the strikes and the crime and the civil disturbance which normally follow great wars are not so much due to the lethal training which has been given to the surviving troops (according to the commonly accepted theory), but to the wandering dead who still seek some outlet for their pugnacity.

Towards the end the communicator gives his idea of what constitutes Communism. It would be quite unrecognisable by any modern practitioner of that doctrine.

The gem of the essay is contained in the last line: "This is the first place to love enemies—the garden fence at home." In re-reading these last few messages I cannot avoid the personal opinion that the communicators, in their elation at their release from the shackles of physical life, are recommending a course of life and conduct which is beyond what is reasonable to expect that humanity in its present state of evolution can attain.

As regards capital punishment, I am personally in complete agreement. I don't think it is ever right in any circumstances deliberately to kill a human being in cold blood; but, apart from the ethical point of view, I think that we bring quite unnecessary ills upon our own heads by sending out into the astral souls filled with hatred and a desire for revenge.

But when it comes to saying that no man should sit in judgment on another, that no man should be deprived of his liberty by being imprisoned for his crimes, that no man should actively and physically resist an enemy engaged in invading his country, and so on, we shall arrive shortly at a condition of anarchy. For if it is wrong forcibly to oppose a body of attacking foreigners by means of an army, it must be at least equally wrong to oppose a gang of English criminals by means of the police when the former are engaged in an attempt to rob a bank. And what holds for a gang of criminals holds also for a single criminal.

When we have reached the stage when humanity throughout the world is engaged in a competitive effort to give and not to take, anarchy may or may not be an acceptable system for the world as a whole to adopt, but there are few sane people who would regard it as practical politics today.

I think that we must regard it at least as a possibility that the 'Commandments' (to use rather a crude word) change with man's developing power to live up to them. I recall a picture from the Akashic Records of the very remote past which we were given some time ago in our Circle. It included a scene in a temple where human sacrifices were made by the priests in conditions of revolting cruelty. I suppose

Chang could see my thoughts, for he explained: "*Thou shalt not kill* is a new commandment; it was not such a great crime then when man was less developed." In any case, as I have said, the point of this series of communications is that they offer us continually fresh problems on which we may exercise mind and intuition.

It is not for a moment to be supposed that these are infallible dicta to be uncritically accepted. There will be a still larger question mark in my mind in connection with the next chapter, which deals particularly with animals.

The undercurrent of the rest of this chapter is Love.

Not merely human affection or the strong attraction between sexes, but the great principle which pervades the Universe; for without this principle neither man nor angel can move in closer to the Light.

Let us start with Richard Home's little essay, and not overlook its principal jewel: "because wisdom is so dazzling in dark places that people forget to love and think only of being wise".

Let us try to consider this line of wisdom, which is what we in our group all belong to.

It is in this line that we find happiness because nothing pleases us more than to hunt out things.

In the proving and trying of wisdom is this line begun, but it cannot be followed except by love, for love is the true wisdom under everything.

This is what we try to show men, but it is only a few who can, with wise love, become the leaders of wise thought, because wisdom is so dazzling in dark places that people forget to love, and only think of being wise.

This is I think this brightness that dazzled me, though I was truly aware that I ought to love first, and be wise the truest way, but I was too interested in little things, and the wonder which was in this little world of sense, that I forgot I lacked the one thing necessary.

Try how I would I could never get rid of the knowledge that my line was weak, and being withheld by me from its true beauty, but I tried not to see because I was wise in my work, and did not want to be on the beck and call of people.

But people are this world's inhabitants; they try to find help and look to those who are wise for it.

I think this is felt, that wise people should be loving. I think this true type of wisdom which this line impels to is very beautiful and joyful and loving as well as wise.

This is true wisdom we try to bring in this writing. Try to love all you meet; it is trying which makes you able to succeed. This enables us to infect them with wiser thoughts while we try to be planners that help to bring peace.

We need love rays to work with. This is the kind of bright wire of current which can bring this wise idea home to people.

Richard Home.

Borthwick was another who thought that the intellect was everything while he was on earth and for a time afterwards. Then he found out "that love is not a vague impression felt between people, but an immense power and: "now I see it is the truest wisdom man can find, to love and to be loved.

We think this is the true tale that will be of interest to some. But perhaps this is the bright idea that is only interesting if people already know how we help each other in this land that is the land of spirits.

I am the spirit who had the bright brain that tried to find things hidden, that could not be found by all. But this brain was no true spirit brain, but only an intellectual one.

This I thought was the highest type of human which I could be, for I thought these fine thoughts that most could hardly understand. But I thought all wrong, as I soon saw.

I tried to be an attender of brainy discussions here, and this was so boring to me, for I could not understand these ideas that love helped, but true thought could be bright without intellectual brilliance, and so on. These ideas just seemed senseless to me, for I thought I had more sense than all these discussers.

But I found after a time that they all did things, and I did nothing but just discuss with people like myself, who all just liked to hear their own thoughts.

But I tried to hear theirs as well, for I truly loved to consider fresh ideas, but all their ideas seemed poor empty ideas in the bright land where such ideas were clearly out of date.

Still some kept working to find how to build a brick house in this kind of material that was like light, but solid.

This was not brick, and could not be treated as brick, so I became bored with such ideas too.

This boredom is trying, for I was never bored in earth life; but this heaven was boring, for I was not in wealthy enough waves in brain to be able to think at all.

This slowly began to dawn on me that love is not a vague impression felt between people, but an immense power. In fact the greatest dynamic I could imagine, but in a different dimension, and much more penetrating than light, but in men's spirits, not in their physical make-up, or even in their minds.

This was a real shock to me, for I had the idea that the mind was the measure of the man, and not his heart, as we call his love seat. This is true, but it is not so literal as I had thought, for it is the centre of his physical system, and corresponds to the centre of his spiritual system. This is how it is the true seat of love. He even feels it warm.

This is strange if he thinks of it, for no other organ feels emotion in this way; but his heart feels warmth and intense love that almost bursts it.

I know this because I really did fall in love, but I did not try to understand this phenomenon, though it was the greatest experience my life held.

This must be the case for most. When this type of love is the brightest thing life holds, may it not be the strongest power known to man or spirit? This is the case, and in spirit life love becomes visible, but only when it is looked for.

I did not look for love till I was bored by human intellect, and did not think this could help, but tried to understand how these thinkers talked this way about love rays that made this or that help possible in this or that way. But this was the truth, as I saw when I looked for love.

But I had to look truly. This was not easy as I still had this intellectual approach, and could not just long to see love because I loved too.

This was hardly my idea of the dignity of human intellect.

But now I see it is the truest wisdom man can find to love and be loved. He has all he longs for. Here is his wealth and kingdom.

This is the line I found, but I had hardly found it at all.

If I had never been in love, and remembered how my heart filled with power. This was the memory that really was the key to my problem of survival, for this was the only thing worth remembering in all my life of intellectual activity.

Though of course I had exercised my faculties, which was good, and would have made me a very intelligent horse or dog if I had altogether failed to look for love.

Happily I did not fail, so I still have my identity, though I expect no one I used to know would recognise me now.

But I was Borthwick. This is only one name; I think I do not remember another. This is the name I tried to be bright with, but I hardly remember now. This is the truth. I think I do not even know how I earned my living. Perhaps I was rich in earth wealth; this would make it harder to remember. This is the whole I can say.

Lilian Lightfoot was a lady who ended her days in a home for the aged. There she not only found but dispensed Love. "Love all", she says, "and your love can light any who wander near you."

We hope to write of the experience called being dead. I was a tired woman in a home for the old and feeble, and this seemed to be a bad thing to me as I longed for someone to care to be with me, and hear me tell of old times.

But it interested no one, and it would have helped me little, for it was old times I had given up, and be ready to understand the idea that there is more before than behind, and that a true time of preparation was a boon to be accepted thankfully.

I did not understand any of this, but on looking back to see how I found my line I think it is true that I found it by being made to think I was alone, and would have to die.

I tried not to think, but to be interested in those of the Home. They all wanted a listener, and I tried to be such a listener, but I had no interest in these stories of past details and pettiness, and willed to know why I had lived at all.

And I thought I could see a kind of light in me that tried to lead me to love these old people, and make them think a human love is a truth in action, and is not just a thing that is given and taken and nothing remains.

I had a true feeling that this was a fact, and worth believing, and tried to hear the stories with love for the tellers, instead of a feigned interest in the stories.

Then a light came to me that I was love, and therefore a bit of God, and I hoped I thought truly, for this almost had a flavour of blasphemy to me, and I did not dare to say such a thing, and only hoped, for it made me happy and warmed my heart so that I felt no loneliness any more, for I was a part of love, and could not be alone.

It made me a help in the Home, as the old women told me their stories, and I listened with love to them, and it made them happier, and helped them to look to be more contented to die as I thought it was a happy thing to do.

This I found was true, for I lay ill, and suffered pain, and one day I found I had no pain, but had got up, and helped to be a bearer of cups of tea to the old women. And then I saw they seemed sad and wept, and I asked what it was, and they said I was dead.

I thought a little in fright that perhaps this was true, but then I found I could see light all round where these women loved me, and it showed a long-lost loved one that I hardly remembered before, holding out hands to lead me. I loved to hold this hand, for this was a true grasp of love that I felt, and no hand of flesh, which is a shadowy thing to us, for it does not fully reveal the love that it feels.

I held this hand with joy, and went away to a place with trees and flowers and little animals which were not afraid, and found time to rest and grow strong and young again.

It was such a lovely place, for it all seemed like a home that I had loved before; and so it was, for I had a long think of old dreams, and it lay in these dreams; but not in the fringes that I had thought were my whole dreams, but in this lovely reality which lay outside the life I had been shut up in.

I was in a heaven of happy living things, in freedom from fear or oppression of one another, and this made me love to be with them, and hear them laugh and sing. This is true; every animal can laugh and sing inside, if it is happy as it ought to be.

This rest lasted a time, till I was ready to see what lay beyond, and found a place in a hill, of light bright long trees, like an avenue of aspens in light, that led to a sort of temple, as it was a pillared building in a bright stone that seemed to be shining in itself. And it was the thought of those who loved old people, but it is not easy to describe, for it is not a building as you know it, but a form of home built by thought.

I tried to enter, but found I was unable to climb the steps—or it looked like this in thought to me—so I looked to see if I could get help, and found a host of people all ready to help as soon as I looked, for I could not see them till I looked.

I tried to talk to them, but I could not speak words. I found instead that I was making pictures in the air in the manner of a picture show, but much more truly lovely and living in effect. It was like the best of the bits of dreams you can remember, for the real dreams are in the spirit only.

I tried to think of my old friends, and at once I could go in, and then I could see their spirits reaching out to me to tell them I could see and love them still. I held a light to them, in a spirit sense, and it was a true help, for I knew they felt it, and did not cry for me any more.

I loved to be a bearer of cups of comfort to them still, for I heard them longing for love, and trying to know I loved them, and it truly was a help, for I often saw a smile on the faces of their spirits—which are like the expressions on their human faces, but much more dramatic and expressive.

It is difficult to write, but I long to tell of how I tried to help one of them to die. This is a true story.

She was ill for long, and lay unhappy and unaware of any love, for only of a great longing for a bright love to hold her hand and be her leader. I came and loved her to be the true spirit I knew she could be, for I could see a shape of her spirit, larger than her spirit's face, and I found I was trying to help her to be bigger in heart, and she tried to hope more to be a bigger heart, and bear her troubles without complaining.

But it was too hard to bear, and she presently became, as you would say, unconscious. This helped to give me a chance to prepare her to look for help; for it is at such times that the spirit is free to meet other spirits, and be spoken to in words, or a sort of thought that seems like words and the language of dream symbolism that spirits use.

I spoke to her and tried to tell her of a love that is eternal, and which could not let her fall, for its arms are everlasting, and that I knew because I had found, this true, and now could come to lead her to find a rest and a place for thought of love and beauty and joy.

She had had little of these bright things in her life, and hardly thought they were true, as she was always working for food and clothes, and had no time for enjoyment of earth.

I told her to be ready to look to my love to help her, and then she died, and she did look to be helped. If she had not been ill and unconscious I could not have led her to look for help, for she had no other thought of looking.

This is true, and shows how our bits of comfort and love can help each other, and it is a great help indeed if we can lead each other to die gladly, with a thought of looking to be led, for then it is easy to be led and to see help.

Otherwise the spirit is lost, and wanders unhappily trying to be led by human hands which do not feel its entreaties.

Love all, and your love can light any who wander near you. They can see a light which is not human, and it encourages them to look to see if there is more such light, and they begin to see there is—but I cannot write any more.

I was a lady by birth, but lost all I had, and tried to forget this was a loss, so it became a gain.

I loved to think I could work too, though I did not be taught in youth. But I had a happy free childhood; this was a great wealth.

I was in London in both wars.

My name is Lilian Lightfoot.

Lionel Pocock's contribution throws light on the recorded saying of Jesus about laying up treasure in heaven.

I always had a subconscious idea at the back of my mind that this was only a transfer from material to spiritual selfishness—something on the lines of the hymn,

> Whatever, Lord, we lend to Thee
> Repaid a thousand fold will be;
> Then gladly will we give to Thee,
> Who givest all

But Lionel (and some other contributors whom I have no space to quote) make it clear that this treasure is not hoarded but given away again and again and again.

His rich old woman "gave a little bit of money to her maidservant to help her to live when she was old Now she can give very little help as she "has no more treasure than this little".

Yes: I think this is a true wish to recognise this wish of the spirit. I am in the true line that most of these spirits are, so I hoped I could try to give a message.

I am this kind of spirit who loves to interest himself in the wills of people. I only mean the true will, not the false will which wishes to be ill, or to accept other ideas than those of its own line.

I wish people realised how strong their wills are, and how bright the world would be if a few of them willed peace.

I do not know how it is they do not try, for they say that only the will to make peace can succeed, and yet they seek to give offence in all sorts of ways. This is of course the one way to be hopeless, to give offence.

I think it is true fear that paralyses hope, but if only a few will will peace, there is enough power to leave the outcome to the army on this side who only long to help the world, for this is the very reason for which they have given their lives. And lives always bring what they are given for; this is an axiom in the spirit world.

I wish people knew it. I think they would not give their lives for such foolish and selfish things, so that they are the unhappy spirits who have no treasure, but only illusion of earth things which does not satisfy.

I think I can tell of a true case of a brave tramp who tried to help others to be covered in the cold. I know he could hardly be able to find a coat, but he gave away all he had that he could take off. And now he can give warmth to poor shivering spirits who feel lonely and loveless, and he can let them feel a warmth of true covering that makes them feel confident that love is this being who is God, and they can take fresh heart.

I can perhaps tell too of a rich woman who gave a little bit of money to her maid servant to help her to live when she was old. Now she can only give very little help to old people who need much help, but she has no more treasure than this little. Though the maid can help all manner of needs of people for she gave her life to working for others.

The loving willing service of men is the highest treasure a man can save; but I think he will not know he saves it, for he spends this treasure, and himself saves nothing.

I hope no one who spends their lives for others will think this is a lie, for they may suffer want in old age, for this want is only a true willingness of the spirit to be poor, which is the training men need to be ready to strip themselves of earth comfort, and be free in spirit.

Long illness is a true preparation, but not necessary if the spirit has no ties.

I think I have said this letter I wished to.

I am the bringer of trees that blossom. This was my work, and now I show how trees bear fruit.

I am Lionel Pocock.
I do not know the place, but think it was this land near this place.

Hotfoot was one who refused to hate, but did not refuse to fight. His contribution is memorable from the sentence: "I am the breath of wind that blows a spark but I am not the match that kindles this spark; this must be done by man himself or he could not be free."

My name that is the kind of thing that eludes most spirits is a thing that holds interest for me. This is because it has meaning. This is my name; Hotfoot. Yes; it always made me hasten, for I liked to feel I belonged to a tribe that had earned its name, and I would be a hotfoot too.

This is my tale.

I lived in this land before the last war but during the first.

This time I lived the two kinds of love tried to pull me both ways, for I felt I ought to love enemies, but I loved my land and enemies did not, but even learnt a hate song.

This was the kind of song that led me to think how I should be a hater of such people, but I thought this is exactly the thing they try to be, haters. This is the thing that makes me dislike this song, but if I hate them it is because I too am influenced by their song. This made me love to be the true refuser to hate, but I hardly loved, for this was not possible to me. I was a fighter that did this because it seemed the only thing to do. I think it never occurred to me that I could refuse to fight as well as to hate. I hope I loved truth, but I loved truth as I saw it.

This I could not see, that love can really conquer hate.

This is a thought that is the result of a true love for man that is the high result of thought, and I did not think such thoughts. But I refused to hate. This is my little point; because I did not hate I can help people not to hate, for I love to help haters not to be hated, then they cannot hate successfully if they are not hated, however hateful they are.

Perhaps this is a truly strange idea and makes little sense to a listener, but I can listen to these haters and hear them hate someone; then I find this person and try to help them not to hate. This is perhaps easy and perhaps impossible, for I can only help if people can let me help them. I am not able to force an idea on anyone, only to fan a love that is the beginning of true love that makes a fire of love. I am the breath of wind that blows a spark, but I am not the match that kindles this spark; this must be done by man himself or he could not be free.

I love to blow the spark into a flame, but I have not the strength I could have had if I had gone further and loved enemies.

But I learned never to hesitate in my actions, so I can at least act quickly. This is the impulse that strikes very swiftly, though still it may not succeed.

I think this is all I have to say. My name I have told except the Christian name. I cannot think clearly of this name; perhaps I loved the other so do not remember this.

Leopold Phibs was a man of narrow sectarian ideas who bound them upon his mother and his children, thus injuring all concerned.

11.4.49.
I think this is the next tale, for it is a tale that longs to be told.

I was a bringer of evil in the horridest way on his children, for I liked my own bright thoughts, and thought my children must like them too. So I made them think this was the only true thought, and they could not have any hope for themselves in this spirit world unless they believed the things I told them.

This I did not understand was the exact opposite way I could help them to be happy in heaven, but I had no imagination, and did not try to think how such things could be true, that a god who loved could damn those who failed to believe the things their father taught them; especially when this father was only a stupid beer-drinking fat man who liked his own comfort more than any real love, or even belief. This is the real description of myself.

This time of which I tell was a time of peace before any thought of great wars came. This I thought would never happen, and made a bright boy of mine be a bringer of this war nearer by being a fighter in his trade. This he hated, but I said he could only be a true lover of me if he obeyed his father. This he did, and became a truly unhappy man who hated his work, and hardly enjoyed living his life at all. This I knew, but was too stupid to understand, and thought he could be provided for this way, and made a brave lad that people admired. So I made this foolish plan for him with no freedom for him to choose.

Then I became old, and made the discovery that I myself had nothing to hold on to and was terribly afraid to die.

This was a true condition, for my belief was a hollow inheritance, not even a true belief of my own.

Then I was in misery, and tried to find some way to be assured that this lift I was going to was in truth the lift I expected where a god would himself welcome me, and I should have a throne and a crown and all sorts of good things. But I had no assurance.

Then I died. This was in truth a terrible event. This dread I had was a real foreshadowing, and must have at least loosened my mind a little. For the shock I had was terrible, for I was simply lost.

No one met me that I could see, for I did not look for love, only for a holy welcome.

This had a dreadful effect on me, for I then looked down to see how I could be helped by men. This was terrible, for I could find no help, though I tried to make them hear my cries of longing for help. This lasted long, but I did not know it was long. It seemed truly brutally horrible to me that I who believed so much should have been so deceived. But so it was; I had deceived myself, and had to discover that I had only believed a hollow sham.

This came by degrees, for I had to find it out by watching people who professed as I did, and people who professed nothing, but loved their children and their friends, and left them free to be the people God meant them to be.

Then I tried to see my own children, and they were loaded with chains that I had put on them, and had no freedom or help to loose them, for they tried to be the good things I had made them to be, and not question anything. I had a horrible despair that I had damned them too, and had a love for them that hated myself. This lighted my mind, for then I found a true parent waiting to lead me. I had no love for him, but thought him a bad father as he had not believed these things, and had never taught me to believe them, for I had only been my own gaoler.

This parent led me to a place of haven for my tired heart, and comforted me by trying to show me my mistake.

This I now had already seen, but not as this kind parent knew was still necessary. I did not wish to be further instructed by him as he had never known the truths I knew; so I had a thought that perhaps my heaven was a true heaven, but I was lost in some unfortunate way, but now could be the revealer of bright truth to my father.

This I proceeded to try to do. I made an illusion of some bright place with psalm singing and harps, but it was hollow, and I could hardly bear to be in it myself, and my helper did not wish to come into such a foolish place. He had a truly honest wish to help me, but

I tried not to be helped and went to my heaven and tried to be in happy bright love there.

But this was not possible, for love is a truth that can never be found in illusion, and this found me the key; for I tried to consider that God was loving.

This was the truth, but only a little of it, but it helped me, for I looked for love, and saw! love everywhere. This made me see that perhaps this was a thing I had half expected. This truth that God is love then came to me, for I had thought this was a truth that I had believed; but I had never believed it, for I did not understand the breadth or height or depth of even an earthly love. This love that I now began to see was only spirit love, but it became the beautiful thing that helped me to be loving at last.

I longed to help my children but could not make them hear me, for I was dead, and must not be thought of as approachable, for this was a thing I thought forbidden, to meet the dead, or even to pray for them. This was a truly strange belief, for I believed that all were one. This really had no meaning for me, but was just a form of words that I had made my hard rule.

Then my mother, who had never had a true love of this type of thought I had, but who had been led by me, attempted to be in communication with me. This was a truly curious attempt, for this true lover of her child was an old frail woman in a little home that had small comfort but had to do for her. Then this true love of hers became a light to her mind, and she asked me to help her to die as she was afraid, and thought I could lead her to my heaven.

I did not know how to lead her, but asked my father how I could be this leader. He told me that only love can lead, but since I loved her I could perhaps try to lead her. But it did not help me, for I had no place to lead her to.

Then I tried to be truer in mind, and became a learner to find some place to which I could bring my tired old mother who looked for help to me. This was a real help, to have to help this love that loved me. Then I found help that showed me a true place of rest that was there all the time, but not visible to me, for I had not looked for simple love that helped each other. This they now showed me helps all who look by being loved, that love creates the rest and loveliness that the spirit needs for its bright haven of refuge that the child can enjoy and the old man lead him to, but all are the same in love.

This kind home that this father had led me to now became my home that I led my mother to, for she had asked me to lead her. This came as a true surprise to me by now as I had begun to know how unfit I was to lead. But I was asked, and I led. But I had no home of my own to lead her to, only her old love's home where she had never been happy, for he had not loved her well.

This then was the best home to take her to, and she had a feeling that all was different from her expectations, and that I had changed and had no bright heaven to welcome her to. This was true; however she was tired and glad to find a home that made her welcome who had been so lone.

My life had been the only true life of her life.

This is a help, to be the loved son of a true mother.

This was the love that made me free.

I am Leopold Phibs.

12.4.49.

No one can possibly imagine how happy this was to be in a home. This is a different thing from an earthly home because this is not just a shelter but a true home that gives hope to the mind and help to the spirit.

This hope is the hope of being secure that nothing can hinder the individual from his own line. This was the truth. I had hardly perceived mine at all, but now I found I had a true line that led me along a path in the mind that taught me to be patient. I think this is perhaps the truth that I was trying to be patient in holding on to my forlorn belief, now brought into bright will to perceive for myself the true patience, that waited to be preferred to all other virtues in my mind. It found a hold in my mind like bright lightning that patience is the loveliest thing that is known.

To be patient is to be the possessor of a true kingdom in the spirit; this is to be the patient helper of people who try to wait to be perfect in this trial of hope that many must endure, for patience is the line that helps the struggling people to hold on. This is the patience of the saints that says 'How Long?' This I now see, for I am this patient spirit at last. But I could not again try to be patient to wait till my children found release from the chains I had put on them. I tried in every way to be their helper not to be patient, but to be truly rash and free and hold their own lines that had had little chance against my patience, for this was the line I had imposed on them, though I had hardly recognised it myself.

I think I thought it high to be patient, so perhaps I had to a small extent known it; but now I tried to waken them to rebel, for this was so necessary to help them to free themselves.

Then this true love of the boy that had to be the fighter tried to tell me he could not be patient in this trade, but must leave it. This pleased me for I hoped he could then be more free. Then I tried to help his mind to think to be led to a high idea of how to be himself. This he heard, but of course he did not know I told him, but almost feared he became a traitor to me. But he tried to be true to hold this idea of being true to the highest he could see. This made him look to see the highest he could; then he became the truly inspired man who found the reason for his own life, and became a true teacher of boys in the loving way that led them to find their own line that each had.

I think I was truly proud of this loving work, for I loved this man that I had tried to chain. This true being became the helper of his brother that was also chained, and both were loving beings that had reason to be bright spirits. I think this is all I can tell.

I am the truly brutal man that had the name Leopold Phibs.

It is a strange thing, but the ordinary man is no more ready to talk about Love than to discuss his belief in God.

There is a sort of idea that Love is either sexual and, as such, not to be discussed, or else something sloppy and sentimental—all very well for women, but something of which the all-conquering male should be ashamed.

I have been looking up my old Circle notes, and this is what Chang has to say on the subject.

The conversation started by a discussion of a dictum of Chang's to the effect that, of all Governments in the world, that then at Westminster (1947) was the best intentioned but the most muddle-headed.

Chang said that in his country, before it was known as China, there was a proverb to the effect that the stones on the path leading down to the darkness were placed there by those whose hearts were good (cf. our own proverb).

"A good heart is not enough," said he; "with love you must have the wisdom to direct. In the West there is a great cult of love, and it grows upon me how foolishly they are who prattle so—always of love that is soft.

"You have not yet learned in the West that love is very sharp, strong and powerful—not meek and mild. Love without wisdom is like a wife without a husband.

"I may seem critical of your system, but it seems to me that before you can talk of Love you must first learn what it is and see that those who prattle of love and kindness are unfit for the tasks they have taken on. Love is the casket which holds the jewel of wisdom, and here it is empty.

"You cannot do much to avert the Karma of your country. Events are the outcome of seeds long since sown; but you can learn the lesson. This is a very small chapter.

... It is so necessary for the people of the West to give up this shibboleth of Love. How you have distorted the message of the great King of Peace. How dare you so belittle him that you would call him weak? "Love is mighty; you prate of it all ye foolish ones. You must walk through fire! Love and Wisdom are the two sides of the coin. Love is not Love till it is joined with Wisdom, and Wisdom is not Wisdom till it is joined with Love".

CHAPTER 8

MAINLY ABOUT ANIMALS

T he communications quoted in this chapter deal principally with animals; but a number of different subjects for discussion arise in this connection and, as two or more of these subjects may be broached in a single communication, it is difficult to isolate them in order to deal with them separately.

There is, for instance, the question of using animals as food and their skins for clothing; the question of their physical mutilation in order to render them docile, or to check their rate of breeding; the general question of the way in which man's treatment of animals reflects upon subsequent generations of mankind; and the theory, so frequently expressed by this group of communicators, that an unsuccessful human life may be followed by rebirth in an animal body.

I am much surprised by this last idea. As a general rule, the doctrine of Metempsychosis includes the idea of human reversion to the animal state, whereas the doctrine of Reincarnation excludes it.

If only one or two of the messages had put forward this theory as a fact, I think I should have ignored them, and not troubled to include them in this book, but there is such a consensus of opinion among this particular group of communicators that I am putting to you this point as one of those upon which we may well exercise our minds as a result of reading these messages. I confess that the extent of my own reading is very limited, but I have regarded Metempsychosis as a purely Eastern idea, and I have not come across any Western authority, incarnate or discarnate, who puts it forward as a possibility, still less as a fact of comparatively frequent occurrence. 'Imperator' in Spirit Teachings states categorically that the Egyptians' doctrine of transmigration through vast ages and cycles was an error which symbolised and typified eternal and unceasing progress. Most people would, I think, read this as a statement that reincarnation does not occur; but, according to some definitions, 'transmigration' includes reversion to the animal state, whereas 'reincarnation' does not. It was explained to me (by someone whose opinion I have no special reason to value) that Imperator' was hedging on the reincarnation issue by using a word which included in its scope the wider issue of reversion to the animal state.

Of course, the more one learns about these things the less one tolerates the idea of watertight compartments and sharp lines of division between states of evolution. There is no sharp line between the mineral and the vegetable, nor between vegetable and animal. Some of the lowest forms of life are difficult to place in either category, and there are plants, which catch and eat insects, which may almost be regarded as anchored animals.

At any rate, it seems to me that the difference between human and non-human animals consists very largely in the power of intelligent speech. In the Astral, where animals are not subject to this limitation, but can converse in thought-language, the dividing line between human and non-human is much more tenuous.

I should say that the essential difference between the human and the animal kingdom is the ensoulment of the physical body by the Ego, the True Self, the Individual, or whatever you like to call it—the point at which the creature ceases to belong to the Group Soul of its species, and develops a conscience, or at which it attains the power to distinguish between good and evil.

This power is possessed in a large measure by many dogs who become faithful and loving to human beings (who are to the animals what God is to us).

Perhaps it begins farther back than that, where mother love ceases to be purely instinctive, and becomes deliberate and self-sacrificing.

The main point of this book is not to set out a number of hard-and-fast conclusions, but to offer subjects for the exercise of the mental faculties, both higher and lower; and I put it forward as a matter for serious consideration that the most highly developed animals may be essentially human before they are equipped with a human body.

If this idea can be accepted without an attack of apoplexy, it means that the sharp division between human and animal has been broken down, and that human animals may exist as well as animal humans.

If this were so, it would help to explain a difficulty which has puzzled me for some years. We are told repeatedly (and not only by this Group of Mrs. Roberts) that it is a human responsibility to bring forward the higher animals towards the human state by kindly and intelligent treatment.

This is all very well for dogs and cats and domesticated animals, but what about the wild animals whose contacts with humanity are few and painful? A herd of African elephants or of Indian black buck? Might it be that human beings return to them as leaders in the same way as Avatars and Masters have returned to help humanity? An odd thought, but perhaps not too grotesque to hold in the back of the mind until further evidence or illumination comes our way.

The person with the 'scientific' turn of mind will be impatient of these speculations. He will say, "Well, you talk a lot about your Circle and your Guides who have been with you for so many thousands of years; why don't you go and ask them, and settle the matter to your own satisfaction, at any rate?" A very pertinent scientific question, to which I can give only the unscientific answer that this is not a part of the bargain between us. The schoolboy who makes unrestricted use of the crib saves himself a good deal of work, but he is not learning the art of learning, and what he gathers does not remain in his mind.

I find that the mere act of analysing my ideas to display to you is helpful to me. There is no hurry to arrive at a conclusion on these matters, but all this kind of mental spade work is going to be of great value to us later on, when we shall have access to new sources of information and a more precise thinking-mechanism with which to work.

First I give the message of Irene Rouse, because she speaks for her group in saying that they work to help those who are in danger of reverting to the animal.

I think we know more about people who revert to animals than other spirits on this plane because we work with ways to help those who are in danger of reverting. It is unusual, and this is only when no line whatever is found. This is rarely the case.

I think few animals have been human, but it can easily be, for the brain is the measure of the spirit's occupation.

This means that the spirit rests while it occupies an animal, like a player in an orchestra with only a small part on a simple instrument.

I think this is always the case. There are unlimited possibilities of development if man discovers how to use his unconscious. It is truly a great leap that is possible for him if he tries to, find his line.

Man is groping successfully, we think, for his wise intelligence grasps the necessity for some such thing as a true individual pattern waiting to be found by an individual himself, without imposition of this wise truth from another.

I wish we were able to help psychoanalysts. We could help so wonderfully, for I think this science is truly a thing which tries to see with spirit eyes. This is impossible as yet, for it requires a previous life to evince in any permanent degree a true clairvoyance of the spirits of human beings. This is only just possible to us. The true thing is that the spirit hides in the body, and is beautifully "veiled in flesh" as it is said.

I think this truth is obvious as this life is to teach man to be an individual, with a brain of his own in spirit, and this he must build for himself out of his solitary puzzles and troubles and courage and love, till he has found his reason for wishing to be an individual, which is finding his line.

I wish I could explain how brains are built, but it needs a student of psychology to understand what I should try to explain. I will wish you goodbye, for it is not easy to reach you.

Irene Rouse.

Next comes Edward Locke. Only the latter part of his message concerns animals, but the first part is very interesting and important. What would some of the 'great minds' of today think if they were told that tomorrow they will come to be helped by a window cleaner?

Yes, we will try to write while we can; there may be little more opportunity. I think we long to keep in touch with people, but the urge to try to rise higher is irresistible.

Man is urging us as well, for we can help him more if we can link him higher. It is true that each generation is able to span a wider gap than the one before.

We try to bridge the gulf in ways in which the work we did as men has fitted us.

I tried to bring light by cleaning windows, and now I can help by trying to clear darkness from the windows of people's minds. I thought that love must be the best thing in life, so I am now able to work with this group who were more developed than I, but had not found their line any better, for education tried to make them think that mental development was what counted.

It is true that they could have been higher if they had found both, but generally the best mental development hardly finds a line at all.

It is very pitiful to see great men unable to realise that they are no longer great, but very weak indeed. It is part of my work to clean their minds of cobwebs of earth values, but it is extraordinary how they cling to these notions of class and rank and party and church and ideas of what they think I ought to do for them. It would be funny if it were not sad.

I long to warn people that this story of the rich man and Lazarus is quite true, just because poverty makes people humbly ready to welcome what comes next, because earth has no ties for them save ties of love.

Lazarus was the type of the man who was ill and alone.

This makes a person very eager to find a home when he dies.

He tries to find some spirit who once loved him; there is generally someone. If there is no one the group spirits of his race take him home, as in this case. Then he is at rest indeed in the bosom of his fathers who look after their child. I saw such a one. He was old and alone, but hoped it might be better when he died. He waked to such a welcome, and was a happy child in this home of the spirit.

This is because he did not quite despair.

I know it seems unfair that despair should be punished.

It is not punishment, it is choice. Man prefers to give up to keeping on hoping. I think it is best for him then to slip back and have his weary spirit revived as a happy puppy or kitten. It is just a rest for his spirit, for these true loving animals can do little more than love and enjoy life; then the spirit has fresh courage to start again.

It is the other way round with the rich man. He cannot be happy as an animal for he wants to have things of his own. If he is an animal he is truly a sad beast, for he thinks he has lost something, and cannot love freely in consequence.

But the life of the animal is cleansing, for he can possess nothing, and knows no harm that can without a true reason bring wrong and brutal treatment. This makes him ready to trust till the master who illuses him wills his death, and he can start again.

But it is not such a good start. He was not a happy animal, and there are sad memories in his unconscious memory which will dog his steps. He may often hate dogs unreasonably, or whatever animal he was, or he may wish to love them, for they need love.

This will help him more almost than anything, for he tries to redeem his own beastliness in the beast he loves.

Sometimes the love of a beast will save a man from going back, for it wakens real love to find the animal he loved still loving him, as true loving animals ready to become human do.

I think many people know they will meet their animals again. I hope they will not have to ask too much forgiveness for wrong and cruel injustice.

With true love comes the will to be kind, and many animals are kind enough to forgive grievous wrong that will make their human life difficult and perhaps a truly unhappy one, for such unhappy truly miserable shame producing memories lurk in their unconscious as will haunt their dreams and be the cause of mental instability and insanity, which will mean a fresh reversion to animal life.

I wish it were possible for forgiveness to wipe out suffering; perhaps it reduces it in some way; I hope so, I do not know enough to say.

I wish people could love and be fair to their animals, for every animal is a human spirit in the making. People should love them all the time, not only when they feel like it. Animals need so much love.

Try to get people to understand that lunatic asylums and prisons are filled with unhappy spirits who were ill treated as animals, and cannot forget it.

Edward Locke.

We might perhaps underline the words: "I think many people know they will meet their animals again. I hope they will not have to ask too much forgiveness for wrong and cruel injustice."

Next comes Arthur Neilson, a turnstile man at the Zoo. He writes:—

We think we can write another letter.

I was the turnstile man at the Zoo, but I do not know which Zoo.

This was beautiful work because I loved to think the people loved the animals. Now I can see this is true, but that it is also very wrong indeed to cage the animals. They come back to animal life, or even to human life, with bars on their minds.

It is sad when truly beautiful animal spirits are prevented from freedom. It is wonderful how the spirit grows in a wild animal, for it ranges freely, and reaches out in finding its food and home, till its spirit knows how to manage for itself. I wish it were possible to find a way in which animals could be really free and also loved. Perhaps man will devise such ways when once he realises the importance of the development of freedom and resource in people, and that it is by true understanding of the needs of animals that such beauty is insured.

I think it is much to be deplored that there is no inkling of these truths; though people often will say what animal they used to be, they do not really believe it, but it is a genuine impression from the unconscious memory.

We long to be personally interested in the future of animals, for these are our young brothers, and all so true to their God-given instincts. It is truly sad to see these instincts denied expression. To people they appear happy, but we can see how cramped their spirits are. I hope someone will see this with a present thought that this may be why he finds his mind has bars, for then he can know the reason, and be determined to be free in truth to brave adventure of the mind, for this is his rightful heritage.

This is the barred mind which dare not challenge all which others have found, for it must find its own food for thought, and shelter for its heart in this lovely world which the God of Love and Freedom has devised for His true and free sons to replenish and subdue.

Arthur Neilson.

He puts his finger on the difficulty which man must have in influencing by love the animals with which he will never come in contact unless he subjects them to an artificial life of captivity.

Perhaps game-reserves may supply an answer; but the problem still remains that herds of hungry elephants and lions and antelopes will not be able to live cheek by jowl with civilised agricultural inhabitants in the new Africa— when the Dark Continent is transformed into the Continent of Light. The result will be extermination, except for a few herds maintained in Reserves as samples of fauna which are otherwise extinct, like the American Bison.

And the same process will go on throughout the Earth, as humanity expands up to the limit of the fertility of the whole earth to support it. Animal life, except parasitic and domesticated, will tend to disappear from the Earth.

And then what becomes of the idea that animal life is the antechamber of the human? I'm sure I don't know.

Now a few words from a woman who used to cook for two rich (and presumably selfish) women.

> I would like to write, as I was the cook that got the meals; for two women who used to have this stuff men call riches.
>
> They try to be free, but I must work for them still, or they may go back to animals. This is true.
>
> I loved to try wise ways of preparing food, so am in this group, for I was not educated, only loving.
>
> Lizzie Mallinet.

Now I have to draw attention to the fact that a number of these messages inveigh in the strongest possible manner against the practice of castrating animals for human safety and convenience.

This is such an integral part of herding and shepherding and farming and horse mastership, and has been so for so many thousands of years, that criticism of the practice will be generally regarded as unreasonable and impractical in the extreme.

I do not record an opinion myself at this stage, but I wish to put on record the very strong feeling which exists against it, in this group, at least. They maintain that a great deal of sexual perversion and mental disease is due to this cause.

I give one of the letters in full and extracts from three others.

> No time can be better than this to make clear the question of how children can help to be the true bright thinkers that make the race more truly high. For this animal question is largely in the hands of people who must be the kind trainers of their spirits, for they will come back to life in human shape.

This may be their very next step if their spirit is ready.

But too often it is the truth that a spirit is ready mentally but has had too little love, or has suffered the brutal wronging of some vital instinct.

This is terrible, and a truly horrible handicap for the brain in human life.

This tying up all the time that happens to some dogs leaves a feeling of restriction, and many cannot believe themselves free in spirit; for they were not free when their spirit was being formed.

Tying always to a lead is also very bad, for the spirit cannot easily be independent, but looks to be led. This harms them very much, for the line that every individual must find is free from all others, and the feeling that the line belongs to another is terribly literally misleading.

The truest cruelty of all is to deprive the dogs and cats who love to be true fathers and mothers that love each other and their children of this great training. I think this is the real life the brain needs.

To be hit is the next cruelty to the mind. I do not understand how people can hit little puppies that are only little tiny babies, but not so bright even, for their spirits are less developed. But nearly all little puppies are hit by men who think they train their spirits. This is true; they train them to fear blows that drop upon them from a mighty hand, that hurts because it likes to hurt, with no true cause. This makes them submit to things in the mind that ought not to be submitted to. Then they like to be hidden, to escape, but are dragged out. This too is terrible, to be dragged out, for a puppy that hides is frightened.

This is already harmful, but can be helped if he is comforted.

I think people could be so kind to puppies if only they thought of these possibilities even; for they are certainly possibilities that may be true.

This is the most likely means that they can have to be the trainers of the race. It is not a truly animal race they train, but the human race.

I love to think I may help some little puppy to be a happy dog, praised by his loving lord that holds his lordship lightly, and does not blame the little baby for only being a baby. This is generally all that is wrong, and this time can cure.

A dog loves to please, and can learn all sorts of things by praise, for he loves to hear these loving words that call him 'Good dog'. This he tries to deserve. Thus his spirit seeks love in higher life than his own, and this draws his love to higher levels as a man. I love to hear this word 'good' myself, for I try to love in higher ways, but am not always good. It is a bitter hopeless life for a dog who never hears these kind words. He may be made a criminal.

His human life can be so unhappy and loveless, for he has learnt no love that looks for loving return, but only fear.

I think surely some can let their dog be happier if they think this is a possibility. I think they cannot fail to see the beautiful idea that a lovely spirit full of freedom loves to be a loving bright companion. This is the life a dog should lead.

I think I always knew that I had been a dog for I was so fond of dogs, and hated to see them hit and tied up. But I did not realise how cruel this is, not only to the dog, but to the child and man he will be.

I love to hear a kind man love his dog; for I can hear love. This is music in spirit like pealing bells that make happy chimes. I think many can recognise this truth as truth.

I cannot remember if I even lived, in this land, for it does not make much difference to me which land I loved, but I know my old friend that lives here with me; he is the dog I once had who loves me still. Though he is the most forgiving dog I have much to ask him to forgive. I think many can hardly bear to be an asker for forgiveness, but they will have to be. Judgment is a thing each must pass.

This is justice, to be one's own judge when all is open to all.

This is all I had better say.

I hope I am the true lover that helps a few dogs to be happier. I think my name is Wright, but I do not know what else. I think I lived in this land, but how long ago I am not sure. This is clear, that I loved dogs, but not in a truly high way.

Pastor Hastres: I thought all animals liked to follow their instincts and be the true kind of hunter or fighter, or hunted that had to flee. I never knew this could be a constant discord that man has planted. But I know now it is, for I have seen the spirits of these animals, and they are not fierce but loving to play the long games of lovely animal life that enjoys sun, and loves leaping and chasing and harmlessly looking for herb food. I think the description of the holy mountain is this heaven, for all animal spirits behave in this fashion and play with the children.

But this kind of base instinct that besets them in bodies is the base brain that man imposes on them. This is a strange thing, but it is so.

I think now they are having trouble in nervous traits that are the direct result of having restricted the loving instincts of the animals that are the forefathers of their own children; and this is a terrible crime, for it makes criminals of them, or idiots and insane. For these traits are deep and not easily outlived. This kind of repression is the direct result of tampering with love, that creates and tries to be master of men's true development, but is instead directed in the opposite extreme, and becomes lust. This is horrible, and no lust can become love for they are opposites. I think this is obvious, for lust kills love.

This is true, for love is free and pure and has no lust for power, or greed. These things distract people from their lines, and bring wars and horrible fears on the race of men.

I think I am hardly able to write strongly enough that animals should be free to follow their best instincts. These always include sex. This is fundamental in earth life, and this is obvious, that tampering here with such deep instincts leaves deep repressions, for the traits left are hideous fears and perversions, instead of honest creation that loves the mate.

This type of wrong is hopelessly moving men to more and more crime and insanity. This is, as they know, a bad thing, but how to check it they cannot tell. It is very hard that they cannot see these truths, for I can see them but am helpless to prevent more spirits being doomed to this kind of wretched existence because they have made these animals the poor mutilated half-brained creatures that they chose.

I am strong in this letter, but this is too horrible a subject to mince. It is truly awful. But the people responsible are stupid ignorant people who cannot be reached by our letters I think.

I am the true lover of animals that always loved them.

I think my name was Pastor Hastres.

This is team writing, but I have the feeling that this is not the name. This is a title that I had, perhaps. I think it may not be the true name that follows. I have no sure memory, but I think I lived in the land of France. I loved this land, and was sad that there was so little kindness to animals.

Henry Calverley: I wish I could see what psychologists mean when they speak of all downward pull as being sexual. It seems as if they themselves do not think clearly, for sex is one of the most elevating true attributes of man.

This is not in his animal ancestry to love and work faithfully all his life for a fellow-spirit in fleshly form. When animals are similarly faithful one says they are almost human, and this is often true, but such devotion is one of the things man comes to earth to learn.

He is the wonderful helper of God in sex, for he tries to consider how he may rule himself that his children shall be free and happy. I wish people could try to think thus of sex, and not attribute all the awful memories in the subliminal mind to sex repression.

This is sometimes true when man has polluted this unconscious memory by cruelly mutilating these lovely animals, which will be his children, so that they cannot obey their instincts, which train them for life as man.

But truth is true, whether men like it or believe it. They are brothers to their animals, and in them make or mar the race. I hope this will make a few stop to think how animals should be treated so that no terrible memories linger in the unconscious.

Henry Calverley.

He continues:—

Man is hurting his own race when he treats animals unnaturally. This is sadly true. This greed is terribly strong in countries where animals are treated by man as nothing but food producers. This is easy to see in this land where people think so much of food, and things to bring them comfort and escape from thought of how to find things out for themselves.

I think this is reasonable to explain for much of the conflict in each individual, for it is only a terrible conflict that man has brought on himself. Now this is showing itself in exploitation of man by man, which is partly outgrown since the animals have not been kept specially to fight each other. This is noticeable, for the higher animals are now much gentler than they were even a short time ago.

This is truly terrible that man tries to think the animals are only food. It is the cruellest blow he can strike at his own children, who are trying to find true ways to follow their instincts faithfully so that they will be equipped for human life. I think no one can fail to think how terrible the effects of unnatural mutilation of the body are. This is the cause of undue sexual desire which has lost its right use. We try to help the spirits of these animals to be eager to love, for this is the truest thing to help them, but man should know how he wrongs God in distorting the instincts of animals.

Nellie Ingram was little more than a baby when she died.

I append a short extract from her letter dealing with play between children and animals in the Astral world. I think that this is a common item in the education of children there.

This little girl was about as big as I, and she held my hand tight in such a nice way. I thought how much she loved to play with me, for I was the littlest and did not always be able to play well, for I was only a baby. But this was no baby although she was little too. We went to such a lovely place on the tall hills and played with animals that loved to play with us. I thought how funny it was we had never done this before, but thought animals would scratch or bite.

But none did. They loved to jump over us and be in our laps.

This was the great play place for newly dead children I afterwards found, for they have fears to meet, so meet first little animals with no fears, and this makes them bolder. I became bolder and we went into the wood that was near and found bigger animals, but all were friendly, but had fears to some extent, especially big wild ones. They feared us, but not much as we were little, and not angry as they remembered men might be.

This is sad that animals fear man, but this is only because man has made them fear him. This is not a true part of animal spirit, to fear; but they fear each other too. And this too is no true part. That this has come about is because man has been cruel and fights himself, and this is the result and cause, for he dictates what he will be and has his own ancestry made to fit him.

There are no vivisectors in this group; perhaps they are to be found in a different stratum of Astral society, but there is one John Priestley who experimented on animals. Here is an extract from a long letter of his.

This is the kind of thing I did. I liked to be an experimenter in practising how to find the reactions of these poor animals to various illnesses. This was a truly brutal thing to do, but I thought

I served man by leading him to better health if I found out these things.

I had this type of mind that enquires into causes, but I thought all causes of physical troubles were physical. This brighter idea that I see you have now in the world was hid from me, though others began to think these true animals should never be sacrificed that man by their suffering might be better.

Now I see I was the cause of brutal traits in the spirits of several men, but happily not so terrible as the one you have just heard, but so very bad that I was horrified to see the result of my work. This brightened my spirit to try and love these poor wronged spirits. This perhaps has helped to some extent; but this is a true brutality which persists in spirits which have been wronged thus in the place of the love that should have been given them by man.

This is the bitter tale I tell: I liked to experiment with beautiful mice that suffered in bitter silence, for they do suffer, even in brain. This is a mistake to think that animals have no brain suffering. I think people have little idea how a beautiful animal can suffer if it feels fear. This is always the reaction of brutal treatment, for the animal even shows fear. This is easy to see, but men do not try to encourage them, but consider their fear is automatic, as it is; caused by their brutality. I think this is known, for animals where man has never been are not afraid of him, and often not of each other either. I think savagery in animals is largely created by man. This turbid brain, that only tries to kill and be killed is not a true creation.

I was the truly bright man in a brain of earth, but tried in vain to create myself a bright spirit, for I did not love.

This is true. I think I am the doctor that was called John Priestley.

Yes; Priestley, I think. I knew this kind of work in being the founder of medical brutality; for this is the truth, though I could not guess it.

I lived in London; I know this is the truth, in the time of this Queen, but I cannot say how long ago.

I was a bright brain that may be still known. We believe the name is John Priestley; this is the name we hear.

You will remember that the query arose as to how wild animals could be kept in existence after populations, primitive at present, have become civilised and spread over areas of country which are at present untilled.

The same sort of difficulty would arise in connection with domesticated animals if mankind were suddenly to adopt a vegetarian diet and refuse to wear leather shoes. As vegetarians, we should have to plough up all our grassland, for a mental revolution would not change our stomachs so that they could digest grass.

What, then, is to become of the herds of cows accompanied by fierce bulls? (If you are going to be consistent, you cannot continue to drink milk, because this involves calf-slaughter on a large scale.) Are they, together with the millions of the pig population of the country, to roam at large as non-contributory pets devouring the crops which are destined for our sustenance in their place? Of course not. It is quite obvious that cattle and pigs would cease to exist in a vegetarian Britain. Sheep might be tolerated for their wool, but the keeping of sheep without using their carcases for food would make wool a very expensive and uneconomical commodity, and some synthetic substitute would probably soon be provided.

With the disappearance of wild animals, and of cattle, sheep, and pigs, we should have to rely on pet dogs and cats and on vermin such as mice and rats as the antechamber to humanity.

I think we should allow the Lords of Creation to work out their plans at their own tempo, and that we should not spurn animal flesh, provided that cruelty in every form is excluded from the process of their slaughter.

Incidentally, my wife tells me that in visits to the animal spheres she has seen beautiful new types of animals which are to inhabit the earth, so the problem is not being overlooked by the Authorities! I have not seen any message which deals with cruel methods of slaughter of domestic animals. This is strange, because there is a great deal of absolutely unnecessary cruelty in, and especially outside, slaughter-houses in this country.

I believe that in the comparatively near future (in geological time) man will have ceased to kill animals for food, or in order to use their skins for clothing. In the meantime the practice is in consonance with man's present state of development and, it seems to me, perfectly permissible.

What is not tolerable is that unnecessary suffering should be caused to these poor creatures either in the preliminary stages or in the killing itself.

Inside our slaughter-houses orders are in existence that all animals shall be stunned either by electricity or by the humane-killer before the knife is used. Jews and Moslems are excepted from this order at the time of writing (Spring 1950).

But outside the slaughter-houses no such protection exists, and more than half a million poor animals are killed with the knife in full consciousness every year—often by inexpert slaughter-men.

As the group are silent upon this point, I will quote my wife. She has always been a devoted animal-lover, and her love has, if possible, increased in the thirty years since she died.

In 1946 she wrote: "I have got some new work. You know you have slaughter-houses and send animals over to us in a great agony of fear. When they arrive they are put in pens—they wouldn't appreciate complete freedom.

Some cows have never seen a field. We take them into a pen—we talk to them, and they talk back.

"Then we open the pen and let them walk out into a field. I just couldn't believe it—some people never let cows out of sheds.

"I think that the American and English are the cruellest and nastiest people to do such cruel things.

"Chang took me to see. Perhaps I could help. The poor dumb animals can't do anything about it.

"When the animals are getting afraid, some of us go and talk to them and soothe them and lead them away.

"Their souls are smaller than human, but still they have got souls. Every kind of animal comes over here, even scorpions; but they have no stings."

Chang says that all life must go through all stages." Before I finish with this group I must just relate a comic incident which arose through the attachment of one of them to Mrs. Roberts. (He was not one of those mentioned above, but a minor character from the Shakesperian party.) Mrs. Roberts records the incident thus:— While considering what to give for Christmas. Helpful Voice: "What about gloves? Or an account book? Or hair brushes—a pair of good stiff hair-brushes?" "But these are baby girls." (Solemnly.) "Oh! this is another matter. Hairbrushes would not be suitable then. No. I see; I see." In order to carry out the ideas expressed in Chapter 1, I have endeavoured to find out from Mrs. Roberts what sort of personal life the members of this group lead, what clothes they wear, and what sort of houses they live in, if any. I haven't succeeded in getting much information: they say that they don't live in houses, and they don't seem to take any interest in clothes. One of them said, "I wear only very poor ideas", and one of the stories which

I have not reproduced dealt with a very haughty nobleman who created a replica of his ancestral castle, and used to wear his coronet all day and sleep in it at night; but the emancipated souls who constitute the bulk of the communicators don't seem to think about these things at all. This is odd, because elsewhere (as for instance in Vale Owen's principal book) we are given to understand that there is a mystical significance in the robes and the gems of order and degree of ministry which each person wears.

If these communicators have any common denomination, it is that they are all approaching the stage of progress where direct communication with earth is becoming difficult.

Although I have perhaps devoted a disproportionate amount of space to the messages of this Group, I have had to put aside a large number of interesting and educative stories which I would gladly have included had space permitted. Those interested are referred to Mrs. Roberts' book, particulars of which were given on page 105.

CHAPTER 9

CONVERGING PATHS

I propose now to deal in what must be a very superficial manner with some of the different paths which people follow as a means of reaching a common goal.

Of course, in a sense, every religion is such a path; but I do not propose to make any attempt to offer potted versions of the various religions of the world. I have, in fact, found it rather difficult to find a common denominator for the systems of thought that I do propose to outline.

I suppose I can say this, though, that the systems which I propose to touch upon accept the continuity of conscious life after death and have an intelligent interest in acquiring fresh knowledge concerning the conditions under which that life is carried on.

My object is to give to people, who have only recently begun to take an interest in psychic or occult affairs, some sort of idea of the various schools of thought which deal in these matters, so that the enquirer may find a channel which is congenial to his or her personality and habit of mind.

May I begin by quoting an extract from a message received by a friend of mine who is intermittently the recipient of communications from the invisible world? "Torch-bearers sometimes lead processions, but at other times they stand and light the way for others to follow the Path which, without them, they could not find.

"In either duty they give of their uttermost in His service, asking not why or when, but only to be His followers." She saw two pictures;

one of a procession of people marching through a dark landscape and headed by a group of torch-bearers, and another of people finding their own way along a dark road illuminated at intervals by single torch-bearers.

And so my idea is to give a brief sketch of the 'processions' which I happen to have encountered, so that the neophyte may make further enquiries along the lines which appeal to him, or else, like myself, may elect to make an individual search for the road, preferring to risk making his own mistakes rather than to follow the crowd irresponsibly along highways and, possibly, byways.

The four most important Organisations of Spiritualism are perhaps the Spiritualist National Union, the Marylebone Spiritualist Association, the Greater World Christian Spiritualist League, and the London Spiritualist Alliance.

I will not bore my readers by enlarging on the work of these very well known bodies, but for those unfamiliar with the movement I may perhaps mention that the first-named is, *par exellence*, an organising body, deeply concerned with the legal aspect of the protection of honest mediums against persecution and the discouragement of fraud of every kind.

They have a countrywide membership, their Headquarters are in Manchester, where their paper, The *Two Worlds*, is published. They have many churches.

The Marylebone Spiritualist Association is a body very active in practical Spiritualism. At their Headquarters at Marylebone House, 42 Russell Square, almost every form of practical Spiritualism is in active operation. They have twenty-five mediums attached to the premises. Healing Circles, Group Demonstrations, Psychometry, Development Classes, Obsession Circles, etc., are all in their weekly programme. Private sittings are given every day, and each Sunday a big service is held at the Victoria Hall in Bloomsbury Square. They have a little monthly periodical called *Service*, which generally contains one or two interesting articles, as well as a full programme of the month's activities.

The Greater World Christian Spiritualist League, lays more stress on keeping contact with the Christian tradition than perhaps any other Spiritualist body. Their Headquarters are at 3 Lansdowne Road, Holland Park, W.II, where services, circles and classes are held. The king pin (or rather queen pin) of this organisation is Miss Winifred Moyes, who, in spite of constant pain and ill health, travels about the country every Sunday giving trance addresses from one 'Zodiac', a teacher in the temple at the time of our Lord, and later a convert to Christianity and a martyr in that cause. His weekly talks are recorded in their journal *The Greater World*. An important feature of their work is the provision of shelters for homeless women in London and Leeds.

The London Spiritualist Alliance, of 16 Queensberry Place, S.W.7, was founded by Stainton Moses in company with other early stalwarts of Spiritualism.

If I say that they would perhaps wish to be thought of as intellectual Spiritualists, that remark is not intended to be derogatory to any other section of the movement. They rather specialise in lectures and discussions, but maintain a staff of mediums for group and private sittings. They have (so far as I am aware) quite the best library of any Spiritualist organisation, and are the publishers of *Light*, the most sedate of Spiritualist journals.

I do hope that I shall not get into trouble for sins of commission or omission in the above little thumbnail sketches, or for inferring that these four are necessarily the most influential or important sections of Spiritualism: I hope I may say that I am on friendly terms with all, and if offence has been given in any quarter it has certainly not been deliberate.

Now I want to turn to some other smaller Societies and Circles, not because of their size or present importance, but because of their beliefs and teaching. Three of the four that I have already mentioned are too large to have a sharply canalised canon of belief; even if they wished to do so, they could not tie all their members down to a common creed.

There is perhaps less divergence of opinion among the Greater World people, because, as I have said, they hold as closely as they can to the Christian tradition, and, apart from that, Zodiac is their prophet and Miss Moyes his mouthpiece.

The 'Greater World' teaching is quite definitely against Reincarnation, as is the opinion of the headquarters of the London Spiritualist Alliance. And I think that if today a ballot were to be taken among all Spiritualists, the vote would be decidedly against the acceptance of the principles of Rebirth.

If I was going to string along with any of the torchlight processions pictured at the beginning of this chapter, I think I should probably choose the 'White Eagle Lodge', because it so happens that the teaching which they receive is very similar to that which was given to us in our own Circle. Their headquarters are at 9 St. Mary Abbot's Place, W. 8. I should quite definitely recommend it to the seeker after a teaching which will satisfy the heart as well as the brain. I think I am right in saying that White Eagle gives a trance address there through Mrs. Grace Cooke about once a month, and I feel sure that an enquiry, accompanied by a stamped and addressed envelope, would elicit the date of the next address.

The organising head of the White Eagle Lodge on the physical level is Mrs. Grace Cooke, best known, perhaps, as the authoress of the book *Plumed Serpent*, which is well worth reading by anybody, be he tyro or old hand in the world of Spiritualism. By her permission, endorsed in the kindliest manner by White Eagle himself, I include hereunder a sample of his Inner Teachings.

White Eagle's Inner Teaching

Invocation

Great White Spirit, All-enfolding Love; Source of all light, all wisdom, all truth; we Thy children earnestly seek knowledge, love, and clear vision of the purpose of life.

We seek to be servants of Thy Son, the great light of this universe; we wait upon Thee; and we call to our brethren in the spheres of light, angels and archangels and all the company of the Great White Brotherhood, to send upon this gathering the power of love and peace; and all our love and thankfulness we humbly bring to Thee. Amen.

We are continuing our talk on the subject of the Aquarian age, or shall we say the future of mankind on earth? We would remind those who listened patiently to our last talk that we roughly explained the purpose of the last age, the Piscean age, and enlarged upon the bearing these great ages had upon the spiritual evolution of earth's humanity.

Now you will be looking forward to hearing something about the wonderful and beautiful things likely to come in this new Aquarian age. You do right to look forward to better conditions of life and to greater happiness and harmony on the earth. We would, however, remind you that nothing is attained lightly, and humanity must work for any happiness which is likely to come. We say likely to come. Man has been given power of freewill choice.

Man likes to think he can choose this path or that, and proudly, will sometimes go to any lengths to assert this freedom. We would remind you here that life is subject to law. Therefore while man possesses free will it does not operate quite as the majority of people think Man certainly has power to choose to live in the God-way or the way of the spirit; or to follow the way of the earth, the way of flesh. In the old terminology, we would say that man has free will to choose between God or the devil.

This sounds forceful, does it not? So we will put it in another way, and say that you can choose between following light, love, goodness— all the qualities of the Christ man— or the qualities of the earth man, the materialistic man.

These two possibilities are within you, so you are all dual personalities in this respect. The actual events or the karmic lessons which the soul has to learn are there waiting, and you cannot escape the debts of karma.

So we want to point out clearly that while this new age of Aquarius will bring mankind opportunities, man himself can either use or abuse these opportunities. This statement applies to every individual, as well as to the world as a whole. So we say again that man has to work for happiness, and for the blessings which the law of God is showering upon humanity if he will obey the law which these blessings bring.

The great thing in this new age is going to be a two-fold development of both the human and the divine nature, the human being and the divine being. You will have already noticed that powerful mental development has its dangers; side by side with this development there will be the opportunity for great spiritual unfoldment. Thus the first thing to be attained by man in this new age will be self-realisation —realisation of his own soul-powers. Some of you will accept this truth, for there are today many groups who are doing pioneer work in preparation for this new age of Aquarius. Because they are pioneers, they are liable to be criticised and scoffed at by others who are not ready to accept or even to comprehend the measure of soul development which is already taking place in the world. These groups of pioneers are agents or representatives of the Great White Brotherhood behind the veil. This Brotherhood is composed of men and women who have attained to a degree of mastery over physical matter. Having passed through their training, they have acquired a spiritual degree. They draw close to the earth to help the younger members of the community to develop certain qualities and soul powers. Together with development of these soul powers must go development of character and of spiritual qualities.

We shall deal as far as we can tonight with the spiritual as well as the material advancement which you can expect in the new age. First will come this consciousness of man's spiritual or soul powers. For ages past man has been going through a rather dark cycle, which has immersed him deeply in physical matter. He is now just rising from this state of darkness and beginning to see a glimmer of light. In the future this spiritual consciousness or God-consciousness will grow. Possession of these soul-powers will be realised by the majority of people. Man is both divine and human.

Neither aspect must be neglected. It is of the utmost importance that the human side of the nature should be utilised in the right and true way, as well as the divine nature, which also must be encouraged to grow in stature.

The Master Jesus came during the last age, the Piscean age, to give man this clear teaching. He came representing both the human and the divine man. It is gravely important for man to realise this same truth when he is tempted to say, "Oh, well, it is only human nature!", or, "Man is only human". This applies to only half of man.

Man is divine as well as human, but you must have that wonderful blending of the two.

This is going to be brought out clearly in the Aquarian age, for this is an age of mind and spirit, or of the unfoldment or manifestation of the divine and the human. The human provides the vehicle for the divine. In the Master Jesus can be seen a lovely manifestation of these two aspects.

Here was the man who could enter into the sorrows and joys of his brothers; here was the man who found in the simple things his greatest joy; here was the man who worked in the fields not as a beast of burden but as a son of God, with his face towards the sun, and who served his brother man not with greed in his heart for satisfaction of his own desires, but whose joy was to serve life, to serve God, to serve his brother man. This brings his divinity right through his human nature. This is so important.

You are living here on this earth, not to escape at the first possible opportunity in order to float away into higher worlds; but you are here to live as God-men, to live nobly and beautifully. You are here so to live as to glorify your Creator.

These same simple truths will be manifested in the new age—not all at once, because we have to realise that there is a great deal of soul-work to be done before man can demonstrate the qualities of the Aquarian age. To you who listen we say how lovely it will be! Scientists will discover further the secrets of Nature; we shall have a wondrous mode of lighting and decorating our homes, which will be beautifully warm, being heated by concentrated rays of the sun in various forms. There will be no dirt in the home, and so the housewife will have a good time. We shall not have to work nearly so hard. How beautiful this new age is going to be! Yes, but pause a little and think: all things of this nature have to be earned, and they also bear a penalty. This may not be quite the best way of putting it. At all events, we can say that these reforms, these inventions which will come forward in this new age will have to be paid for, in some form. For that matter, everything in life must be paid for. Spiritual things cannot be paid for in money. They have to be paid for by man himself. Man has to learn in this new age the art of giving himself. None can give a greater gift than himself or herself. This is what the Master Jesus demonstrated.

Hold the picture before you of the life of the Master Jesus, and you will see he gave himself without measure. The race in the Aquarian age will have to do likewise if it wishes to enjoy the gifts which are waiting in the invisible for man to bring forth into the visible. Man must therefore learn to give himself without stint. This does not mean that man has to crucify himself, but that man has to surrender the selfish demands of the mortal man. He has to see things in a truer perspective. He has to develop discernment, discrimination between what is worthwhile and what is worthless. He has to select, to choose his way, and to choose the better way. As the Master Jesus taught, the better way is the narrow path. It does not appear so inviting; it means discipline; it means restriction of the appetites of the flesh; it means the controlling of the thoughts and the speech and the actions in life. These things mean self-discipline.

The many beautiful qualities within human nature are going to be brought forth in this new age. Let us consider only the material things which are likely to come about.

There will be a further overcoming of time and space— this is happening today, is it not?—and consequently a lessening of distance. Before very long transport will seem so rapid that distance will disappear. Man is already beginning to extend his term of life in the physical body, and there will come a further prolongation. Life will become longer, because as man evolves he will touch divine wisdom. He will not recognise at first that he has touched divine wisdom. This divine truth will percolate through the mental body, and this mental body will grow very powerful at first in the new age. You are seeing indications of this already in the worship of the intellect, and the achievements of the brain and the mind, but this will pass and there will come development of the spiritual qualities, the Christ qualities, and a breaking down of mental arrogance. This is of the utmost importance and necessary because without this other influence to qualify the strong mental development, man would destroy himself through the uncovering of the secrets of nature. Today, you see, mankind has arrived at a certain cycle in his spiral of evolution on which he is getting more spiritual balance. So these destructive powers of the mind will in time be held in check, but not without work and effort, as we have already reminded you.

You people are pioneers of this new age. To you and groups like you the powers behind the veil are looking to bring to the earth this supreme light, this spiritual quality which must hold in its place the great mental power. We might almost describe the two as force and energy, two opposites necessary to the development and the keeping in place of physical matter. Yes, a very great age is before you in which there will be advance in television, in the reception of sound, in interplanetary communication, and in knowledge of the wonderful secrets of the invisible world.

There will be also the discovery and very great use of metals and the discovery of new metals. Yes. We do not know how to explain, but can tell you there will be most wonderful new materials. Even buildings, houses, all these material things will change and will become, as you say, "streamlined We see at first not very artistic (from the heavenly point of view) architecture. We do not think the points, squares and hard lines at present in vogue attractive, but this is only a phase. We look forward to the greater beauty of curves and beautiful lines in building.

These will come with development of God-consciousness, when man begins to get beyond his mental plane to the celestial. Then he will bring through something of the beauty of the heavenly spheres. Do you understand? A great difference exists between the mental and the celestial planes. When your vision is open and you look into the mental spheres you will see triangles, squares and points—sharp, hard lines. When you get to the higher and celestial plane you will get beauty in curves, gracious and soft colouring, a greater harmony of line and form. This is what you will expect in the later part of the Aquarian age —a manifestation in matter of this more heavenly state of life.

Let us return to this development of the soul-qualities.

First, man will become aware of his inner powers. Then he will begin to develop them, and the veil between the visible and the invisible will be swept aside. Except for a very few people, there will be no division between the two states. That is to say, man in his body will develop his vision, his certain knowledge and understanding of an extended life beyond death of the physical body. This will be known far and wide. Instead of being laughed at for holding extraordinary ideas, those people who have not got there will be the more criticised.

It is one thing to acquire mental knowledge and power, but another to apply or to use what you have wisely. You see what we are driving at? Unless man follows the path outlined by the Master of the Piscean age, man will prove his own destroyer. He can destroy himself. We do not think he will, but he can. In individual cases this destructive power can be seen at work in the life. Every person has to learn his infinite possibilities, has to develop his infinite powers, and then must apply or use them as God meant him to use them. To this end we have the wisdom of the sages through the past ages teaching man the correct and wise way of life, showing him the path of his soul. In a way it does not matter much if people are wilful and insist on taking the left-hand path. It is only like a man banging his head against a brick wall. The wise man does not batter his head to pieces. He follows the quiet and orderly way of progress and takes the right-hand path. The sooner humanity recognises the fact that it is subject to divine law the quicker it will enter into this state of harmony and happiness. The object of life here is that you may realise, may find, may create your own heaven on earth. You do not depend on outside things, if you are a true candidate.

You create your heaven. Then you are in your heaven here and now.

The natural process of evolution brings humanity into ages which offer to mankind certain opportunities, qualities and gifts. You are really now on the cusp of a very great age of beauty, harmony and power and spiritual ecstasy.

Before we finish we want to refer to the people in this mystic isle. This is a very favourite topic of ours. This mystic isle has great potentialities. We cannot go fully into this. It would take too long. In this land lie buried the secrets of a great early age when the world was controlled or directed by angelic beings, by Sun-Gods or Godmen. These great ones came from another sphere, another planet which is invisible, and were known as Hyperboreans.

They travelled south from what you call the North Pole, a magnetic centre, to this mystic isle and to other parts of Europe. These great Sun-Gods have left their secrets buried in the earth of this isle. In the

Aquarian age development of man's mental and spiritual qualities will enable your scientists to penetrate these secrets of what we call the "lost world". Even now in the not too distant future some very remarkable discoveries about these ancient centres of power in this little mystic isle will be made. The White Brotherhood are drawing closer to those who can be used for this purpose. This divine fire is going to grow and develop in man; it is going to rise from the very ground upon which he lives.

All this will sound far-fetched to many of you, but we are unconcerned. What we say is right and true; and to those of you who can accept it, we say, continue faithfully and patiently with your work of resuscitating these centres of divine light and power; because in this isle lies the secret of creation, the secret of moulding etheric matter and the building again of the beautiful temples of the Great White Light of the past.

There are still so many things we have left unsaid.

May we tell you what part music is going to play in the future, and also speech? Even now the stimulation in people of the love of music has begun. The power of music is going to increase. Beauty is going to increase.

You have passed through a period of rather unpleasant music. This has been a time of noise and conflict, which has had its purpose in breaking down unwanted things, like the builder who gets to work with his pick to clear away old buildings. More beautiful music will stimulate the mental qualities, and will gently open the heart centre.

The music that is coming will raise the vibrations of the earth.

All that has finished its usefulness will be cleared away.

It is even now being cleared away. This is not altogether pleasant, of course. This age is going to see an increase of brotherhood, but at the present time some misunderstanding exists as to the meaning of brotherhood. Brotherhood means recognition of the needs of all others, not only of one person or of one class. The true brother is only too willing to help his brother to be satisfied and to receive that which is necessary to him. The spirit of love and brotherhood amongst men is surely, surely coming to you, my children.

No man can crash the gates of heaven. He must proceed according to law and gradually unveil the rose which is his heart; and you are all on that path towards mastery over the lower nature and mastery of physical matter.

Q. What part will speech and dancing play in the new age?

A. Movement and Speech and music are all connected with ritual, and ritual is connected with the utilisation of invisible forces. When speech is correctly used it means that invisible forces are gathered up and built into form or are directed to a certain centre or place on the physical plane. This certainly has an influence, for it is a creative power. Speech is a great agent for the control of occult force. Dancing, of course, was much used in the temples of the past. If you could see clairvoyantly what takes place with the movement of a trained dancer, who is working from the spirit, and not only from the mind, you would see most beautiful designs of light. Everywhere he or she went they would create certain forms, and you would see all these forms build into the ether, being built of light. Forms built of light in the higher ether will in due time gradually crystallise, and be brought through into matter. All this is somewhat beyond you at present. We can only give you a hint, an idea.

Movement will have a great deal to do in the new age, not only with the body itself, with the prolongation of life and health, but also with the creation of life. Movement and speech are very important.

Much harm is done ignorantly by bad speech. Good speech, the correct formation of words, clear diction, precision in speaking, is really very important. Few of you use your speech in the correct way. People are apt to become slovenly in speech and use a lot of words which will create a state of chaos. In the temples of the past rhetoric was one of the subjects in which the candidate was trained. It would be a very good idea to have a speech-training class and movement in the White Eagle Lodge. You may be amused, but this is all part of spiritual development.

Q. In the Aquarian age will there be one common speech?

A. Of course; spiritual language is a common language.

In the higher spheres there is just one language. In time unification of all the races on earth will necessarily bring one common language of the spirit, which will be interpreted in the same speech through the lips.

Q. In the higher worlds is speech by sound?

A. Not as you understand it. Speech is almost like a flash of light. It is speech, but not as you understand sound on the earth. There is sound, there is spiritual vibration. Speech is very much finer and more musical than you understand speech.

There will be many unexpected happenings in the new age. Miracles, my children, the world will call them. From many quarters a flash of light will come to illumine the darkness of the earth. The effect will be like a revolution, but not of the kind you think—a revolution of thought and ideas which are going to flood in before very long.

Benediction: We thank Thee, O Great White Spirit, for Thy blessing, which is upon us now. We thank Thee, Great Almighty Presence, for life, for love, for all the gifts which Thou dost so freely give to Thy children. We thank Thee; and may Thy peace, Thy tranquillity be born in our hearts and remain with us evermore. Amen.

I propose to take this opportunity of saying a word about Guides. A good many people who are new to the ideas of Spiritualism are repelled or moved to ribaldry by the prevalence of American-Indian or Egyptian or Chinese Guides. The reaction is perfectly natural; I experienced it myself.

There is a good deal to be said in explanation of this state of affairs, but the basic explanation is that there is nothing to explain. We 'white' people are so abominably arrogant, buried as we are in our present Personalities. We happen to be in a 'white' body at the present moment, but there is no guarantee that we shall be so next time, and the more we despise the 'inferior' races in this life, the more likely is the law of Karma to operate, so that we find ourselves in an inferior position in the next.

But in any case our superiority to the Red Man was mainly material. We had mastered the use of metals, and he had not. In spirituality, in endurance, in honesty and in service to the one Great Spirit, the uncontaminated Indian compared very favourably with those who drove him from his heritage by methods which still bring a flush of shame to the cheek.

As Belloc makes his hero, Blood, say:—

> Whatever happens we have got
> The Maxim Gun, and they have not.

The Indian lived in close touch with the Spirit in earthlife, and is by that the better qualified to act as an intermediary between the quick and the dead.

Then you must remember the 'mechanics' of Communication. When a spirit has reached a certain stage of development, direct contact becomes impossible—or rather it becomes impossible for the Earth-mind to receive consciously any communications from such a source. One of the various devices which can be adopted to overcome this difficulty is for the spirit to recreate out of Astral matter one of the Astral bodies which he has occupied in past lives.

Some, therefore, of the many Indian Guides may be highly progressed spirits who are using the Astral Indian body purely as a telephone exchange.

It should not be inferred, however, that all Indian and Chinese Guides fall into this category. Many of them have no pretensions to be anything more exalted than they appear; they often specialise in healing work, in which many of them are skilled, but they may have little knowledge of the more remote vistas of our life to come.

My own idea, for what it is worth, is that we all have a Guardian Angel—a very highly developed spirit who is linked in age-long friendship with the shining Individual who is the essential 'I' of each one of us. Very few of us make conscious contact with this Angel in this life, or perhaps for a long period after physical death; but he has his deputies and assistants at various levels, and perhaps it is not unreasonable to suppose that we may each have several friends who are specially charged with our welfare, the least developed of whom is known as the Door-keeper, who is constantly with us to protect us from invasion by obsessing entities.

Perhaps this idea may seem a little fantastic and farfetched to some people, but the professing Christian, at any rate, should not jib at it; for Matthew tells us that, when the devil was quoting scripture to our Lord in the wilderness, he said, "For it is written, He shall give his angels charge concerning thee, and in their hands shall they bear thee up, lest at any time thou dash thy foot against a stone. This I regard as substantially true, as are so many passages in the Bible which materialism looks on as poetic abstractions.

Well, I must get down off my hobby horse and come back to the Groups and Societies which I was describing before I embarked on this digression on the subject of Guides.

There is a smallish but not unimportant group of people who base their ideas upon the Ancient Wisdom of the Egyptians. *The Book of Truth*, which is the canon of their beliefs, is not readily available, but preliminary books entitled *The Teachings of Osiris* and *The Book of El Daoud* can be found in some psychic libraries.

There are some people who, consciously or unconsciously, have very strong links with past Egyptian incarnations, and such people may find that this Society (which is in continuous receipt of fresh inspiration) will appeal to them, whereas others who have no Egyptian links may be put off by the strong remnants of the Ancient Religion that persist in the modern version.

Unfortunately, at the time when this book goes to press, the Centre of the Crown is undergoing a reorganisation.

This prevents me, for the time being, from giving information concerning enquiries or applications to join the Centre.

It may come as something of a shock to the unthinking to be told that this group is still in direct touch with Osiris.

This is such an extreme statement that it is a good peg upon which to hang some thoughts about the exclusiveness of Christianity—the idea that, because Jesus came into incarnation as perhaps the greatest of World Teachers with the loftiest code of teaching, therefore all teachers who had come before him must have been false prophets who came to lead the people astray into the paths of heathendom.

Let us take the Lord Buddha, who lived only five hundred years before Jesus, as an example. He was certainly a historical character, and his life and teaching have affected the lives of more people than have the life and teaching of Jesus.

It is true that his teaching has been twisted almost out of recognition by priests; but so has the teaching of Jesus, if perhaps to a smaller extent.

Jesus lives, as the hymn truly says. But The Buddha also lives, and today inspires millions of his followers.

And so do other World Teachers upon whom the mantle of the Christ Spirit has descended.

Now, just in the same way, Osiris was a mortal man, suffused with this great Cosmic Spirit. He came to bring wisdom to the Egyptians; we call it the Ancient Wisdom now. Osiris, like others of his kind, was deified after his death, and the priesthood took it upon themselves to build legends about him and to fit him in to their elaborate pantheon.

It is this tiresome habit of deifying our teachers which leads humanity into so much trouble. We say:— "Our teacher is God (or a God, as the case may be), therefore what we believe is divinely inspired and correct, and all other forms of belief are incorrect and lead inevitably to eternal damnation." And so, just as we may sing "Jesus lives we may also state it as a parallel fact that Osiris lives. Of course it is always possible that he might have chosen for himself a path of progression which would lead him away from Earth and its interests; but it is surely reasonable to suppose that a Great One who came into incarnation to teach and help humanity would choose to 'stay with the ship' until at least the end of the period of illumination by the Spotlight which I described in Chapter 3, and which we erroneously think of as the 'End of the World'.

Osiris lives—yes. But does Osiris speak and, if so, does he speak truth? That is for those to determine to their own satisfaction who have their roots buried deeply in the Egypt of olden time, and are thus attracted to this Group.

It occurs to me that, in my efforts to be completely open minded towards those who look to the Lord Buddha, or Krishna, or Osiris, or any other Avatar, for their primary inspiration, I may have given an impression that my own allegiance is half-hearted or divided. That is not so.

My immediate allegiance is due to the Beloved Master.

Jesus we call him. But remember that Jesus was merely the name of his Personality in that particular lifetime of his of which we are fragmentarily aware. The word 'Jesus' in Hebrew is merely another form of 'Joshua'. He has another name, as an Individual, which we do not know; and it is that Individual who is my Master and the Master of millions who, through him, try to worship and to serve the Ultimate Unnameable One.

Then there is a book called The *Winds of Truth*, printed by Butler and Tanner, Ltd., Frome and London.

It consists of writings received in trance by the 'Group of Solar Teaching' which operates, or used to operate, at Glastonbury. The instigator of the writings is stated to be the Archangel Michael.

The names of persons, planes, rays, etc., jar on the modern sight because an attempt is made to transcribe Atlantean or earlier words in English lettering, and one gets words like MLUNHISIA, MLYHYHIA, FRANCHILIA, etc., etc.

There are two chapters in the middle about King Arthur which rather appeal to me, but apart from that I am not much attracted by the book. I mention it here, however, because it has a great fascination for some people (possibly those with strong Atlantean links), and I want to give some account of the different paths which different' processions' follow towards the Light, even if they are not processions which I personally should be tempted to join.

I have dealt with Vale Owen's book, *The Life Beyond the Veil*, at great length in my book *Many Mansions*, and I do not propose to repeat myself here. Personally I think that it is one of the best and most comprehensive books which has ever been written on the earlier stages of the next life.

It is corroborated in essential outline by R. J. Lees' books *Through the Mists* and *The Life Elysian*, which are classics of Spiritualism (or rather it corroborates them, for they were written twenty years earlier).

One does not associate any particular little 'procession' with these books; I think they may be regarded as guiding lights to the average run of Spiritualists.

All the 'processions' which I have so far mentioned can fairly be included under the umbrella of Spiritualism, though perhaps some of them might not readily apply the label to themselves; but there are certain other frames of belief, which do not constitute religions, upon which I ought to touch. I must say a word, for instance, on the adherents of the Qabalah, which has its roots in the ancient religion of the Hebrews. These include the Rosicrucians and (I believe) have certain links with Freemasons, though, not being a Mason, I have no knowledge of their Mysteries.

I have industriously burrowed my way through a book called *The Mystical Qabalah*, by Dion Fortune (Williams and Norgate, Ltd., London), which was kindly presented to me by the Librarian of the Society of the Inner Light, 3, Queensborough Terrace, W.2, from which source those interested may obtain more reliable information than has resulted from my own uninstructed gropings into the system.

The central glyph of their doctrine is the 'Tree of Life'. From KETHER, the Spiritual apex, to MALKUTH, the earthly base. There are ten such Sephiroth, or stations as they might be called, indicating the various stages of spiritual progress. They are arranged in three columns, and are connected by thirty-two paths.

The system has links with Astrology and Alchemy, and with Divination through the TAROT cards.

It deals with Numerology, based on the numerical value of the letters of the Hebrew Alphabet; but this is apparently an optional section of the philosophy, because Dion Fortune has stated in her book that she was not a Numerologist.

I gather that the cult is concerned with ceremonial, ritual and magical practices, but these, of course, are not included in books available to the uninitiated public.

There is a good passage in the early part of the book. It deals with choosing one's occult system and making an adequate study of it. "After this has been achieved," she says, "we may, not without advantage, experiment with the methods which have been developed along other Paths, and build up an eclectic technique and philosophy therefrom; but the student who sets out to be an eclectic before he has made himself an expert will never be anything more than a dabbler." It is a strange thing, but I have an instinctive aversion from prediction in general in so far as it affects persons and their actions; and perhaps that is why I am not attracted to Astrologers and operators of the Tarot cards.

I cannot defend my point of view except in that I have met a number of people who seem to me to rely unduly on the element of prediction in their lives. It seems to me that it saps their power to make decisions for themselves, and it does not seem to matter how often the predictions turn out to be wrong, they are just as ready to be guided by them in the future.

Of course this does not apply only to Qabalists and the followers of Astrology; some Spiritualists are just as prone to this attitude.

For myself, if I am told (for instance) that I shall visit Japan next June, a resistance to the idea is automatically set up. It is a sort of challenge to my freewill, and I subconsciously set about asserting my self and making the prediction go wrong. I do not say that the resistance would necessarily be so strong as to cause me to refuse to go to Japan if circumstances should strongly indicate the desirability of the journey, but the tendency would be there.

I think that perhaps in some life I may have been a Black Magician and used for personal gain the power of seeing into the future, and suffered accordingly.

When I consider the subject rationally and not instinctively, I fully appreciate the value of a hint as to the nature of future work, so that one may be prepared for a call when it comes.

As an unseen friend said to me some years ago: "Since when has loving companionship been denied to man? I offer myself as a companion, who, having trod the roadway a little ahead of you, may perhaps be permitted to say, 'Here is a Pit—Go round—Beware'. 'Here is a grassy plot, rest awhile'. And when the time comes when I must stand aside while you battle on alone, my love shall follow you, for such is the law." There are some people to whom the path of Yoga may appeal, and to such I may be able to give some limited help and guidance. I say 'limited' because the Yoga path involves the seeker in search for his guru or spiritual instructor. The guru normally accepts a limited number of disciples who live as his chelas or pupils, sometimes for many years.

The aim, as the word Yoga implies, is the eventual union with the infinite, which is brought about through the process of self-realisation;

and the guru gives personal instruction to his chelas both on general lines and also in those physical Yoga exercises by means of which the process of self-realisation may be expedited without incurring the quite definite dangers which accompany the uninstructed practice of Yoga methods.

A book called *The Autobiography of a Yogi* was published in the United States about 1945, and has been published in 1950 by Rider & Co. in London. It gives the life history of one Paramhansa Yogananda, who, after a prolonged training in India, was sent by his own guru to become a guru for the people of the West. He travelled to the United States, where he has built up a very considerable organisation.

During his subsequent travels he lectured in England, leaving behind him a smaller organisation operated by deputies under his general supervision and instructions.

Of course the intimate personal relationship between guru and pupil cannot be maintained under a system of this nature, but I think that quite a number of people are attracted by the results obtainable by means of Yoga exercises and undertake experiments without any guidance or safeguards beyond that which they may find in the books which they have chosen for their instruction. As I have stated above, this practice is not without its dangers, and such people may be glad to know that the English Headquarters of the Self-Realisation Fellowship, as it is called, are at 33, Warrington Crescent, London, W.9, where the Secretary, Mrs. Gertrude E. White, will reply to enquiries.

I want to make it quite clear that I am neither recommending nor disparaging this organisation; I know little more about it than I have learned from a study of the book and a visit to the London headquarters. It seems quite obvious that the ideally intimate relationship between guru and *chela* is unlikely to be attained by such wholesale methods, but it does seem at any rate that a definite degree of protection may be afforded to those who decide that the Yoga path is the path for them.

I shall finish this chapter with some thoughts on Theosophy. As I said in *Lychgate*, I am not a Theosophist, I am a Dowding-ist, if I am any kind of an-ist at all. (In this connection, you may be amused to learn that I received a letter from a lady who wanted to become a Dowdingist and "put Dowdingism on the map so to speak, doubtless with a headquarters and a staff and an annual subscription.

It just shows how difficult it is to escape from the organisers.) In pages 109-112 of *Lychgate* I gave a rough outline of the ideas of Theosophy, and, though I have many friends among Theosophists, I have only been challenged over one of the statements which I made there, and that was the statement that the attitude of the Theosophist is one of rather lofty indifference towards proselytisation.

I am genuinely sorry if I have given offence in this connection. Its context was a warning to enquirers to be prepared for this attitude, of which I formed a (perhaps erroneous) personal impression from some of Leadbeater's writings. As a matter of fact, I think that a certain restraint in this connection is by no means a bad thing. One cannot "go out into the highways and hedges and compel them to come in" to Theosophy. The mind of the enquirer must have attained to a certain degree of receptivity and must be reaching out for knowledge, if its contact with Theosophy is to be a fruitful one.

The particular point with which I wish to deal in this book is the attitude of official Theosophy to spirit communication. Theosophy is one of the most broad-minded of philosophies, and allows a very wide range of belief and action to its members, provided that they subscribe to their Three Objects, which are as follows:—

1. To form a nucleus of the universal brotherhood of humanity without distinction of race, creed, sex, caste or colour.
2. To encourage the study of comparative religion, philosophy and science.
3. To investigate unexplained laws of nature and the powers latent in man.

Many members of the Theosophical Society are personally believers in spirit communication, and some of them participate actively therein; so I must be careful not to overstate my case. Instead I will make a deliberate understatement to the effect that the Visible Directors of the Theosophical Society do not to my knowledge practise this communication and do not encourage others to do so.

And I have seen comparatively recently a statement in Theosophical News and Notes by a prominent and responsible Theosophist to the effect that everything which it is necessary for a Theosophist to know is contained in the *Secret Doctrine* and the *Mahatma Letters*, and that there is no need to seek other sources of information.

I think that this is an unfortunate point of view, for two reasons. One is that it would put Theosophy into the category of 'closed-book' philosophies where revelation has ceased to be continuous (as in the Christian Churches), and an art or science or religion or philosophy which has ceased to go forwards and begun to go backwards.

The other is that Madam Blavatsky in her writings and the Masters in the *Mahatma Letters* adopt the view that spirit communication is a dangerous fallacy, that as a rule those who do so communicate are really in touch only with undesirable creatures, such as shells, spooks, murderers, suicides and such like.

Now, here I find myself in a serious quandary, because I believe in the existence of the Masters; they are very real to me, and, if it be not presumptuous for me to say so, I hold for them a very real affection. And yet I know, in so far as any human being can be said to know anything, that they are either wrong or have misreported in this connection.

This is not just an academic point; it means that Theosophists as a whole have cut themselves off from the conscious cooperation with the unseen which adds so immeasurably to the efficiency of occult work.

I leave out of consideration all physical mediumship and all communication which has for its primary object the assuaging of grief at the loss of relatives or friends (except in so far as this latter goes to prove that the Astral is a state of existence very necessary for the progress and development of the human soul, and not a region occupied only by undesirables).

But there remains a vast field of work in which the labourers are pitifully few. Take Rescue Circles as a case in point. There may be adepts and masters who are capable of doing this work single-handed; very probably there are, though I don't happen to know any of them personally; but in any case they must be comparatively few and far between, whereas very commonplace 'men of goodwill' can take their part in this kind of work under the leadership of the Invisibles.

Somebody has to decide who is ready to be brought to the Circle, somebody has to do the bringing, somebody has to take the patient away afterwards, either on towards the Light, or back again to his own place, to try again later.

It seems strange that human intervention should be necessary in such cases, but we have been told on more than one occasion, The regeneration of Mankind must come through Man". We can act, as it were, in the capacity of transformer stations to make contact with those whose faculties are too dulled to resonate to the high frequency waves of the real Rescue Party.

Then again, take the work of the Obsession Circle, already described in this book. Jesus was able to cast out unclean spirits without the use of a trance medium and a Wimshurst machine, and so were His disciples, intermittently, when His Spirit was upon them.

I think that there are probably individuals living today who can do this. But, if so, are they doing it? And, even if they are, the volume of results must be the merest trickle.

Here is the double work of saving a patient from the asylum and setting the occupying entity on the upward path; and this work can be done by quite ordinary people, plus an electrical machine and a trance medium, if they are working with the Invisibles.

I have sometimes sat by invitation with groups in occult societies engaged in sending out combined thoughts into the world, aimed at some worthy objective. Of course I have never been invited into the inmost circle of any such society, and I cannot speak of what occurs there, but in those groups which I have attended I have felt a disunity and dissipation in spite of the most genuine and strenuous efforts to attain to uniformity; all the various minds are wandering along their own channels for lack of a directing influence.

The difference from the proceedings of our own Circle is most marked. To begin with, the object of our mental exercise is selected for us by someone to whom the immediate needs of the world are an open book; and, furthermore, our thoughts are visible to the unseen director, who can check them, correct errors, and so secure uniformity.

I remember on one occasion we were concentrating on producing a healing ray of a certain shade of blue, and the director said "No, F., you are thinking green. Think of the pale blue of a summer sky" (or something of the sort; I forget the precise details).

The point was that the different colour, which she was emitting by means of her thought, was instantly detected and remedied, so that the final product was homogeneous and (we hoped) effective.

On another occasion four of us were asked to visualise a white temple standing on a platform and each of us to visualise a flight of five steps leading up to the platform from our own quarter of the compass. I was the note-taker, and I am afraid that my efforts at step building were adversely affected by my scribbled recording of what was in progress. The director remarked in a pained tone of voice, "I wonder what can have happened. I can only see three flights of steps." So I had with shame to put down my pencil and paper and take a proper and attentive share in the work. (I have said, "The director remarked—the director said—etc.; but you will, of course, understand that the director was invisible and inaudible to all of us except the clairvoyant medium.) Now, of course, to the ordinary materialist, the above must seem the most absolute nonsense. Four people sitting round on hard chairs and trying to influence affairs at a distance by sending out coloured thoughts and mental images! If the materialist were on the staff of a mental home, he would say to us, "Come inside".

But I am not writing for the benefit of materialists, mental, scientific or religious. I am writing it for the eyes of members of societies who know that these things can be done with practical effect; and I want to put it to them that this kind of work can be done more pleasurably and much more efficiently if we are privileged to operate in conscious cooperation with the Invisibles.

As a member of the Theosophical Society, as distinct from a Theosophist, I am distressed at this rather paradoxical situation—viz., that I should accept and venerate the Masters, that I should have an overwhelming sympathy with Madam Blavatsky for her whole-hearted devotion to the Masters and for her sufferings in the service, and yet that I should have the hardihood to maintain that I know from personal experience that 'My Truth' and 'Their Truth' differ in this particular respect.

I think that if one wishes to make up one's mind about the personality of a historical character (and Madam Blavatsky is a historical character) it is a good thing to read two books about that person, one written by a fervid admirer, and the other by an implacable enemy. Miss Neff is the fervid admirer chosen by me, and her book is the *Autobiography of Madam Blavatsky*. The implacable enemy is V. S. Solovyoff.

You have guessed him a Russian shrewd reader at sight. And I think altogether, shrewd reader, you're right.

(Gilbert adapted.) His book is called *A Modern Priestess of Isis*.

The thing that struck me most forcibly after reading these two books (which are by no means the only ones which I have read concerning this most outstanding woman) is the remarkable similarity of the impression which remains after making allowances for the points of view of the writers.

It seems that Miss Neff has not been able to gild the lily nor Solovyoff seriously to besmirch it.

What is abundantly clear from both books, if words have any meaning, is that Madam Blavatsky was a medium.

Theosophists may think this a dreadful accusation to make, but to me there is nothing dreadful at all in it: in fact, I will go farther, and say that, in my opinion, if she had not been a medium she would have been of no use to the Masters.

However that may be, Madam Blavatsky was a medium, and while she was in America before the founding of the Theosophical Society she made no bones about it—in fact, she and Colonel Olcott were for a time engaged in the investigation of activities of other mediums. The particular entity who habitually manifested through Madam Blavatsky at that time was one John King, who was supposed, for some reason which is not explained, to have been either Sir Henry Morgan the pirate, under another name, or else another incarnation of the same individual. He also had the distinction of being the putative father of the celebrated Katie King.

John King appears to have been a typical séance-room spirit, not a bad sort of creature, but not far above the level of the Earth-bound, perhaps. Later on it became necessary to account for John King in accordance with the crystallised Theosophical doctrine, and two opposite explanations are given in Miss Neff's book within three pages of one another.

One is that he was a low personating elemental, and the other is that he was a great soul on a level with the Masters, if indeed not a Master himself! But this frightful quandary does not arise for those who believe the Astral to be a condition through which all souls pass, and in which the majority of souls spend many years of our time engaged in the process of the purgation and sublimation of the Emotional Body.

Any attempt to canonise Madam Blavatsky as a saint in character or behaviour seems bound to lead to artificiality; and surely it is sufficient to think of her as a benefactor to humanity who, by her absolute devotion to her Masters and her triumph over pain and disease, gave to the West so much of the wisdom of the East.

We must remember, of course, that in writing *the Secret Doctrine* Madam Blavatsky acted in a purely secretarial capacity to the Masters; what she wrote came through, and not from her brain, when it did not come in written or 'precipitated' form through one of the Masters' *chelas*.

And indeed even the Masters did not perhaps originate so much of *the Secret Doctrine* as is often supposed. Poor Madam Blavatsky is accused of wholesale plagiarism from books which she probably did not know existed, and certainly never had any opportunity of reading.

The astonishing thing about *the Secret Doctrine* is the way in which information from the rarest books in the libraries of the world appears to have been collected and arranged and given to the world by a poor sick old woman.

Poor she was, and old she was, and very, very sick, but her devotion was indomitable, and her body and soul were held together by the Masters until she had finished her work.

Her tragedy, to my mind, was that she could never altogether give up the practice of physical mediumship— 'the Phenomena' she called it. It was this that eventually brought her reputation to ruin in the eyes of the outside world. When she was accused of cheating in India, her friends in the Theosophical Society maintained that she had been condemned by falsely manufactured evidence, and I believe that they were correct, but they dissuaded her from facing her accusers and defending herself, and therefore her case went by default in the eyes of the world.

As for the Masters, they are great and evolved souls who voluntarily submit themselves intermittently to the limitations of human bodies in order to serve humanity. They say themselves in *Mahatma Letters* that they are not infallible when subject to these bodily limitations, and if anyone deliberately takes the contrary view in spite of their disclaimers, and indulges in the practice of Mahatma worship I can recommend a detailed study of the *Mahatma Letters* as a wholesome corrective.

The decision to publish certain letters which were expressly marked by the Masters 'Not for publication' is nowhere explained. I have sometimes thought that this and the abandonment of Madam Blavatsky in her hour of need may be factors which account for the drying up of this flow of knowledge and inspiration from the East to the West.

To my mind, the outstanding feature of Theosophy is that it gives an intelligible idea of the creation of this planet and of the Solar System of which it is a part. It deals with world history in millions of years and with the involution and evolution of the human race.

It looks into the future and foresees the so-called 'end of the world' with untroubled eyes as a minor and perfectly normal event in the evolution of the Solar System, a System which is itself a speck of infinitesimal importance in the grand progress of the Universe.

It shifts, or should shift, Man from his geocentric and egocentric view of universal existence. It blows like a blast of fresh air through the musty crypts of Western religion and irreligion.

Its function, as I see it, is not so much to lay down the law concerning these matters, as to dynamite the so-called educated man out of his groove and to say to him, "Now get your teeth into that, as a beginning, and start to think for yourself, for a change." I have little to say of certain offshoots from Theosophy, such as the cult known as Anthroposophy. Its founder, Rudolf Steiner, was a Steiner-ist, and started up a Society of his own, with a literature which is available in occult libraries to those interested.

I should, in addition, mention the work of Krishnamurti.

He was 'discovered' by Mrs. Besant and Leadbeater, and brought up in India as the coming World Teacher.

Quite an elaborate organisation was built up around him, with picked disciples and an institution named the 'Liberal Catholic Church' (which remains in existence today).

A castle in Holland was bought and occupied by the organisation, the property being in his name.

And then one day he said to himself: "No. This is not right." And he walked out, with nothing but what he could carry in a suitcase, and went to California, where he has built up an organisation of his own.

He is one of the solitary torchbearers, but he has many pilgrims who look to him for light and leading.

It may be that Mrs. Besant had a true vision of him as a World Teacher, though the method of his ministry did not turn out as she expected.

Quite apart from his teaching, he is one of the men who have a profound, if unseen, effect upon the course of world events. His headquarters are in the Ojai Valley, California.

There is another Society also which is worthy of mention.

It is called the Arcane School. It is in no sense a direct offshoot of Theosophy, but it makes the claim that up till 1949 it was receiving regular communications from a Tibetan Master. Not from either of the Masters Morya or Kuthumi, who were the Masters mainly concerned in the communications coming to and through Madam Blavatsky, but from one Djwal kul (the spelling varies), who was a chela or disciple in Madam Blavatsky's day, but has since attained to Mastership.

Voluminous communications were received by a lady named Mrs. Bailey in the United States. She died in 1949, and at the time of writing I am under the impression that another recipient will not be chosen, for the time being at any rate, pending the assimilation of the great mass of material which has been transmitted.

I should like to give one of the Invocations which they use for the spread of light throughout the world:—

An Invocation or Prayer.

From the point of Light within the Mind of God
Let light stream forth into the minds of men.
Let light descend on Earth.
From the point of Love within the Heart of God
Let love stream forth into the hearts of men.
May Christ return to Earth.
From the centre where the Will of God is known
Let purpose guide the little wills of men—
The purpose which the Master knows and serves.
From the centre which we call the race of men
Let the Plan of Love and Light work out
And may it seal the door where evil dwells.
Let Light and Love and Power restore the Plan on Earth.

So far as I am aware, they do not practise nor encourage personal communication by means of mediums.

The address of their headquarters in England is 38, Broadwater Down, Tunbridge Wells, Kent.

So that completes my little picture of the bands of seekers, each headed by their own torchbearers, marching on resolutely through the twilight of earth-knowledge in search of the white light of Truth. All will find it some day, all the bands and all the solitary seekers, and then they will realise the words of another Master, "And ye shall know the truth, and the truth shall make you free."

CHAPTER 10

AN IRISH INTERLUDE

I think it may be of interest if I now give an account of some experiences of mine in Ireland a year or two ago.

I must begin by explaining that I have altered all the names of people and places. I don't think that my host and hostess would have any particular objection to being mentioned by name, but there is one character in particular who might get into trouble with his priest if he were to be identified through my story. If I have invented Irish names which are etymologically ludicrous or which actually exist, I hope I may be forgiven as an ignorant Englishman.

I must start by going back a hundred years to the time when a wealthy Guards subaltern came on a short fishing visit to this part of Ireland; he was so shocked and horrified at the existence led by the local peasants, that the course of his life was diverted to an attempt to improve their living conditions. Bit by bit he bought the land, till he had acquired a large estate; and the welfare of the people became the primary objective of his life. Sir Gerald Lock was his name, and it still remains a name to conjure with in that countryside.

Sir Gerald's son was not sympathetic; he thought that there were better ways in which the family money might have been expended, and he held aloof from the estate and everything connected with it during his lifetime. Sir Gerald's grandson, General Arthur Lock (who was my host), however, took up the work where Sir Gerald laid it down, and, although the estate had been compulsorily acquired by the Government of Eire, he still regarded the people as his people, and spent his time going from cottage to cottage, talking to people, bringing medicines for the sick, and tobacco and snuff for the aged. He owned the salmon river which flowed through the estate, but during the ten or twelve days of my stay he never touched a rod. All his time was given to his people.

The Locks are old friends of mine, and I accepted their invitation to pay them a visit without any knowledge that there might be psychic work to be done, though I did know that Mrs. Lock was often the recipient of inspirational writings. These came from various sources, but most commonly from her father, who will be designated simply as 'Father' in this story.

While I was staying at The Lodge a communication was received almost every day, generally in the hour before dinner, and we developed the routine that after dinner Mrs. Lock would read over to me her script, illegible to anyone else, I would take it down in shorthand (sometimes illegible to everybody including myself), and then the next morning I would write it out in longhand, keeping a carbon copy for myself. This record I now give to you substantially unaltered. As I have said above, I have invented new names, and I have modified some of the very polite things that courteous communicators have said about me personally; one or two irrelevant passages have been omitted, but broadly speaking the messages are given as received.

One other point before I begin. There was in the neighbourhood a peculiar sharp-pointed volcanic mountain, quite different from the surrounding gently rounded hills.

This mountain was called *Slieve Mish*, and turned out to be the focal point of the work which we had to do. It was about ten miles from the coast.

The first message was from Sir Gerald. So far as I remember, it came on the day of our arrival.

Yes. I have come to write with you, my daughter. I am very glad that Arthur and you have come back to Dunroe and have brought your friend with you: we welcome him to Dunroe, and are very grateful to him for coming. It is a great deal to ask, even though the travelling is better than it used to be in my own day.

Yes—I know you want instructions. I am very glad Lord Hugh (I must call him that, it is his name) has the desire to climb our Mountain. It will make him one of our band more easily than anything else. He has been influenced into coming here for a purpose, which is to put him in touch with all the big natural and spiritual power centres on the whole of this coast. The one on *Slieve Mish* is in contact with and mainly in charge of the rest, partly through geographical and partly through historical associations and other powers. Go to the top and, if you can, write a little at the top. So few go there that the Devic atmosphere is intense, and you may contact teachers of enormous value. (Anywhere else?) Yes, any places will welcome his presence, but *Slieve Mish* is the centre of the great outpouring of force for the whole of this coast.

(Question.) Yes, the Devic and Nature-spirits are all over this place, and we see them and use them for our different purposes.

(Question.) Yes. I am still working here continuously, and so is Parsons (the old Vicar). We are not fitted for any other work yet, and we both enjoy a delightful life.

Healing is one of our most interesting works. You will need to help with that in Dunroe. Lord Hugh always has a large following of R.A.F. boys with him. I have been taking some of them and introducing them to Dunroe. So you see that it is not only Lord Hugh himself, but also the men, who want to see Dunroe and help it. I have one here called Taffy: I do not think Lord Hugh will remember him, but he has been with him before, and now goes on many journeys with him. It is very like a large Staff, and sometimes for fun, they tell me, they dress up and pretend to be very official, and use up-to-date office language, which makes us feel very old-world. Of course it is all a game, but it impresses the new souls over here; and they often come and help, too, partly because they want to, and partly because it is for the R.A.F., and they like the earth feeling of working in an organised body again.

The Staff say this is a very good place for them. Many of them have never seen fairies or Nature-spirits of any kind, and are immensely entertained. I wish you could see them. The R.A.F. lads have brought with them many preconceived ideas, and it is very disturbing to find that your young brother's story books can on occasions come to life.

I took a party into the hills this morning to discover and enjoy the vibrations of a former age, while some others were enjoying the islands. One boy has not been to the sea since he was a child, and is delighted with all the things he can do and see in the water. I think they are all exceedingly happy, and I will tell you more tomorrow. In the meantime Taffy wants to try and write a little. My respectful greetings to Lord Hugh and my welcome to Dunroe.

Taffy. Yes, Sir, I am very glad; this is something quite new. I have been about a bit, but always with our own push. Here it is different, and we can go off on our own.

The people are very nice to us—I mean the ones who used to live here in the body and now live here in the soul.

They do not leave often, as far as I can see; they are all about here, living in the queerest little houses—very comfortable, I'm sure. I do not use houses nor food any more, but many of them are still living like they were. It is all very strange to me, and they keep on talking about evil spirits, and seem afraid to sleep outside, as some of them still do sleep. I do myself sometimes; but this is such a muddle.

If you can believe me, the people over here and the present-day people with you all seem to be living in the same sort of way. I think it is because they came over here without much idea of what would happen, and they wanted above all to have food and shelter; so here it is, but nothing more. I have been trying to talk to some of them and so have the other fellows, but they do not seem to take it in.

Simple-minded! One of the other chaps has been into the mountains, and he will write now.

Yes, I took a turn up and into the hills; it's grand country! Just what I've always longed for. I was always going to find something like this, but I never did till now.

It's fine flying up these gullies and then walking up the hills. I love walking here. Of course there's no fatigue for us, but we can take part in life easier if we are on the ground.

I saw a lot of other kinds of beings that I have never seen before; some very large and some very tiny. Too big a job to explain them today, but I'd like to try later.

Thank you. I salute my Chief.

(Who are you?) Oh, I'm just one of the Fighter Boys.

Next Day.

Father. Yes, my dear. I am so glad you have made direct contact with Sir Gerald. He is a splendid person, but I do wish he could be persuaded to leave Dunroe. You know, even here one needs a change at times, and it is so easy to get one. No arrangements to make, no money to spend, and, as time is not, we can use some of what does not exist for our own education. Revitalising is not necessary, but education is, and that comes to very much the same thing; and this visit of Hugh's will, I hope, stir Gerald to move away and see how the world is going elsewhere.

You are thinking this is the first time I have ever complained of anyone over here; but I am not complaining, though I see the one-track mind hampering one on any plane, and I was always averse from that, as you know.

It is very good of Hugh to come here, and I am going to tell him what he is doing. Gerald has told him of the big power-centre, but that is another subject.

Gerald works ceaselessly with the people, mainly those of his own time and earlier who, as the R.A.F. boys explain, have got stuck here, and they, by their friendly comradeship, have 'knocked them off their perch' better than anything I can think of. Some are actually going to try to do without a house, in consequence: this is a very great advance.

Fear, fear, fear has kept them tied to the plane of this Earth-life, and the very bond they had with Gerald has held them tighter than ever. They dare not go without him, and he hates to leave any behind, so progress is extremely slow; but this visit of Hugh's has changed the tempo all round, and Gerald is thinking of making a journey with some of his people. Others (R.A.F.) are staying here till he comes back. It has done marvels already for the past generations, and once we can get them on the move it will be reflected on the living.

Ask Hugh to concentrate on light and freedom entering into all those homes he was shown today. I was very glad you went for that drive: the whole country is much alike, and it gave him the grey outlook of people on this coast.

Of course those who have passed over do not necessarily see it as grey.

Here is an old woman who is pressing close to me and wants to write.

Old Woman. Oh, indeed, I have not good English, but I want to tell you I am all right: I have got back my memory and I can see you and the General coming as you do back to Dunroe. I want them all to know that I am happy and young again and upright too. I live in a house partly, it is the real house on the Coyne, and the other is just not really there at all. This is real. And another thing, it is always warm and sunny. No gales, no rain: but the burn flows all the time. I want you to know that, my dear. Bridget B. (Later identified by the estate agent as a woman who used to live on the Coyne—the piece of land between two adjacent lakes.)

Father. You see it is sunny here for some and warm, with food, shelter and water. What more can they want! Now comes in education; it is not only for this life that you lead—so, when children learn things at school, it is for all time. I want Hugh to feel he is in a huge nursery where immense numbers of very young souls are being held back through lack of desire. They are quite happy in a negative way, but their happiness is of a semi-physical nature, because the whole of their mental bodies are quite unevolved.

Life in the earth-body was so hard that they clung to their negative existence rather than adventure forth again into life.

Gerald took on a very big job and, refusing to acknowledge defeat, he has struggled on, but it is a very slow victory.

All honour to his grit. Gerald is immensely pleased that Hugh has come, and if you could send him the thought to expand his own personality and go forth for a little time himself, it would be a great step forward.

Gerald has become slightly influenced by the fear of change, and the habit of routine has taken hold of him.

Try to see Dunroe expanding to the light of the Mental Sun, and the inhabitants in strength and beauty. I will tell you more tomorrow. My love to you all. Father.

Next Day.

Father. Yes, I have been reading what you wrote yesterday and the day before: I think that is all correct and gives you a picture of the place and the position of the people.

But now comes the direction of the influences, and these are very complex. So I have brought with me several people who have more knowledge about this intricate work and who can explain it better than I.

Bagot (R. C. Priest). Can I write? It is new to me. I want to explain the various lines of mental expression which have been fighting for existence here. It is a curious position, and the lack of development among the people comes through the neutralising of two great opposing forces. I was a priest here many years ago before Sir Gerald came to Dunroe, and the land was then under the sway of a very evil power.

It was an old, depraved kind of devil-worship coming from good-ness knows where, and, owing to the real results shown, we had a very tough fight, and I fear in the end we became allied together in the minds of the people.

This worship was a Nature-worship of sun, moon and stars, with a deeply seated belief in fairies, good and evil, coupled with terribly cruel rites which I found in full but secret swing. I invoked the pow-er of the Holy Spirit with all my strength, and I think I restrained the evil, but I could not demonstrate the good, so the neutralising influence set in. Many of our priests became imbued with some of the evil forces, and used or misused them, with the direst results; but the position of Dunroe was very terrible at that time. All this tended to make us jealous of our converts and deeply, passionately keen on grabbing the souls from the devil-worshippers.

The worst and most potent of their centres were around, and on the lower slopes of, Slieve Mish, so we tried to draw them to the coast. We set up our Chapel, and worked as far away as we could from the Mountain, which was our strength and our decay all in one.

I think we have done the spade-work, but in doing so we have become besmirched with some of the power, too, and it has meant everything that not only Lord Dowding himself but his following should, in a sense, sweep the country. By bringing their positive vi-brations, they will cleanse and remove many of the negative ones. The Trap* and the Place of Battles have given so much work, and of course the Mountain itself because of its misuse.

Father. Yes, now that is quite a good point. He has explained the evil workers, but the end is not clear. All humanity must go through these stages of evolution, the animal, and then the sub-human over which the fairies and Nature-spirits exercise immense influence. Sex begins to play a part, to inspire or corrupt, and at this point the men-tal body should begin to evolve; but that growth has been stunted

---

* The Trap was a narrow valley which I explored the next day. About half-way up I found a place which arrested my attention as a marvellous setting for an outdoor theatre. At the back a vertical black rock rose to a height of fifty feet or more. In the front of the rock was a smooth green sward as big as the stage in a large theatre. At the front of the sward was a black rock that looked like an altar; and on both sides were sloping banks which could accommodate an audience of several hundred people. As will be seen from the opening sentences of the next day's message, this was one of the places of sacrifice. The Place of Battles was about eight miles from Dunroe, and I visited it at the first opportunity. In fact, I covered as much ground as I could in my wanderings.

by the neutralisation of forces. The Church did well to obstruct, but was not strong enough to construct, so no progress has been made upon the ether. These souls that your R.A.F. boys are meeting and talking to are almost centuries behind them and, what is more important, confidence has been eliminated from their make-up. Gerald has worked like a mountain of force. He has brought into the ether a complete prototype of *Slieve Mish*, and by the most astonishing methods transmits through it beams of the purest radiance: but growth must come from below as well as from above, and so, to his passionate demand for help, Hugh has replied. I hope you have this clearly explained.

Bagot was the priest; a very tough fellow. He has never written before.

Olga (a friend of Mrs. Lock's). My dear Althea, what a work! I am glad you have brought Lord Dowding. He will be able to remove mountains of distrust. I have been with old Bagot and seen something of the devil-worshippers —I mean on this side. It is most astonishing, and I quite see why all this country has been held back. But the point is that now we cannot afford to have places like this, in a negative state, when the new powers are about to be released, on these shores. The new powers must have free play in cleansed areas, and this part of the country, because of its strength, is a powerhouse even now in its semi dormant condition.

My love. Olga.

Next Day.

Father. Well, Hugh had a walk over the country today, and we helped him to find one of the places of sacrifice.

Yes, that was one of the many, but he recognised it, and through that one others can all be cleansed.

If you can, go with him to this place and climb up on to the highest rock and, facing all four directions in turn, sweep the horizon with your prayer to cleanse and reinstate the Christ Ray upon all the altars of sacrifice.

I have told you about the Etheric planes and something about the physical planes, and now we will enter into the gnome kingdom within the Earth.

Wherever you have volcanic centres of this kind you have direct touch with the beings within the Earth belonging to the gnome kingdom. That is why Mrs. Randall saw them on the Mountain. (Mrs. Randall was a lady who lived opposite *Slieve Mish* and could see the gnomes tumbling on the sides of the Mountain. It was generally, but quite unjustifiably, accepted that she was a little cracked.) The gnomes are similar to fairies, but they have more developed mental bodies—in many cases more developed than some of the human beings, and this has been a great and troublesome subject, because they were enormously amused at finding that they could in many cases 'possess' human beings and make them do exactly what they wanted.

That was another stumbling block for poor Gerald.

It is not without its humorous side, too. Nothing is more completely comic than to see, as I have seen, one of these rather undeveloped humans, perhaps slightly drunk, under the complete control of the most ridiculous rollicking gnome. It is funnier than I can possibly describe.

Gerald takes it all in his stride, and sees the funny side, luckily, or he would have given in long ago. I think it is owing to this gnome influence that you have so many demented and simple-minded people. Of course this is a very difficult thing to deal with, and extremely bad for the race; it is a type of perversion. Two entirely different lines of evolution meet, and one controls or possesses the other. It is like sex perversion on another plane.

So far we have no solution to this wastage of human energy. Perhaps your R.A.F. boys, Hugh, will provide one.

But on this particular point we feel powerless until the growth can be fostered from below.

The gnomes come pouring out of the Mountain: they are not in the least evil in their way—just reckless, thoughtless little people—and the amount of trouble they cause throughout Ireland is beyond belief. The gnomes have got into the blood of this race, and their inconsistencies are everywhere. From another point of view the humans sometimes help the gnomes, but usually it is a case of the gnomes hampering the humans.

These other lines of evolution are very interesting, and sometimes beautiful; but not in the case of gnomes: they do not belong to the human race, and should never be allowed to influence them to anything but laughter. And when they do this—when the human being laughs at the gnome and ceases to take him or her seriously—the spell's broken and, through laughter, humanity gains its release.

This country is a Battlefield between gnomes, fairies and man.

The next day Mrs. Lock and I climbed the Mountain.

We had a stiff climb of about 1500 feet from where we left the car. Three sides were so steep that heather could not grow on the rocky slopes; the back where we came up was not quite so steep, and we had to use our hands only in a few places. The top is very sharp, with twin peaks connected by a narrow ridge about twenty-five yards long.

At the top Mrs. Lock suggested that we should 'bless the land' according to the previous day's message; so she took one peak and I the other, but, from the next day's letter, it will be seen that we exceeded our instructions.

Afterwards Mrs. Lock sat down to write—not an easy matter on the sharp summit, with a cold little breeze blowing the paper about. This is what she wrote:—

Father. We have been with you, and the Mountain has received you. This writing with us now forms the shining bridge between us and you. Through this Etheric substance we can transmit the rays which are most needed in order to quench the flow of lower vibrations and raise those of the upper. I am now going to hand over.

Then (very slowly)—"You are now among the devic people, and the great Devic kingdom receives and welcomes the Earth-leader. We cannot describe this but as a welcome."

Father. That was one of the Great Spirits who are at the apex of the beam, where the Etheric and the physical, the fairy and gnome rays unite.

The method of his speech is not to be taken, only the form of his vibrations; meaning that you are both received into the ray-vibration of the devic power in order that your work to free Dunroe may become more potent. This is in a sense an initiation. You have given of your effort and you have given of your power. This is enough.

(While we were at the top it was clear and we could see all round; but five minutes after we had left, the top was covered in dense cloud.)

Next Day.

Father. Yes, we are here. Now, about yesterday. You were surprised and disappointed that you were not able to write more freely on the Mountain or to have the feeling of contact like you do here. That was because we had to protect you. I never urged you to bless the land from the top of the Mountain and then write. (Not that it really mattered.) But if you throw out your desire to cleanse and vitalise, and then in a depleted condition turn to take in all messages, the result is dangerous.

Your aura has two layers or rings. In the outer is the perceptive, gold, which you are often reforming. The second is blue, the protective. The yellow draws in, and the blue sifts the rays. In this way I can use my power to strengthen the blue filter and to refuse passage into your finer bodies of any ray which may injure or possess you: but with the devic power all round I was not in a very good position to protect you. Luckily, many others were with us, and we formed a ring round you. (A little impatiently.) Yes, Gerald and Parsons and Mrs. Randall were among them.

All we asked was for you to make the contact; that was quite enough. When you wrote in Scotland it was quite different: the atmosphere of Iona and Holy Island was strong enough to remove all negative power. That is why those islands form such ideal places for awakening.

Here on *Slieve Mish* it is quite a different matter. If you had not had our protection you might have got into serious trouble through various old sources.

Now, I want to try and rebuild the picture for you. The devas are seldom in complete harmony with mankind in the physical body, so we invoked a higher power, and that power overshadowed you and held the vibrational direction of the pencil. The words meant welcome: that was the best I could make of them on paper. This Being was formless light, colour and sound. I cannot think how you could fail to sense so great a presence.

The peaks had already been prepared for you with vibratory colour and power, and the devic-keepers, two great and most beautiful beings, presided. They were the personification of the positive and negative in all Nature, and their ray-auras were glistening like a thousand jewels of colour. They do not have round auras like humanity, but their surrounding circles seem to be fashioned out of a million million dewdrops. I do not quite understand how this comes to be so, but the beauty of their swiftly changing, iridescent colour is beyond description. We who held you within our protective aura felt very small and weak within this vast devic stronghold, but when the Great One came we fell back and listened to the teaching which he gave us all. I am trying to put that into the next letter, but the words are difficult. We stayed and listened after you and Hugh had left the circle. We stayed withdrawn within the cloud cutting us off from the world of men, in order that we might absorb the new teaching brought to us by this Great One.

Next Day.

Father. Now we are here again.

First I want to thank Hugh for following out our orders so carefully and going to the place mentioned (the Place of Battles). He has covered many centres of power, good and evil. Now we want to tell him more about them. I have tried to take the subject in layers, and now we come to the men who have become earth-bound here—the inhabitants who belong to the land but have served in the Forces, either in this war or in the previous one. They return to the land and, following the habit of their grandparents and great grandparents, they have stayed on here, living in the Etheric belt, happy or content, but searching subconsciously for something better: and now here is the chance, they are all throwing in their lot with the R.A.F. boys, and some of them have changed considerably during the past week. They in turn are influencing their families, and the change is becoming very rapid among the last two generations.

There is one man here who looked after Hugh's horses at one time, and when he came over he brought the horses with him; they are all living together. The horses do not want to go any farther just yet, and, though he has explained the position, they are not willing to leave, so this will break up their happy home for a time. It is delightful to hear them speaking. Of course it is very like children, and they cannot see any point of view but their own. The horse has naturally a hard halo.

Other animals are here, too, cats and cows and calves and a few dogs, but they are not usually ready to stay over long, and leave with immense delight to start life again in human circles.

Paddy has come through several wars; he was in South Africa, so we have a link together, and he has been showing me over the place and explaining this and that in the vernacular. Even his speech is unchanged. I think I shall put him on to look after Jim Reed; he wants a job, and this will just suit him. (Jim Reed was a man who committed suicide under pressure from an obsessing entity. Mrs. Lock had been able to do much to help his widow). Now to return to the subject of circles and the *Slieve Mish* meeting. How I wish I could form the words to express the manner in which we were caught up into the clouds of vision. That was the method of the teaching—no words or rules, just a sense of ecstasy imparted to the listeners, and we found ourselves transported into a plane within a plane. We had not moved from the Mountain, but all our perceptions were changed. The devas, once so great and terrible, appeared suddenly beautiful and benign.

The gnomes whom I had been reviling became as the roots of a million flowers, uniting with the fairies and forming a complete column of Nature-spirits. The sounds of harmony were everywhere, and the sense of all evil completely banished from our minds.

And so we remained, held within the cloud of superb perfection until the Being who had given birth to this ecstasy relaxed his grasp upon our minds and we, in our primitive condition of evolution, were resolved back to the stage to which we belong.

That was our experience—our payment, if you like—for the effort and patience we had expended. I have never been through anything so wonderful. The colour-waves enwrapped us, the music of ten thousand harps delighted our ears, not as music delights you, but as it affects us. It is like a match, kindling and bringing to life part of the dominant substance of our human minds.

My love to you all.

Next Day.

Father. Thank you, my dear, for that welcome and the thanks you gave us. We have the same things to say to you: one side cannot do without the other.

Tonight we have all our circle, and Hugh's wife has also come to join us. She is delighted with the little people, and cannot be dragged away from the shore and the river.

She says Hugh will remember how she longed to play with real fairies and the other things she had from Ireland and always wanted to know more about.

Hugh's questions are before us:**

(1) What is the Etheric plane? Answer; The one nearest to you, the most physical.

(2) When do you leave it and go into the Astral? Answer: There is no time limit, so far as I know; you go when your desire to go somewhere else becomes conscious, and not till then. These people have no desire for change, so I cannot tell you how long they may have to remain here. The Astral is the ordinary plane whereon we learn the why and wherefore of our lives and actions, and most of us stay on this plane for a long time, and then reincarnate directly from here or go farther on into the Spirit planes.

There are many, many planes, and there is no fixed moment to reincarnate unless one has the desire to do so.

Desire is the motive energy, and the desire-body of this plane is intersected with the mental bodies, and they correspond with the Astral and Etheric of the personality.

(The meaning of this is not clear to me.) The question was: "Do we have fresh Astral and Etheric bodies for each life?" In as far as I can tell you, and it may only be my own experience, the Ego incarnates in a different physical and etheric body each time. The Astral body remains in the form of an Astral shell which is renewed by fresh Astral tissue as the Ego gathers understanding through the past life. While on the Astral plane, time is set aside for the refitting of the Astral body. Once that has become thoroughly restored, the overflow of knowledge begins to filter through into the higher mental bodies, who decide whether, and if so how and when and where, the Ego will reincarnate. Once this decision is taken, the etheric and physical bodies must be reassembled.

For the physical it takes nine months, for the Etheric, I am told, seven. The one is the reflection upon the ether of the other. They are the twin bodies of Earth-life, but they do not synchronise until the quickening of life takes place by the fourth and fifth months. At that

** There was a slight misunderstanding here. I had not put my questions quite in this form. After this message I wrote them down, and they were answered on the next day.

182

moment the two bodies synchronise as one and the mother becomes overshadowed by the Etheric body of the child, which has hitherto been within her aura. It now passes within and without, making contact simultaneously with the physical body and the ether of its own dimension.

The Lady Clarice has just come, and says, "How like Hugh to want to have it all made clear to the last fraction." She sends her love, and asks to be sent a direct message for herself at Dunroe: that it will make a real contact for her work.

That's all for tonight.

Next Day.

Father. Yes, my dear; we are very very sorry that your time is over here for the present, but you have made the necessary links for Hugh, and his R.A.F. boys have done marvels.

Now to Hugh's questions, which have sent Clarice into peals of laughter.

What is meant by an earthbound spirit? This is a fairly wide field: let us put them under headings.

First. Those who bind themselves unwillingly by their acts—suicides, murderers, torturers and so on. Almost any violent or cruel act binds the one who inflicts it to the spot for a varying period until it has been expiated.

Secondly. Those who are only anxious to be with human beings—who yearn to experience the human appetites again. These are the people who often take possession of weak minds and use them to gain coarser sensations of material life.

Thirdly. Those who, like your folk at Dunroe, bind themselves voluntarily because they have no desire, no motive power, to carry them farther. The first two categories are bound against their will and better judgment; the third are not really bound at all, but they have no motive force with which to free themselves.

Now to the Etheric body. This again is in various categories. The main part dies with the physical body, but that again varies enormously according to the time, and if the Ego (Consciousness) craves to hold on to the Etheric, they can, as I have seen here, revitalise them through the astral until it is hard to say whether they are astral or etheric, the one has become such an exact replica of the other.

It means with these people that the link with the mental is only in embryo. All their mental actions come from the old physical source and gradually, as they cease to struggle for life or use their brains at all, a vacuum grows in the Etheric-Astral body which gradually seeks fulfilment by a desire for mental development.

When that stage has been reached, the motive spark for action is created which frees them from the Earth and they flit away among the rest of us. I think that utter and complete weariness often causes most of this delay.

There are many delightful spirits among these people who have long ago received their freedom and have returned here to try and help in the real advancement. These are only the residue, the clods as it were; others have gone far away. Some are working with the fairies, others learning to control the gnomes (which is one of the most useful things they can do).

The people Hugh mentions who have been lost in the mist are quite a different vibration. These 'ray-deficients' create their own Etheric conditions, and in this country you will find many who have never known the mists, or the sense of loss and confusion. There are very few rules that can be laid down.

Now the Lady Clarice says, "Surely that will satisfy Hugh." She also says that you are not to go from here feeling that it is a desolate or primitive land full of captive souls. That impression is wrong. Many have very little sense of purpose, but they are gay and happy spirits, and play on their little pipes, some making verses and dancing with the fairies, or playing in the odd crannies of this indented shore. These people will return here again once they have made contact elsewhere, and they will form a huge band of human links, with the friendliness inherent in them. They emit a lovely soft ray which will absorb and distribute the new power once they have advanced a little farther.

This land has been blessed since creation, and even where a centre has become defiled like the Mountain, or the one you visited this morning,*** the natural force can always be tapped again and a free outlet be given to the white rays which can gush forth to cleanse and renew.

Sir Gerald. Thank Lord Hugh for his work. I am deeply grateful to him, and I shall keep in touch from time to time.

*** Mrs. Lock and I had visited the natural amphitheatre at 'The Trap' which I have already described.

Father. My love to Hugh. Goodbye, my dear. Well done.

P.S. Clarice says that I must tell you what happened at the Trap when you stood on the top and blessed the land.

She was there, too, and was uncertain which Nature-spirits she loved the best—the gnomes who were crawling all over you or the fairies who were thick in the air and on the ground.

When you came the hill was wreathed in its usual ruby glow, but before you left white and gold and other colours were coming out like whiffs of smoke. She says she does not know how the veil had been drawn over the evil power, but there was none there today, so the R.A.F. boys must have done it.

That finished the Dunroe messages for the time being. There was a strange sequel which I will relate in a moment, but first, to round the messages off, I should like to say that I wrote to Mrs. Lock to ask if Sir Gerald had returned to Dunroe after his excursion, and what his experiences had been. The following was received from him about ten weeks after the last of the messages recorded above:—

Sir Gerald. Althea, I am home again. You may say that I have not been away for long, but time does not affect me.

The point about leaving was to go away from Dunroe to break the continuity that had begun to bind me to the place.

That was a mistake.

In order to lead one must be free and able to make contact from outside. It was good for us all that I should make this journey. I was not alone, I went with several others, Mrs. Randall and Parsons, whom you know, several doctors and the old schoolmaster who was first instrumental in my coming to Dunroe.

We left by the mountain of *Slieve Mish*—that was important. We moved away through the magnetic stream that flows through the Mountain to the higher spheres. I felt the whole burden of Dunroe leave me as we rose, and the sense of pleasure, amounting almost to ecstasy, which I had quite lost, returned in full measure. I saw more directly and moved with the lightness of ether. In fact, I became once more an Etheric being of pure joy, which is the design for all creation, unburdened by responsibility and despair.

I see now that I have been a burden to Dunroe through my intense desire to shoulder alt the problems. The divine plan is not to place all responsibility on one person but to use them all as links.

It was so easy to forget that the responsibility was not mine, but God's.

He has a plan, and we either help or hinder, but each individual part is small and trivial. I wanted to be able to finish all the work myself and to enlarge it, so that it covered the whole land. But now I have learned that one must stand aside and let God work in His own way.

We left the Mountain and joined the upper spheres.

Your father came with me, and he was eager to go far afield, but I wanted to see the other physical conditions from the Etheric plane first, so he took me to the Western Isles, and I was able to feel the difference between the light rays there and those I knew so well on the Mountain. In this way we passed through the semi-physical to the Etheric, and on beyond the Etheric belt to the spiritual spheres. Only beings of pure light inhabit them, and it is only on rare occasions that we can hold our minds in a condition of sufficient harmony to allow us to enter and experience conscious communion with them. The power was so great that I felt shattered by it and at the same time renewed. Then suddenly it felt as if Gerald Lock had been flung into a million atoms and another Gerald Lock of a different type had been reborn. That is exactly what had happened: I had outlived the usefulness of my Etheric skin, but I had held on to it in the same way that many people do on Earth. I was ripe to leave this phase and to put on the next body, which is nearer in substance to the body of pure light. And so in this manner the act of rebirth was carried out and I became a new being with extended powers.

I was entranced by the change, and wanted to return here at once; but they would not let me, and for a further period I moved through the spheres of training and creating, through the garden of essences and the lakes of sound and so on.

I cannot tell you of the beauty I enjoyed; there are no words that I can use to express all that I have seen and heard and touched.

Then I returned to the Mountain which holds the beam through which we re-enter the physical plane of the lower Etheric, and came into direct contact again with Dunroe.

Here I found everything had changed towards me, as I had changed towards them. I see now the meaning and the tendencies and the plan behind the slow scheme which had formerly been an insoluble problem to me. I saw and I loved where I had only seen and hated. Now I know that only Love can ever heal or teach or create.

Now about the strange experience which I mentioned above.

Two or three days before I left Dunroe a lady, Miss Rose by name, drove over from her house, about thirty miles away, for an afternoon visit. She told us that her chauffeur, a young Irishman called Denny, had been having some remarkable night-experiences.

He would find himself (apparently) flying through the air at a great rate, though perfectly able to see the country below him. He generally broke his journey, at a place which he supposed to be Gibraltar, though he could not give any reason for his supposition, except that it was a big rock near the sea and he could see swarthy folk working in the fields.

He would then resume his journey, and would find a dark-skinned man waiting for him, sitting cross-legged on the ground, and clad in scanty white cotton clothing. He always had an affectionate reception, and when he woke again in bed he was able to see words written in the air in English writing, but in a language which he could not understand.

The words persisted in letters of light till he had written them down.

Miss Rose had no idea what the language was, nor had any of her friends to whom she showed the messages.

The moment I saw them I recognised them as being written in Hindustani, though my knowledge of the language was more than rusty, as I had not been in India since 1910.

General Lock had also served in India and, by putting our heads together, we made out what seemed to be the general sense of the messages; but what with the boy's possible errors in transcription and our rustiness in the language, the result was very woolly. Some of the messages were later sent to an Indian at Oxford, and he didn't make much more of them than we had done, so the main errors must have been in transmission and/or in transcription.

It is strange that the transmitter should have apparently been ignorant of English, yet familiar with English script; for of course Hindustani has a script of its own, derived from the Arabic.

Miss Rose was referred to as The Woman (Aurat), and Denny would sometimes receive somewhat embarrassing instructions, such as, "Go to the woman's room; the power will be stronger." (This at 3 a.m.) The messages were generally signed Malik, which means Ruler or Master.

Miss Rose asked me what I thought they ought to do about it (for the messages went on long afterwards, and are in fact still continuing;

and I said that as, apparently, nothing was coming through which was of any use to anybody, and as the lad was losing a good deal of sleep, which a healthy youngster needs, they should perhaps do nothing to encourage a continuance of the messages, though they should not refuse to accept them.

It seemed to me that there was probably a very strong Karmic link between Denny and his unknown mentor.

They had probably been very close in previous incarnations.

And now this 'Malik' was trying to keep the link alive by occult methods, quite unaware of the (to him) peculiar conditions in which his protégé was living.

There seemed to be no danger to the lad, no Black Magic or anything of that sort; a strong and genuine affection seemed to run throughout the messages; but, as I say, they didn't seem to be doing any good to anyone.

Later on the night-journeys seem to have ceased, but the messages continued to appear in luminous letters, and remained until they had been written down.

The latest development (March 1950) is that the words have begun to appear in the sky as Denny is driving the car.

Miss Rose can see streaks and flashes in the sky, but cannot see the words.

Other people, I understand, cannot see anything. I don't think there can be any suspicions that these phenomena are not genuine. Both Miss Rose and Denny are transparently honest, and neither of them knows enough about Hindustani to recognise it when they see it.

CHAPTER 11

RAGBAG

Now I must have a Chapter to deal with various loose ends about each of which I have not enough to say to justify a chapter of its own.

The first of these is Spiritual Healing; and of course not only chapters but books might be written on this mysterious subject. I mean only that I have no great contribution to make beyond what I have already said in my former books.

I have, in fact, to confess in *Many Mansions*, for instance, I wrote with the enthusiasm of a very incomplete knowledge. I have been looking up what I wrote on page 21 of that book, and, while I don't think that I made any statement of fact there which was not literally true, I feel that I gave the impression that these so-called 'miraculous' cures are a good deal more common than is in fact the case, and also that their existence is recognised fairly widely by medical men and scientists.

These 'miracles' do take place, but, unfortunately, I am not the only one who exaggerates their frequency. I was invited to sit on the platform of a Brains Trust the other day which was to deal with this question at a public meeting.

I am beginning to acquire a certain amount of caution in my old age, and so I said that I would rather be at the receiving than the transmitting end of the proceedings—that I would rather ask the questions than answer them.

They very kindly accepted several of my questions, and one of them was: Have statistics been compiled of the proportion of successes to failures in cures of patients treated? If so, what are the proportions? The question-master was a prominent Spiritualist who, in accordance with his office, refrained from expressing his own opinion, but I thought that he seemed to be a little shaken by the answers received—I know I was. For, out of the five Brains (all active healing practitioners) who replied, the most pessimistic gave the percentage of successes as 80 and the most optimistic as 95.

The only place I happen to know of where strict statistics are kept (including inquiries into after-history) is Lourdes, and their percentage of instantaneous cures is about two and a half.

Of course the Brains were counting all those cases which yield gradually to continuous treatment, and the Lourdes figure does not include the high proportion of clinical failures whose whole outlook on disease and pain is nevertheless altered by the atmosphere of their pilgrimage; but, even so, the discrepancy between the figures is enormous.

My own little personal experience as a member of a healing circle supported the Lourdes figures, but perhaps we were abnormally inefficient.

However that maybe, there is no doubt that certain patients show no clinical improvement, whereas apparently similar cases are successfully treated by the same healer. Harry Edwards has told me, and has stated in print, that he was unable to cure his own best friend who was dying of cancer, whereas he had been instrumental in the cure of other apparently similar cases.

I put forward the tentative hypothesis that some diseases are Karmic in their origin; that the soul accepted this physical handicap before birth, as a condition of its next tour of duty on Earth, and that the key-purpose of that particular incarnation would be frustrated if the disease were to be cured.

I say that I put forward the suggestion; I do not mean that nobody else has propounded the theory, I only mean that the idea is original so far as I personally am concerned.

It seems to account fairly satisfactorily for the observed facts, and it also fits in with the story of the healing of the man sick of the palsy. You will remember that Jesus first said, "Thy sins be forgiven thee," and then said, "Arise, take up thy bed and walk." If there is anything in my idea, Jesus first released the man from his Karmic debt, and only then was it permissible to eliminate his disease.

Of course it is not a corollary of this hypothesis that all diseases which a healer or circle fails to cure are Karmic in origin. Healers and circles vary in efficiency, and there is always the contribution of the patient to be taken into account; though it is by no means a sine qua non that the patient shall "have faith". Cases occur where 'absent healing' brings about the cure of a patient who does not even know that he is being treated, and who perhaps would be righteously indignant if he knew of the unorthodox treatment to which he was being subjected.

One of the handicaps to which one is subjected in searching for truth on this most elusive subject is the freedom with which people invent and repeat stories which have no foundation in fact.

For instance, I have heard the following story about myself from three independent sources. It is to the effect that I was on the platform at a Spiritualist meeting when I saw a crippled girl in a bath chair at the back of the hall.

That I walked down the aisle and told the girl to get out of the chair, and that I then sat down in the chair and told the girl to wheel me out of the hall, which she did.

A most circumstantial and romantic story which has only one defect—viz., that it is completely, utterly and absolutely untrue.

Another difficulty is the extraordinary variety of unorthodox methods of diagnosis and healing, some of them mechanical or semi-mechanical. Some of these methods are of very dubious origin and value, and some of them are extremely promising.

As so often happens in human history, similar inspiration seems to be coming independently but simultaneously to people in different parts of the world. This is not a good time to try to write about these overlapping and competing systems; they must be given time to justify or to eliminate themselves by the process of trial and error, culminating, we may hope, in a process of trial and success.

And don't be too critical of the doctors if they do not rush enthusiastically after each new epoch-making 'discovery' in the art of healing. In my own small personal experience I have found doctors much more open-minded to what does not register on the five senses than clergy or scientists or philosophers.

The good doctor's first wish is that his patient shall be cured, and for him the criterion of a method is its success.

But don't forget that the doctor has spent five years in training for his profession, and perhaps half a lifetime in practising it, and complete ignoramuses come along and start to teach him his job.

Ignorant and self-opinionated 'healers' are merely quacks to the doctors, and to others also.

If I may indulge in a good hearty mixture of metaphors, the doctor has but one virginity to lose and, if he backs the wrong horse, he becomes an outcast from the fold.

The next article in my ragbag is a speculation on the progress of humanity which I do not happen to have encountered elsewhere in my limited study of this vast subject.

People say that human nature has not changed throughout the centuries and millennia: that if we look as far back as history can take us, man acts now very much as he did then, allowing for the change of external circumstances.

This may be a very reasonable piece of pessimism from people who believe that every human being is a fresh creation at birth and at death passes away from the earth never to return. In such circumstances there is no logical reason to suppose that the population of earth ever will improve in character and behaviour.

But I suggest that this is a point of view which is unlikely to commend itself to those who believe that, for the Spirit, eternity stretches into the past as well as into the future. It is as if I should go back to my old school and visit the Lower Fifth (or whatever it might be), and say, "Oh, this is dreadful! Here they are, doing Virgil and Homer, exactly as they were doing fifty years ago, when I was at school. They have made no progress whatever in all that time!" It would very reasonably be pointed out to me that generations of boys had learned these lessons and passed on in due course to higher classes and to the University, and had then applied their knowledge in doing their work in the world.

And so, in the same way, mankind is continually learning —not only during the term-time on earth, but during the holidays between lives. The way in which this improvement is manifested depends very largely on the way in which the Lords of Karma regulate the intake and the output to and from the vast multitude of those who are 'bound on the wheel'.

If they throttle down the intake of young souls from animal life and keep the old souls in continuous circulation, that part of humanity which is in incarnation at any given time will have acquired experience beyond the present average, and people will say that the Golden Age has arrived and humanity has improved out of all recognition.

If, on the other hand, they reverse the process, free most of the old souls from the wheel and accept an intake from the animal world limited only by man's powers of reproduction, then the Earth-experience of incarnate humanity will be far below the present average, and it will be said that humanity, far from improving, is rapidly deteriorating.

I am not suggesting that the Lords of Karma are not perfectly aware of this, I am not trying to teach them their business; I am merely pointing out that unless we have some inside information about the 'through-put'—the percentage of souls who are the finished product of the earth life process—we are in no position to form a useful opinion as to the progress of humanity in general.

Also, when some of our less well-informed invisible friends reproach us for our many failures, we may think that there may be something to be said in our defence, although we should not be the ones to say it.

These thoughts lead to somewhat similar speculations on the question of world-population.

For instance, the result of our stewardship in India, whether it be approved or condemned, was at least the elimination of most of the ravages formerly caused by civil war, pestilence and famine and an increase in the material prosperity of the country. These potential benefits, however, which should have resulted in an improved standard of living for the average inhabitant, were completely swallowed up by an uncontrolled growth of the population which increased from three to four hundred million in little over fifty years, and left the average inhabitant no better off as to his standard of living than before.

My eyes turn to China, with its five hundred million of souls maintained in spite of the existence of war, flood, pestilence and famine as almost normal features of national life. What is going to happen there when the lessons of Western civilisation enable the Chinese substantially to reduce the ravages of the last three? I put this point to Chang, and he laughed, and said that as the comfort of people's lives increased, people would be more thoughtful about the number of children that they bring into the world.

I think that this is a very important point, but that there will have to be a very considerable increase in the amenities of life in India and China (for instance), to say nothing of Africa, when civilised conditions begin to impact upon the people, before any sort of voluntary restraint in propagation begins to show itself. After all, there is not much restraint of this kind observable among the poorer classes of the so-called civilised countries of the West.

The very word 'proletariat' comes from the Latin word 'proles', or 'offspring', and defines the proletariat as the class which produces children regardless of any other considerations.

I expect Chang knows what he is talking about, but it seems to me that the world may have to go through a rather sticky time before equilibrium is struck on the basis of voluntary limitation of the size of families.

Our verbal discussions with Chang are generally stimulating. One little point is perhaps worthy of special note.

At one of the last sittings of our Circle before its suspension, he said, "Chang will always be very close. Call upon him if necessary; but, if you do, be quiet for a little time afterwards." I think that we must be very irritating to our unseen friends sometimes, when we send out a thought-call to them, and they leave their work to come to us, only to find that we have at once allowed our minds to wander off into other channels. As he said to us on another occasion, "You human people are so unreliable." On yet another occasion we were given the picture from the Akashic Records of the human sacrifices in the temple (to which I have already referred), and I was rash enough to query the justice of the fact that the harmless and elderly teacher, who was the principal victim of the priests, was today still 'bound to the wheel', while the cruel Chief Priest who had encompassed his death had apparently achieved emancipation.

"Foolish brother," replied Chang, "you are still tied by the Earth-idea."

Only part of the Real Self manifests on Earth. Sometimes the greater part and sometimes the clearer channel....

At this present stage the Earth-conditions are very heavy; and while man is seeking and striving to know, his vision is more obscure, perhaps, than at any time. ... I hope it is clear. Not one set up above another, for the last shall be first and the first last. So it is. So it is. For the king of today is the beggar of tomorrow, and from both of them shall emerge the Man of the future. I should like you in your script to use a capital M for such a one as you all hope to become." Some people have a very fine open incarnation, what you would call a Saint's, and then one with no spiritual content whatever. Progress is only made through the doorway of Spiritual memory.

"I can but drop little stones into your mind so as to set the ripples moving and to disturb you.

"I also am foolish: when I come into the atmosphere of Earth it is difficult to put forward the thoughts that are in my heart. But I must beg of you to break down any idea of inequality and advancement: that leads to Spiritual Pride.

"Those who know that they are on the Threshold, how far from it are they in truth! Those who are do not know; they are as a child, unaware of the cot in which it lies. ...

"And now as the dusks of evening brush out the lights of day, let the light of the Spirit so shine that the stars in their courses shall be put to shame by the Glory of the Creator reflected in you—His handiwork." I have written in *Lychgate* of St. George and King Arthur, and I am not going to repeat now what I wrote there; but I give here an extract from the Monthly Message which I wrote for the Royal Society of St. George at the request of its late President, Lord Queenborough.

"We have in this country, besides the Royal Society of St. George, other Societies and Orders which have Saints and Angels as their patrons; and I sometimes wonder to what extent members of the public in general and of these Societies in particular think of these patrons.

"Perhaps some people think of them as convenient figments of the imagination round which sentiments of nationalism and loyalty may crystallise; others perhaps take a completely cynical view and regard the whole system of knightly orders as a relic of superstition and barbarism.

"And so I should like to write today upon St. George as I think of him.

"In the infinitely complex organisation of the Universe there is a minor Angelic Hierarchy which is concerned with the affairs of this insignificant planet. The National Angels are members of this Hierarchy, and one of these is the Angel who is especially charged with the affairs of England; his name we do not know.

"He, in his advancement, is beyond all form; but we have made a form for him and given him a name, and, with the courtesy of the truly great, he has accepted them for the purposes of his special work with Earth and with England.

"When I say, 'We have made a form for him,' I mean that we have made a thought-form—for thoughts are things in a very literal sense. We have built up a composite entity from a young Roman officer who married an Englishwoman and was martyred for his Christian faith, and a legendary figure who slew dragons and rescued maidens on the coasts of Cappadocia; and on these we have superimposed the trappings and accoutrements of mediaeval chivalry. (By the word 'legendary' I do not mean 'nonexistent'; for behind most legends there lies a truth, distorted though it may be by the lapse of centuries.) "Now I am going to give rein to my imagination, and in all seriousness and sincerity record the sort of message which the Angel of the English might perhaps give to his people today.

My dear people: I have long since accepted the personality which you have built for me by your thoughts; but though you have built the tabernacle of my form with Roman and Syrian bricks, do not think of me as other than English of the English; for indeed my work lies with you, and for your progress and development am I held to account before the Ultimate, the Absolute, the Nameless One.

"'You have built for me (and are building day by day) armour of steel and a banner blazoned with the Cross of the Beloved: see to it that the steel be tempered and the banner without stain.

And yet, although I say that you have built well, you have nevertheless limited me in part. In your thoughts you stress the warrior element, and you hold aloof in your separate pride from my brothers, the Angels of other peoples. In Love and in Unity are your thoughts of me deficient.

Perhaps instinctively you have recognised this failure, for you have built another form which my feminine element may ensoul, that Britannia who has shed the insularity and separativeness of the English, that Britannia who is the symbol of the British Commonwealth and the foreshadower of union and harmony, ever widening until it becomes worldwide.

You have set my figure on your golden coins and hers on your bronze, and behold now is your gold taken from you. Think upon this for herein lies a parable.'" As for King Arthur, I think of him increasingly as the Angel of Britain, whereas St. George is the Angel of the English. If in some remote contingency the English were displaced from this Island and removed elsewhere, St. George might be thought of as accompanying them in their exile.

Arthur, on the other hand, is primarily the Angel of the Land of Britain. We may perhaps think of him as taking up his position on the topmost height when first the land was raised from beneath the sea and while yet the droplets sparkled in the sun.

Between him and our Beloved Master there is a special link of burning Love, and he and his knights, some in the flesh, but all in the spirit, still carry on the fight against the heathen in heart.

Arthur, as I think of him, is especially connected with those mystical power-centres of Britain whose opening will have such a great effect upon the material as well as the spiritual welfare of humanity. He has his roots in the Hyperborean Race which antedated the Third Root Race in Lemuria, and the Devas and Fairy Folk call him Lord.

I want to say a few words about the Society for Psychical Research and its work.

It was founded well over half a century ago by people who were prominent at the time in the field of Psychic Research. I don't know what was in the minds of the founders, but I hope that I shall not be doing them an injustice if I say that perhaps they contemplated making an announcement, after a due period of research, to the effect that they had found no evidence to convince them that spirit communication and/or psychical phenomena were possible and did in fact take place, or else that they had convinced themselves of these basic facts and were going on into the field of study to which these things had led them.

But time went by and no such pronouncement was made. On the contrary, the Society now states that it is no part of its corporate functions to make any such general pronouncement ever, but only to investigate specific cases as they are brought to its notice.

Tell it not in Gath, publish it not in the streets of Askelon, but some of the members are convinced Spiritualists in their private capacity. Other members, and the Society as a whole, maintain a strictly agnostic attitude.

Mr. G. N. M. Tyrrell, a President of the Society, has had the courage to publish his own opinion, formed as the result of his researches, and one of his books, *The Personality of Man*, published in the Pelican Series in 1946, may be described without effusiveness as a classic.

Still, the Society as a whole has adopted this noncommittal attitude for so long that its work is being increasingly disregarded in all quarters.

Spiritualists think of them as unconvincible (as indeed they claim to be as a corporate body), and scientists tend to regard them, in so far as they regard them at all, as a body of people who claim for their work the cachet of the scientific method, a claim which they, the scientists, are by no means prepared to concede.

A short time ago I was tackled by a member of the S.P.R., who said that mediums were not prepared to allow themselves to be watched through an infra-red apparatus (by means of which one can see in the dark) while they were engaged in the production of physical phenomena. That, in spite of the offer of an award of £250, no medium would come forward and submit himself to the test.

I replied that it was not a matter which much concerned me, since I had convinced myself that physical phenomena did in fact occur and had passed on to the more constructive side of Spiritualism; but I did know that some mediums at least were distrustful of the treatment which they might receive at the hands of the S.P.R., and were not at all anxious to collaborate with them, especially as the sole arbiter of the success or failure of the demonstration was to be a research officer of the S.P.R.

I thought that if the S.P.R. would consent to the appointment of a neutral judge agreeable to both parties, then some such arrangement as the following might be made:— The medium claims to be able to make a trumpet rise from the ground and bump against the ceiling. The research officer then lays down the conditions, e.g., the Society's own séance room to be used. Not more than three sitters besides the research officer, the judge and a spiritualist representative 'to be permitted. All persons to submit to search before the sittings. Medium to be tied to his chair. If the trumpet then leaves the ground and touches the ceiling, the award to be paid unless the research officer produces as the result of search the rod or pulley or other mechanical device by which the effect was produced.

The judge to decide on the facts.

If some arrangement of this sort could be agreed upon, I said I thought I could probably find a physical medium to participate in the experiment.

After a few days I received a letter saying that the offer of the reward had lapsed, but that it could probably be revived if I could find a medium willing to accept their conditions. That as the money was being offered by members of the S.P.R., it was only reasonable that they should wish to make their own research officer the sole arbiter of the success or failure of the demonstration.

So that left us just where we started, and I did not feel called upon to proceed farther in the matter.

All the same, though, I think it would be quite a valuable experiment to use the infra-red 'looker' in connection with physical manifestations, quite apart from the question of a reward or the participation of the S.P.R. Perhaps this is being done somewhere, I do not know.

To return to our scientists; personally I should think that there is no question but that physical phenomena are capable of examination by the scientific method. Crookes' work, for instance, when he said to a projecting lever "Be light" or "Be heavy" and measured the change of weight instrumentally, was scientific enough, I should imagine, as was the work of Crawford in the Goligher circle, where ectoplasm was photographed and traced on its return journey by the trail of coloured powder which it left behind it.

The trouble is, of course, that though these phenomena can be investigated by scientific methods, the conclusions are so shocking to the orthodox scientific mind that the subject is one to be avoided at all costs.

But of course these physical phenomena are of no great importance in comparison with the mental phenomena of communication with the unseen, and phenomena of the latter sort are probably not susceptible to examination by the scientific method. The rather one-sided difference of opinion between the S.P.R. and the scientists does not, therefore, much affect those whose main interest lies with the mental phenomena and their further implications.

Mind you, there is something to be said for the scientists, in this connection. A scientist may be a Christian or a spiritualist, or both, or a lover or a golfer or a pianist, quite independently of scientific methods or outlook.

He is perfectly at liberty to say, "In my opinion this matter is not one which can be dealt with scientifically.

As a scientist I cannot interest myself in it: but from other aspects I may be permitted to keep an open mind." There is only one type of scientist or philosopher who is a public enemy in this connection: this is the aggressive materialist who influences weaker minds by flat denial of Spirit in all its aspects.

Solomon dealt with them in the Book of Wisdom, where he wrote: "For if they had power to know so much that they should be able to explore the course of things, how is it that they did not sooner find the Sovereign Lord of these his works?" I can't finish this chapter without putting on record a story against myself which comes from America.

It has already appeared in the Star newspaper, but I think it is worthy of a wider immortality.

A friend of mine was attending a Spiritualist meeting in New York (I think) when the speaker on the platform mentioned my name in connection with one of my books.

A man sitting behind her said to his neighbour, "Say, who is this Lord Dowding? Is he any relation to Sir Hugh Dowding, who fought in the Battle of Britain?" His companion replied, "Why, he's his father, I guess.

You see, in England the son of a Lord is always a Sir." The first man accepted this item of heraldic information without demur. Then he said, "Gee, I wonder what a smart guy like him would think of his old man going off the rails that way."

CHAPTER 12

THE RIGHT IDEA

I shall finish this book with a chapter on Religion: and the first thing I am going to do is to reproduce one of Z's 'sermonettes' from *God's Magic*. This last book seems to have reached rather a different public from that which has been attracted by my earlier books, and many of my readers have not heard of its existence.

So, with grateful acknowledgments to the Spiritualist Press, I reproduce one of these little gems of true wisdom.

They are all on subjects which are generally considered to be hackneyed, and yet they all succeed in displaying new and sparkling light upon each well-worn theme.

MAN'S CRYING NEED, 4TH JULY, 1945

The world today, more than at any other time in its chequered history, needs a guiding star, a vision, a hope.

War, with its attendant discomforts, its physical horrors and mental tortures, can be a power for the growth and development of man, or a power for the annihilation of all that part of him which makes life manifest to him beyond the level of blind, unreasoning instinct, as is the case with animal and plant and mineral life.

Evolving life must struggle always; there must be effort for any lasting progress. Yet man is turning his back on this basic truth—a truth which he will ignore at his peril.

On all sides one hears of schemes where initiative will be taken away, where effort will be nullified. All such schemes are doomed to failure, because they go against the very fundamentals of life itself. But before they fail they will have destroyed much that is valuable and almost irreplaceable.

The scheme of the Universe provides that human life must evolve. The environment of this Universe is confined by the fact that life must evolve through effort. Not a strained, painful effort, but a natural growth brought about by the order of law which says that all effort shall bring greater understanding and greater opportunities.

That the efforts of the few shall be all that is necessary to bring about the salvation of the many is a pernicious doctrine.

The efforts of the few can at best only hold at bay the appalling disasters which the apathy of the many naturally attracts. But a society based on this futile doctrine of allowing a group or a government to do for the people these things which the people must do for themselves, is doomed to eventual extinction. The first and last reason for the existence of life on this planet is that individual Monads may penetrate into its gloom and refine and elevate it.

To do this it is necessary for the human forms hiding the Monadic glow to work ceaselessly to clear the way.

Every individual incarnate has a right to the opportunity to do this very thing. No one individual is privileged above another, except by the greater vision that his own efforts have engendered in him. And that vision brings the responsibility to help others less evolved, not to remove the boulders from the path, but to throw some light so that they may be seen more clearly.

In removing the boulders much superfluous weight and flabbiness is cast aside—the effort calls forth a ray of divine power, and no one has the right to refuse this ray to another by completing for him the task he should tackle for himself.

Respect for himself, that he will be independent yet gentle of spirit; respect for his fellow creatures, that he will concede to them the rights and privileges he wishes to enjoy himself (and this means to all classes of society respect for the life flowing around him in every form, so that he will hesitate to destroy), that is the keynote for the new age.

To gain this respect what must man do? Physically he must be healthy—that means good food, clean habitations and living, exercise and rest.

Mentally he must be alert—that means learning, learning by books, learning by listening to others and learning by experimenting and experiencing for himself.

Spiritually he must be aware—that means that he must realise and accept the Immanence of God in himself and all his fellow creatures. That he must remember that he is greater than all the temptations which beset him. That he must differentiate between religion and true spirit, that he must be prepared by unremitting effort to enjoy to the full the world God has given to him and which he is making— not God—man is creating the earth conditions. That he must have dignity and justice for himself and that he may recognise it for others.

These things he can accomplish by meditation and prayer—meditation on the life of One who led the way, and prayer which is a living life.

Today the earth needs more than ever hope and vision; and these man can have, for the course of evolution is sure, and some there are who, seeing the vision, are helping evolution along.

But the vision can only be realised when each individual accepts his responsibility and works physically, mentally and spiritually with continuous effort and unremitting labour, one to help the other, to treat with courtesy even his enemies, and with respect those with whom he deals.

With love to all in his heart what man can fail to see and follow the vision of heaven on earth? Blessing. And now may His blessing rest upon you all.

May you go forward strong in His work. May you be deemed worthy to feel His presence and be glorified therein.

And unto Him shall all men aspire, and unto Him shall be brought all who are weak, all who labour and all who sorrow, that He may take them in His arms and bring them peace. Amen.

When I say that this chapter is about Religion, I am not referring to the beliefs that people hold, but the influence which those beliefs exert on people's personal conduct and behaviour to one another.

I don't say that it is impossible for a man who is bound by what I may call the 'Sunday School' teachings of the Protestant Church to live a good unselfish constructive Christian life, but the ordinary intelligent educated man is inclined to revolt from these teachings when he arrives at years of discretion, and there is no recognised orthodox authority who can give him anything to take their place.

The tendency then is to throw overboard the Church's theology and philosophy which never were compiled by intellectual men, and are fourteen hundred years out of date at that. This is all to the good; but the trouble is that there is a tendency at the same time to throw overboard Christian ethics and Christian morality and live only for the Personality and its supposed interests.

I am no enemy of the Church; I know perfectly well that there are many modern clergymen who don't believe in eternal punishment for anybody, nor in the resurrection of the body of flesh, nor in an age-long sojourn under six feet of earth waiting for judgment day, nor in a 'knife-edged' judgment between the sheep and the goats, so that if the beam just tips for you on the goat side you remain a goat for all eternity. They don't teach these things, perhaps; but they don't deny them, and they don't teach anything different and positive.

I had rather an interesting experience the other day when I was speaking to one of the small 'highbrow' societies which spring up in London from time to time round the personality of some leader. The society was not particularly interested in psychic matters, but did not exclude them from its field of discussion, and they had asked me to speak, giving me a free choice of subject.

I started my talk by saying more or less what I have said above about the teaching of the Church, and how a revulsion from this teaching started many young people off on the wrong lines, and then I went on to give as much as I could in an hour of my ideas about the plan for human life and for the evolution of humanity.

At the end of my talk I invited questions, and the chairman, who was the president of the society, got up and said: "While Lord Dowding was speaking about the Church, Archbishop Temple was here with Wilberforce. He was much moved. He said, 'I never taught these things. I never taught any such thing!'" So I said, "I am sure I didn't intend to hurt anybody's feelings. I didn't know I had such a distinguished audience; but what I must say to you is that you didn't teach anything different." Now I don't want to make too much of this incident; I know nothing about the chairman; I had no idea that he was psychic. He gave me the impression of being a completely reliable and trustworthy person, but I have no means of checking his story nor the identity of the visitors. I just relate the incident as it happened. And indeed it does not seem to me to be very improbable that a great leader of the Church, immersed as he must be in the cares of organisation and administration, might quite honestly overlook the fact that the Anglican Church gives no constructive lead on these vital matters, but avoids all honest consideration of the subject. As a cynical theologian is reported to have said, "When you come to a difficulty, look it squarely in the face and pass by on the other side." The Wilberforce mentioned by the chairman is more likely to have been the Archdeacon of that ilk than the Bishop. The Archdeacon was (I believe) an active' Spiritualist during his life and (I know) is one now.

Having had a number of letters from clergymen telling me that the Church does not teach the things which I said it does, I thought that I would try to obtain an authoritative pronouncement on the subject from a working vicar who is well thought of in the Church circles and regarded as one of the coming men.

I wrote to him telling him that I had been accused of misrepresenting the Church's teaching, and asking him to give me information which I could quote, so as to be able to say "The Church of England teaches so and so", without laying myself open to a charge of unfairness.

Here are the questions which I asked:—

1.   Is there a Resurrection of the flesh'? (See Baptism service.)
2.   If so, does this Resurrection occur on the 'Last Day?'
3.   Is this the Day of Judgment?
4.   If not, what is?
5.   What happens to souls before such judgment is promulgated? To Abraham, for instance?
6.   Is there such a thing as Eternal damnation?
      (a) For the unbaptised?
      (b) For those who died before Jesus was born?
      (c) For people who have heard of Jesus but do not accept Him?
      (d) For those who die in sin and unrepentant?
      (e) For anybody?
7.   If Judgment is deferred to the end of the world, it would seem to follow that such judgment must be 'knife edged', and that in a border-line case some trivial act of good or ill must tip the beam one way or the other. Is this an unfair view?
8.   Did you exist as an individual one year before you were born into this life? If so, in what conditions?
9.   Will you exist as an individual one year after you die. If so, in what conditions?
10. Is the Garden of Eden story historical or allegorical? If the latter, what is the Church's teaching concerning the arrival of the human race on earth?

11. What is the destiny of mankind and what logical grounds are there for assuming that Good will prevail over Evil as the evolution of humanity proceeds?

In reply I received the following letter:—

MY DEAR LORD DOWDING,

If I don't make an attempt to answer your questions now they will have to wait some considerable time, as my days are very full and I am much pressed for time. I must apologise, therefore, for answers which ought to be greatly expanded and which are therefore inadequate. I found your questions very interesting, but some of them are very big questions which cannot be answered by a single word or by a single sentence.

The Faith of the Church is based upon the Scriptures and upon the Creeds as witnessing and testifying to the Scriptures. On many points the Church does not teach with a single voice. All we can say is that certain Christian teachers have said this and others have said that. This applies particularly to matters concerning the afterlife.

The point of view of our own Church is that our Lord told us very little Himself, and therefore a good deal of latitude is allowed us. On the other hand, the Roman Catholics have everything taped and seem to possess a celestial geography which nobody else knows anything about.

That, of course, has its advantages for the simple-minded, but it is of little use to the rest of us.

1. The phrase "resurrection of the flesh" occurs in certain early versions of the Apostles' Creed, which catechumens had to recite at their baptism as their profession of faith. At one period the word "flesh" was substituted for "body" to emphasise the reality of the human body as against the Gnostic heresies which denied it. The usual phrase in the Creeds is "the resurrection of the body".

The Scriptural phrase is "the resurrection of the dead".

If by "flesh" is meant the body of earth, there is no resurrection of the flesh. At the same time it should be recognised that the belief of the Christian religion is not the bare Greek notion of the immortality of the soul, but the distinctively Christian doctrine of the resurrection of the body.

2. The answer is that nobody knows. Texts can be quoted from the N.T. suggesting that the resurrection will take place at the "Last Day", in which case we must think of the departed as spirits without bodies—a difficulty for me.

On the other hand, St. Paul in 2 Cor. 4 seems to conceive of the resurrection taking place immediately after death, a view which personally I prefer. The main point is that by the power of Christ's resurrection the ravishes of death whereby soul is sundered from body will be "repaired".

Seeing that this is an event which will take place in the eternal sphere, questions as to time are misleading. We, of course, are subject to space-time language—hence our difficulties in a matter of this kind. The Church of England has no official teaching on this point. The Romans, on the other hand, have it all "taped".

3. The Last Day, the Second Coming of Christ and the General Resurrection all relate to the one final event when the time

4. process is wound up and the earth comes to its inevitable end.

5. Scripture distinguishes between the Particular and the Final Judgment. Death is followed immediately by the Particular Judgment, which is the trial. The General or Final Judgment in the sight of all men, when sentence is declared, completes the idea of judgment. Here again we must recognise the inadequacy of time-space language, and remember that when it is all boiled down, it witnesses to the main fact that there will be judgment, and that it will be complete and perfect, in contradistinction to fallible human judgment.

It is the teaching of the Church that the merits of our Lord's death and resurrection extend forwards as well as backwards, in which case Abraham will be a partaker.

This is the meaning of the Petrine text about Christ preaching to the spirits in prison, incorporated in the creed in the words "He descended into hell.'

6. If this means never-ending retribution the answer is no.

(a) No.

(b) No.

(c) No.

(d) This is not a matter for human judgment, but the Scriptures do emphasise the probation of this life and the infinite seriousness of continued and unrepented evil.

(e) There may well be such a thing as the extinction of personality. Personally I could not reconcile Eternal Damnation with the

Christian doctrine of God. I would like to think that in the end no soul will be lost, but our Lord's own parable of the sheep and goats does seem to suggest the possibility of lost souls. Their destiny, so I imagine, can only be the disintegration which finally ends in cessation of being. This is, of course, a personal view. Mercifully the good old C of E refuses to dogmatise. The Romans, on the other hand, know it all!

7. I cannot agree with this quantitative notion of good and ill. In the sight of God I can conceive of no such phenomenon as a border-line case.

8. No.

9. Yes. An immortality which did not preserve individual identity would not be worth having. We are told very little in Scripture about the next life. It is sufficient to know that we shall be "with Christ, which is far better".

10. Allegorical, of course. The value of the myth lies in its profound spiritual insight, viz., that God created beings in His own image and likeness in order to share fellowship with Himself. The scientific doctrine of evolution (now considerably modified since Darwin) does not, of course, conflict with this basic fact.

11. The destiny of mankind is to know God, to love Him and to enjoy Him forever. In technical theological language, it is to enjoy the Beatific Vision.

Our grounds for assuming that good will prevail over evil are the death and resurrection of our Lord.

I think it would be quite unfair for me to comment on this letter without giving the vicar an opportunity for another reply and, in fact, making a regular debate of it.

I have asked my questions and have had my replies, courteously accorded by a busy man. The reader shall form his own opinion on the correspondence as it stands.

Perhaps you have been wondering about the heading of this chapter. I got it in the following way.

At a sitting about six months before the interruption of our Circle, Chang asked us to say what we thought was the most important thing in the world.

One of us said, "Unity", and another, "Brotherhood Chang replied that these were both important, but that the answer to his question was 'The Right Idea'—the embodiment of truth." Anything which goes against these things is the wrong idea. A great battle is still being waged for the Idea. We see the opposite sides, Progression and Retrogression. We see the drying up and withering caused by separativeness.

"We see this in many forms; strongly in the Astral, through the Mental, and right up to the Realms of Light.

It is the battle of the two-sided coin—the Great Idea. We call it the battle of light and dark." I find myself subjected to a strange sort of paralysis when I try to elaborate this idea. The thing is so clear in my mind, and so essentially simple, and yet I find the greatest difficulty in setting it forth in the clear and simple language which it deserves.

Perhaps I may begin with the negative side of the picture, and say how handicapped a person is in trying to live a constructive and harmonious life in accordance with the great Plan for the evolution of humanity if he has the Wrong Idea.

To take an extreme case, if he believes that he is going to be snuffed out like a candle at physical death, why should he put himself out to live in any way other than that dictated by his bodily desires? If he believes that absolute and permanent extinction will follow physical death, he can have no possible regrets for anything he has done in life, except in so far as the results of his deeds may catch up with him before he dies, either through the operation of human justice or through bodily disease, and, just as he can have no regrets for acts which have injured others, so he can derive no satisfaction from memories of his own altruism.

This is, as I say, an extreme case; but there are hundreds of millions of people who have some sort of belief in life after physical death, but are so muddled and confused by what they are taught or are not taught that their ideas afford little guide to conduct. Such may say with Omar:—

> Some there are who tell
> Of one who threatens he will toss to Hell
> The luckless Pots he marr'd in making—Pish!
> He's a Good Fellow and 'twill all be well.

A comparatively small proportion (but a large number in total) of these confused people accept the hotchpotch of religious teaching which they are given in childhood and at their Confirmation, and solve their logical misgivings by forcing upon their intellects the idea that it is positively wrong for them to query what they have been taught, or to make any attempt either to think things out for themselves or to search for direct evidence which might upset the beliefs, to which they cling like limpets with the power of that misguided loyalty which they misname faith.

Such people often lead moral and unselfish lives, though I am afraid that some of them suffer something of an initial disappointment when their eyes are opened upon their new life. They tend to join in the great chorus, "Why weren't we told about these things?" Whereas they have assiduously armoured themselves against the acceptance of any such ideas during life.

One person who had lived a life of unselfish service, but with a very narrow outlook, said to me afterwards:— "The heart was all right; it was the intellect which was at fault.

"Your sledge-hammer thoughts reached me, and enabled me to see more clearly. I was not so 'closed' as might have appeared: I did have doubts now and again. I want to thank you for your help. Stress as much as you can the power of thought in your teaching: so much depends upon it.

"I was able to give joy and light in the slums. It was given back to me a hundred-fold, so that my dim consciousness was stirred.

"In reality there are not many even hide-bound Christians who linger very long in those bemused states. Nearly all can be reached by someone who loves them and has perhaps a little wider vision.

"Where that fails there are guides and helpers over here to fan the flame into a roaring fire; and behind all these is the Lord Jesus Christ Himself, and His patience is never exhausted." The dividing line between the Right Idea and the Wrong Idea is, of course, not sharply defined; there are degrees of truth in error and degrees of error in truth.

Furthermore, mortal man cannot aspire to all truth.

If one has to pick the most critical stage in the journey from error to truth, I should say that it was the point at which a man realises and accepts the difference between the Personality and the Individuality (in the sense in which I have used these words) and the strong opposition of the interests of these two aspects of the self—the fact that the Personality is transient and that only the individual goes on eternally until the time when it unites again with the Source from which it sprang.

All those things which people are inclined to regard as the 'good things of life'—wealth, position, power, fame, comfort and the satisfaction of the senses and the appetites— are things which appertain to the Personality and will perish with the Personality. Material things must be left behind at physical death; lusts, greed, fears and hatreds are disposed of in the Astral; and the indiscipline of the lower mind is eliminated in the mental stage of development.

Mind you, when I deprecate an undue hankering after the good things of life, I do not mean to say that men should become ascetics, or hermits, or killjoys.

We are meant to enjoy the beauties and pleasures of life in moderation, we are meant to laugh, we are meant to be happy and jolly, we are meant to live in the world, and not to run away from it into monastic seclusion.

But we should let none of the satisfactions and pleasures of the world, any more than its pomps and vanities, get a grip on us: we should be able to take or to let alone.

We all start with a clean slate when we are born, and during the course of our lives we make ourselves into men and women of certain types. Some of us, through our inherited bodies and favourable circumstances, have a much easier task than others. Hence the injunction, "Judge not that ye be not judged". No human being is ever in a position to judge another, because he cannot possibly be in possession of all the facts.

Can you remember (it is one of my own most deeply engrained memories) the stage where you passed from your mother's philosophy of life to your father's? From the stage of "Johnnie shall have it: he is the littlest, the weakest, the youngest", to the more 'grown-up' rule, "Tommy shall have it: he is the eldest, he is the strongest, he is the senior." Perhaps the most basic trouble with Christianity as commonly taught and preached is that the feminine aspect of God is entirely suppressed.

While the early fathers were creating their Trinity, they might at least have found a place for woman in one of the Persons. Woman is the builder, the preserver, the cherisher of Life; it is man who is the destroyer.

I think that the Hebrew origins of Christianity have a good deal to do with this. Look at the Commandments.

"On it (the Sabbath) thou shalt do no manner of work; thou, thy son and thy daughter, thy manservant and thy maidservant, thy cattle and the stranger which is within thy gates". Nothing about the poor wife, you will notice.

But when we come to the Tenth Commandment, where a man's property is in question, it is a different story. "Thou shalt not covet thy neighbour's house, thou shalt not covet thy neighbour's wife, nor his servant nor his maid nor his ox nor his ass nor anything that is his." I think that it will be a feature of this Aquarian Age, upon which we are just entering, that woman and woman's outlook on life will be a more potent influence than ever before: not as a supplanter of man in rulership, but as a co-partner and counsellor.

So, as I say, carry your mind back to your earliest recollections as a little child under your mother's influence, and see what you have made of yourself since that time. You may be pleased—I hope you are—or you may be displeased.

However that may be, you will pass over into your new life, when the time comes, exactly the same person as you have made yourself on earth.

There is a Latin proverb, *Nemo repente turpissimus fuit*, which might be translated, "It takes time to make oneself into a thorough blackguard". The parson will say that the voice of conscience tries to restrain; the Right Idea says that it is the glorious shining Individual trying to control the rebellious Personality. It comes to very much the same thing. But the great thing to remember is that no irreparable harm has been done so long as the conscience or the Individual, according to how you look at it, has not been completely suppressed; in other words, so long as one keeps on trying.

While the will to do so exists, it is always possible to retrace one's steps up the hill, and this applies on both sides of the grave.

There is a good deal of loose thinking about deathbed repentances. Some people say that a life of persistent and deliberate evil can be neutralised by a few words spoken at the last possible moment, and others say that it is nonsense to suppose that a deathbed repentance can be of any avail.

As a matter of fact, the deathbed is almost as good as any other occasion for repentance. You can't be spirited back to the top of the hill by magic; you have got to climb back, just as you let yourself down, by stages. And sooner or later you have to become again as a little child, back in spirit under the feminine system, which is the Christ system.

This process is possible either before or after physical death, but it is likely to be less painful if it is at least started during Earth-life, because one can get a good deal of help in the process from decent kindly people whom one encounters on Earth; whereas after death one goes to one's 'own place', where the society is exclusively on one's own spiritual level; and, if the level is very low, then that is Hell.

Man is not *compelled* to make any effort. He has his freewill. If he chooses the way of darkness, there is nothing to prevent his doing so. He may have to wait long ages in the dark regions, but he is never for a moment forgotten by those who are responsible for his progress, and sooner or later the hard black shell which he has built up round his heart softens and cracks under the never-failing Christ love which pours unseen upon every creature.

Then does the current of love begin to circulate again feebly, and perhaps agonisingly, in his atrophied veins, and he calls out on God or Allah or Buddha or Christ, it matters not; for his cry is heard and help is sent.

And as with men, so with nations; and as with nations, so with humanity. Mankind *must* come into the Light sooner or later, but the road may be dark and bitter if man will have it so. The choice is upon us, and the choice is upon us now. I need say no more.

Those who have the Right Idea, however, will not concentrate too much upon their own progress, either material or spiritual. They will be concerned to extend a helping hand to all who need it and will accept it, and in helping others they will best help themselves.

But the respect in which the Right Idea is almost unique in this world is the atmosphere of friendliness and conscious cooperation in the Master's work with individuals in the unseen; with the angels, into whose charge we have been given, and with the lesser messengers of the Light.

It is something which has to be experienced to be appreciated; it generates friendship greater than earthly friendships, and to my thinking this is the way in which humanity is likely to extricate itself eventually from its Slough of Despond.

There are so very few who have opened their hearts to this friendship, or, indeed, are aware of it as a possibility.

I have a strong understanding with and sympathy for people who cannot accept as a reality this idea of the constant fellowship and companionship with the angels. It is one of the strange characteristics of our work with the unseen that what is an intuitional certainty, not subject to any faintest shadow of doubt, on one day shall become a little nebulous and questionable after a period of interrupted contact; and if those who have been fortunate and privileged enough to experience such certainty can later be brought to query the actuality of their impressions, how can they blame others, who only read about these things, if they remain unconvinced? The affection which we feel is in most cases intuitional; we have in our subconscious minds memories of past associations with members of our own Group stretching back into the dim aisles of time, and reinforced by the frequent but unremembered contacts which we make with them during our work in sleep. As Z. once said to me, "You can never be lonely again": and that is true.

I sent across an ocean and a continent to ask Z. if he had any contribution which he wanted to make specially for this book. The following is the result.

Greetings: In the heat and fret of the day, surrounded by the stress and strain of living, it is very often difficult to gain that sense of wellbeing and balance which comes from inward peace. It is more than difficult, very often it is impossible (so one says), to attain inward peace, to raise one's thoughts and aspirations to that point where the Power descending can first be contacted. Yet that sense of peace is the only worthwhile thing that man can gain. From it all other things flow; from it the ability to accomplish all things can be attained.

Men turn their eyes and look backward and sigh. It was so much easier to live the contemplative life in the olden days; life was so much more simple. Or they look around and sigh for the opportunity to retire from the turmoil and noise of the everyday world, to the monastic calm or the peaceful mountain retreat. They forget in both cases the evolutionary scheme. A trite saying, yet none the less true, is that; you cannot turn Time back. The spent minute is gone forever. Only the fool wastes his energies wishing for the return of the past; only the craven shuts himself away in an attempt to recapture it.

The past has played its part. Even in the past that the man of today so longingly covets it was not easy to gain the inward peace which alone is the pearl of great price.

Physical life was more simple in many ways. There was perhaps more leisure to think and contemplate, but the Life Essence was not so universally capable of using that leisure through Its manifest beings as It is today. The forms were heavier and less responsive, more immersed in the material world. The exceptions in the rare souls who sought and found merely point the rod at the infinite numbers who did not.

The mechanism was not tuned for the experiment as universally as it is today. The past world would not have served that brother who, now aware, yet lacking the initiative to move, sighs longingly for what he mistakenly believes was a better opportunity.

Neither would it help him to retire from the hurly-burly of today. The new mechanism is tuned to respond within the framework of the society which has been created. The outward handclasp of material peace can now be only an initial and transitory one. It can be only for the first faltering step to help him who is too frail and weak to break open the chrysalis from within. It is not essential. That thought is important. If the desire is true, the bonds can be, and indeed should be, broken from the sanctity of the Inner Realisation.

A few moments of quiet ere the day's tasks are begun; a few moments of quiet when the day's tasks are over, to give to concentrated thought on the meaning of all existence.

That is the beginning. That is the only essential step. He who sits idly sighing procrastinates—and too many now are doing that.

There is so much to be done, and the opportunity for selfless service to the Great Unnameable One and to the cause of Humanity has never been greater, or its rewards more important.

Humanity stands at the crucial turning point of its evolution. Now, yesterday, today and tomorrow in the limitation of earthly time, and Now in the limitless, timeless realm, is the moment of turning from the without to the within, from the path of outgoing to the path of return; the moment of the Prodigal Son's return to the home of his Father; use what words or symbols you will; there is but one meaning. Now the face of humanity is turning back to whence it came—eyes are searching for almost forgotten landmarks, stirrings within tug at remembrance; the beginnings of the realisation of the dawn of the glorious day of reconciliation are filtering through to the long-enmeshed children of a great destiny.

In turning thus, Man has shocked the evolutionary rhythm which was outward set. Because of his still-uncomprehended capabilities and opportunities, he has been unable to accomplish this first step in return with the harmony and joy it should have attained. Even the few—and how very few they are—who have faint understandings of this great event, fail to hold the harmony uppermost by giving in to the pressure of outward events, and letting fear and discord and anger sway them. Consequently the outward manifestation of this great event, instead of being one of great harmony and beauty and consequent rejoicing on the part of mankind, is one of disturbance and fear. Great truths of the universe are being uncovered that Man might begin to assume his true shape; but instead of being co-operator and true builder with the Great Lord of the Universe who has so unstintingly revealed His Majesty and Might, and made of them an offering to Man, Man has accepted the gifts, and not paused to attain, in the moments of quiet, that inward peace which alone can assure him of true wisdom and vision.

Yet despair not. The shock is mighty, and it reverberates through the universe, and the plight of causes much interest and speculation to those who see.

It is regretted that the rhythm of the spheres is interrupted by discord rather than harmony, but it is seen that the discords in time will weave a new harmony and the purpose be accomplished. For His Law is unbreakable, His Law that ordains that, from the water and slime of the lowest manifestation to the glory and majesty of the full revelation, all shall eventually attain to that true place wherein He dwells. Rejoice, then, even in the moment of tribulation, for in the mighty crucible of discord and struggle the future glory of mankind is shaping. The moment of Return is upon him, and his brothers of the universe rejoice to see his face set once more towards the ultimate goal.

May He uplift and guide.
May He penetrate and inspire.
May He light the path with a flaming torch.
And lead men through the fire—Home.

Blessings unto you my brother, Z.

I shall not take it upon myself to attempt to expound or elaborate this message to the inhabitants of the Dark Star.

The language is simple and clear. All I have to say is, "Read it over and over again, for at each new reading some new facet of truth will flash out." Will you allow me to thank Z. for his message on your behalf, as well as on my own, and let me finish this book of mine with his special prayer? "Cleanse this, Thy servant, from all thought of self.

Stabilise the emotional body, balance the intellectual body, open the Spiritual. And in a completely balanced whole may Love find its abiding-place, that this may be a tabernacle worthy of Thee."

Paperbacks also available from
White Crow Books

Elsa Barker—*Letters from
a Living Dead Man*
ISBN 978-1-907355-83-7

Elsa Barker—*War Letters from
the Living Dead Man*
ISBN 978-1-907355-85-1

Elsa Barker—*Last Letters from
the Living Dead Man*
ISBN 978-1-907355-87-5

Richard Maurice Bucke—
Cosmic Consciousness
ISBN 978-1-907355-10-3

Arthur Conan Doyle—
The Edge of the Unknown
ISBN 978-1-907355-14-1

Arthur Conan Doyle—
The New Revelation
ISBN 978-1-907355-12-7

Arthur Conan Doyle—
The Vital Message
ISBN 978-1-907355-13-4

Arthur Conan Doyle with
Simon Parke—*Conversations
with Arthur Conan Doyle*
ISBN 978-1-907355-80-6

Meister Eckhart with Simon Parke—
Conversations with Meister Eckhart
ISBN 978-1-907355-18-9

D. D. Home—*Incidents in my Life Part 1*
ISBN 978-1-907355-15-8

Mme. Dunglas Home; edited,
with an Introduction, by Sir
Arthur Conan Doyle—*D. D.
Home: His Life and Mission*
ISBN 978-1-907355-16-5

Edward C. Randall—
Frontiers of the Afterlife
ISBN 978-1-907355-30-1

Rebecca Ruter Springer—
Intra Muros: My Dream of Heaven
ISBN 978-1-907355-11-0

Leo Tolstoy, edited by Simon
Parke—*Forbidden Words*
ISBN 978-1-907355-00-4

Leo Tolstoy—*A Confession*
ISBN 978-1-907355-24-0

Leo Tolstoy—*The Gospel in Brief*
ISBN 978-1-907355-22-6

Leo Tolstoy—*The Kingdom
of God is Within You*
ISBN 978-1-907355-27-1

Leo Tolstoy—*My Religion:
What I Believe*
ISBN 978-1-907355-23-3

Leo Tolstoy—*On Life*
ISBN 978-1-907355-91-2

Leo Tolstoy—*Twenty-three Tales*
ISBN 978-1-907355-29-5

Leo Tolstoy—*What is Religion
and other writings*
ISBN 978-1-907355-28-8

Leo Tolstoy—*Work While
Ye Have the Light*
ISBN 978-1-907355-26-4

Leo Tolstoy—*The Death of Ivan Ilyich*
ISBN 978-1-907661-10-5

Leo Tolstoy—*Resurrection*
ISBN 978-1-907661-09-9

Leo Tolstoy with Simon Parke—
Conversations with Tolstoy
ISBN 978-1-907355-25-7

Howard Williams with an Introduction
by Leo Tolstoy—*The Ethics of Diet:
An Anthology of Vegetarian Thought*
ISBN 978-1-907355-21-9

Vincent Van Gogh with Simon
Parke—*Conversations with Van Gogh*
ISBN 978-1-907355-95-0

Wolfgang Amadeus Mozart with Simon
Parke—*Conversations with Mozart*
ISBN 978-1-907661-38-9

Jesus of Nazareth with Simon Parke—
Conversations with Jesus of Nazareth
ISBN 978-1-907661-41-9

Thomas à Kempis with Simon
Parke—*The Imitation of Christ*
ISBN 978-1-907661-58-7

Julian of Norwich with Simon
Parke—*Revelations of Divine Love*
ISBN 978-1-907661-88-4

Allan Kardec—*The Spirits Book*
ISBN 978-1-907355-98-1

Allan Kardec—*The Book on Mediums*
ISBN 978-1-907661-75-4

Emanuel Swedenborg—*Heaven and Hell*
ISBN 978-1-907661-55-6

P.D. Ouspensky—*Tertium Organum:
The Third Canon of Thought*
ISBN 978-1-907661-47-1

Dwight Goddard—*A Buddhist Bible*
ISBN 978-1-907661-44-0

Michael Tymn—*The Afterlife Revealed*
ISBN 978-1-970661-90-7

Michael Tymn—*Transcending the
Titanic: Beyond Death's Door*
ISBN 978-1-908733-02-3

Guy L. Playfair—*If This Be Magic*
ISBN 978-1-907661-84-6

Guy L. Playfair—*The Flying Cow*
ISBN 978-1-907661-94-5

Guy L. Playfair —*This House is Haunted*
ISBN 978-1-907661-78-5

Carl Wickland, M.D.—
Thirty Years Among the Dead
ISBN 978-1-907661-72-3

John E. Mack—*Passport to the Cosmos*
ISBN 978-1-907661-81-5

Peter & Elizabeth Fenwick—
The Truth in the Light
ISBN 978-1-908733-08-5

Erlendur Haraldsson—
Modern Miracles
ISBN 978-1-908733-25-2

Erlendur Haraldsson—
At the Hour of Death
ISBN 978-1-908733-27-6

Erlendur Haraldsson—
The Departed Among the Living
ISBN 978-1-908733-29-0

Brian Inglis—*Science and Parascience*
ISBN 978-1-908733-18-4

Brian Inglis—*Natural and Supernatural:
A History of the Paranormal*
ISBN 978-1-908733-20-7

Ernest Holmes—*The Science of Mind*
ISBN 978-1-908733-10-8

Victor & Wendy Zammit —*A Lawyer
Presents the Evidence For the Afterlife*
ISBN 978-1-908733-22-1

Casper S. Yost—*Patience
Worth: A Psychic Mystery*
ISBN 978-1-908733-06-1

William Usborne Moore—
Glimpses of the Next State
ISBN 978-1-907661-01-3

William Usborne Moore—
The Voices
ISBN 978-1-908733-04-7

John W. White—
The Highest State of Consciousness
ISBN 978-1-908733-31-3

Stafford Betty—
The Imprisoned Splendor
ISBN 978-1-907661-98-3

Paul Pearsall, Ph.D. —
Super Joy
ISBN 978-1-908733-16-0

All titles available as eBooks, and selected titles available in Hardback and Audiobook formats from www.whitecrowbooks.com

www.ingramcontent.com/pod-product-compliance
Ingram Content Group UK Ltd.
Pitfield, Milton Keynes, MK11 3LW, UK
UKHW040635150425
5479UKWH00039B/715